WOMAN IN THE SACRED SCRIPTURES OF HINDUISM

Woman in the Sacred Scriptures of Hinduism

MILDRETH WORTH PINKHAM, PH.D.

NEW YORK

COLUMBIA UNIVERSITY PRESS

1941

COLUMBIA UNIVERSITY PRESS, NEW YORK

Foreign agents: OXFORD UNIVERSITY PRESS, Humphrey Milford, Amen House, London, E.C. 4, England, AND B. I. Building, Nicol Road, Bombay, India; MARUZEN COMPANY, LTD., 6 Nihonbashi, Tori-Nichome, Tokyo, Japan

MANUFACTURED IN THE UNITED STATES OF AMERICA

TO MY FATHER

GEORGE W. WORTH

WHO WAS READY UNTO

EVERY GOOD WORK

PREFACE

THE HISTORY of the status of woman as revealed in the sacred scriptures of Hinduism is like a cable with many strands stretching from the dim past to the immediate present. Some of the strands in this extended span throughout the ages are intricately knotted. At many points new influences came in, thus bringing about momentous complexities. Contradictions often arose. The purpose of the present study of more than fourteen thousand pages of representative passages of the Hindu scriptures is to attempt to show where some of these influences occurred, what they were, and the effect they have produced upon the status of Hindu women. It would seem that today Hindu women, as well as students of civilization, need to have such material in order to test and evaluate it. It is my earnest belief that the Hindu woman herself can most effectively straighten out this knotty problem.

During several happy years of residence in India I had abundant opportunity to observe Hindu women of all types in their actual home life, and I talked intimately with them concerning their religion. I was privileged to visit many beautiful and inspiring homes, but I also witnessed many homes in which there were restrictions which hindered women from their fullest measure of service to their communities. I came to the conclusion that the sacred scriptures of Hinduism had been one factor tremendously influencing the status of Hindu women. These writings seemed to produce much that was wholesome in spiritual exaltation and actual daily living, but also much that was injurious and unnecessary.

Of course the actual scriptures of Hinduism have not been solely responsible for the molding of Hindu womanhood. Some of the knotty problems in this exceedingly complicated question arose because of factors such as climate, geography, legends, and poetry outside the canonical scriptures, social contacts with aboriginal peoples, as well as woman's natural tendencies, customs, institutions, and economics. It is true that by laws the government has alleviated many unfortunate situations in which the women of India at times have found themselves. No doubt such laws will continue to improve adverse conditions. But it would seem that a more thorough understanding of the helpful and the harmful elements in the Hindu scriptures also should be of very considerable aid. A deep religious spirit long has permeated the Indian mind, and it is because of this fact that much stress should be laid upon the advantage of deeper scrutiny of the writings that the Hindus hold so sacred. Certainly in these modern days a religion should not be a blind faith, but one adequately tested by reason and moral experience. No doubt all peoples could be more diligent in reasonably examining their so-called "sacred" literature to find out exactly what exists in it and to consider to what extent that literature is relevant and helpful to modern living.

Many reform movements have arisen in the Hindu religion, three having been so forceful as to lead to the establishment of separate living religions—Sikhism, Jainism, and Buddhism—all of which took very definite positions with regard to the status of woman. In Sikhism the Hindu degradation of woman was repudiated and she was held in higher regard. In Jainism, although womankind was condemned in the scriptures, women were admitted as nuns in a recognized monastic order. Despite the low estimate of woman and the family prevailing in Buddhism, the founder was revered as a liberator of womanhood. Buddhism was a revolt against the Brahmans, who had helped to wrest from woman her liberty as an individual. In addition to these attempts at reform, in the twelfth century Rāmānuja endeavored to bring about improvement in the condition of Hindu women. In the early sixteenth century another Hindu reformer, Chaitanya, urged better conditions for widows. In 1828 Rāmmohun Roy founded the Brahmo Samāj, among the specific endeavors of which was the combat against polygamy and the burning of widows. These are only a few of the religious efforts to improve social conditions among the women of India. So it is that to some considerable extent Hinduism has undergone change; and no doubt more reform movements will arise. The time may come when the chief religion of India may be far different from that set forth in the historical documents of Nature-Worship and of priestly, philosophic, legalistic, devotional, and popular Hinduism. If not a remolded Hinduism, another faith, either one now existing or a new world religion, may be embraced by the Hindus. However, whatever the future may bring, today no less than two hundred and thirty-nine millions [1] of women and men in India cling tenaciously to their Hindu heritage. It is fairly certain that whatever faith the Hindus of the future may follow they will build upon their Hindu culture for sometime to come, if not always. We must not forget the long period during which the Hindus have adhered to their scriptures. The gods of the early Greeks and Romans have disappeared. Today the *Iliad* and the *Aeneid* are not a part of the so-called "sacred" books of any living people; but the Mahābhārata and the Rāmāyaṇa are still considered among the "sacred" books of the Hindus, and they exert a very important influence.

It must be recognized that the acts of many Hindus are the result of blind adherence to the unquestioned authority of sacred scriptures rather than of a testing of traditional doctrine by conscience, practical observation, and experimentation. This over-conservative characteristic is not peculiar to the Hindus. History shows that throughout the centuries much "re-thinking" has been necessary in the world's living religions. To be of practical, beneficial value doctrines often require much revision. Certainly the doctrines of Hinduism are and will continue to be no exception to this universal rule. Increasingly, everywhere in the world, modern scholarship insists upon textual criticism. Although the followers of the Hindu religion have reinterpreted some of its doctrines, far too little re-study and re-thinking have been done concerning those portions of the scriptures directly affecting Hindu womanhood. That which has been accomplished has been brought about only by great perseverance on the part of valiant men and women in the face of strong opposition.

The prime reason that so many Hindu women have no actual reading acquaintance with some of their sacred documents is be-

[1] India, *Census of India, 1931,* I (Part 2, Imperial Tables, 1933), 515.

cause there are religious pronouncements forbidding women to read them and also because the majority of Indian women have been denied the privilege of even the most elementary education. The time is coming when more and more Indian women will insist that no unjust limitations be imposed upon their mental development. A far greater number of Hindus should know at first hand what exists in the writings which they are brought up to revere.

To bring about a historical and scientific attitude toward sacred scriptures is a most difficult task for the followers of any religion to accomplish. All peoples have been hesitant to engage in a rigorous, unbiased attempt to study their revered scriptures in historical settings. Modern advancements in science and in historical analysis have come slowly. It has not been easy for human beings to test reason and experience in any field of endeavor. Certainly, however, all peoples must develop increasing courage to view their sacred scriptures intelligently. Religion is a precious thing; but to modern scholarship and worthful living it cannot be so sacred as to render it immune from reasonable scrutiny. People must learn to distinguish between beneficial theological beliefs and harmful religious superstitions.

If in a small measure this study shall help toward a better understanding of the status of Hindu women as revealed in the Hindu scriptures and in some degree shall aid in awakening greater numbers of Hindu women to a more discerning knowledge of their religious traditions, its mission will have been fulfilled. It is dedicated to the fundamental and universal proposition that human life is valuable. This precious human life of both women and men has power to bring about an increase of the Divine in the world —more and more of that which humanity holds to be "the supremely worthful Power or Powers controlling in the world." [2] It is through developing personalities that the realization of a better world will come. What a pity it is that one-half the population of India—or of any land—should be denied the fullest opportunity for development and service! Surely this modern world should

[2] Hume, "The Essentials of Religion," in World Congress of Faiths, Oxford, 1937, *The World's Need of Religion,* p. 33.

grant nothing less than adequate freedom for women to contribute their full measure of service as intelligent, responsible, healthy, and happy human individuals and members of communities. Care must be taken everywhere by modern religious leaders and followers not to allow so-called "sacred" documents to prescribe indignities upon any living beings. Such a discriminating procedure may demand a complete reconstruction of many theological doctrines.

This study is offered, not in a spirit of antagonism to all Hinduism, but rather with an attitude of reverent inquiry, deeply rooted in the belief that there are to be found evidences of the spirit of God in the sacred scriptures of all living religions. There is, therefore, an appreciation of whatever is ethical and ennobling in the Hindu religion. With relation to the status of women I have found many noble passages. It is because of this very nobility that I feel a true understanding of the passages referring to the feminine should be noted. There should be condemnation only for that which reasonable persons must label "injurious." Extensive reading in the world's so-called "sacred" literature reveals that we mortals often have created unfair human prohibitions and have needlessly injured one another. The time has come when we should note this fact and should seek to weed out whatever is harmful in order that the future may grow richer in service and happiness for all human beings.

In this study from a comparison of almost any individual passage with its full setting in its own original document the reader will perceive that very carefully selected material has been taken from a vast literary field. In this undertaking scrupulous editorial care has been exercised to present the quoted material in clear grammatical form. The reader will find certain variations of spelling, punctuation, and diacritical marks as used by different authors.

I desire to acknowledge the debt of gratitude I owe to Dr. Robert Ernest Hume, of Union Theological Seminary, for his continual intellectual stimulation. I wish to pay tribute to my teacher of Sanskrit, the late Professor A. V. Williams Jackson, formerly of Columbia University. Likewise I am indebted to Dr. Daniel J.

Fleming, of Union Theological Seminary, for helpful criticism. To my beloved parents and husband I gratefully give thanks for their encouragement during this work. To my many friends in India, both Hindu and Christian, I wish to express appreciation for their interest in this study. I also desire to express grateful acknowledgment to the various publishers whose copyrighted material has been used in this book.

MILDRETH WORTH PINKHAM

New York City
February 10, 1941

CONTENTS

ABBREVIATIONS

AIL	Altindisches Leben, by Heinrich Zimmer.
ASL	A History of Ancient Sanskrit Literature, by F. Max Müller.
A.V.	The Hymns of the Atharva-veda, by R. T. H. Griffith.
B.Y.V.	The Veda of the Black Yajus School, Entitled Taittirīya Sanhitā, by A. B. Keith.
HMW	Hinduism and The Modern World, by K. M. Panikkar.
HOS	"Harvard Oriental Series."
HSL	A History of Sanskrit Literature, by A. A. Macdonell.
HWI	Hinduism: the World—Ideal, by Harendranath Maitra.
ITPP	Indian Thought, Past and Present, by R. W. Frazer.
KP	The Key of Progress, by A. R. Caton.
PH	A Primer of Hinduism, by J. N. Farquhar.
PLMS	The Purāṇas in the Light of Modern Science, by K. Narayanaswami Aiyar.
PSIW	Purdah: The Status of Indian Women, by Mrs. Sarangadhar Das.
RRV	The Religion of the Ṛigveda, by H. D. Griswold.
RS	Recht und Sitte, by Julius Jolly.
R.V.	The Hymns of the Rigveda, by R. T. H. Griffith.
RVC	Religion in Various Cultures, by H. L. Friess and H. W. Schneider.
SBE	"Sacred Books of the East."
SLAI	Sexual Life in Ancient India, by J. J. Meyer.
S.V.	The Hymns of the Sāmaveda, by R. T. H. Griffith.
TPU	The Thirteen Principal Upanishads, by R. E. Hume.
V.I.	Vedic Index, by A. A. Macdonell and A. B. Keith.
VM	Vedic Mythology, by A. A. Macdonell.
VR	The Vedic Religion, by K. S. Macdonald.
WLR	The World's Living Religions, by R. E. Hume.
W.Y.V.	The Texts of the White Yajurveda, by R. T. H. Griffith.

CHAPTER I: THE VEDAS

HINDUISM is the oldest organized living religion. Its earliest sacred scriptures consist of a large literature of psalms and magic spells. They are called "Vedas" (from Sanskrit "vid"—to know), meaning books of knowledge. The Rig-Veda is the Veda of Verses. It is not only "the most ancient literary monument of India," [1] but in addition "the most ancient literary document of the Indo-European peoples." [2] The Yajur-Veda, whether in the "Śukla" recension, known as the White Yajur-Veda, or in the "Taittirīya" recension, known as the Black Yajur-Veda, is the Veda of Sacrificial Formulas. The Sāma-Veda is the Veda of Chants. The Atharva-Veda is the Veda of Charms. The poets of the Vedas belonged to the Aryan race, which is the race from which also sprang the Greeks, the Romans, the Persians, the Celts, and the Aryan peoples of Europe.

In its present form the Rig-Veda is conceded to be the oldest document among the world's living religions. It has been dated variously by scholars from about 2400 B.C.[3] to 1000 B.C. Some Hindus believe that it has existed throughout eternity. They consider the *ṛishis,* or sacred poets, who wrote the hymns to have been inspired directly by the Supreme Creator. Hindus have succeeded in transmitting the Sanskrit text of the Rig-Veda "so that it now has fewer variant readings than exist in the present Hebrew text of the Old Testament and the Greek text of the New Testament." [4]

A. A. Macdonell tells us that "the evidence of the topography, the climate, and the products of the country . . . shows that the people by whose poets the Rigveda was composed were settled in the northwest of India, from the Kabul to the Jumna." [5] These

[1] Bloomfield, *The Religion of the Veda,* p. 17. [2] *Ibid.*

[3] Haug, tr., *The Aitareya Brāhmaṇam of the Rigveda,* Introduction, I, 48.

[4] Hume, *The World's Living Religions,* p. 20.

[5] Macdonell, *A History of Sanskrit Literature,* p. 152.

people tended flocks and were warriors. They conquered the black-skinned aborigines. H. D. Griswold reminds us that throughout the Rig-Veda there is an "antithesis between Aryan and Dasyu, the foreign invader and the aboriginal inhabitant of the land. . . . The Dasyus differed from the Aryans in appearance, speech and religion. As contrasted with the white Aryan colour, the Dasyus were dark-skinned. . . . This difference in colour was one of the causes that lay at the foundation of caste, for the very name of caste is *varṇa,* 'colour.' "[6] This same author writes that "the contrast between Aryan and Dasyu in the matter of religion was equally great. . . . For the Aryan the conception of the divine fatherhood was embodied in the idea of Father Sky, the bright heavenly one; for the Dasyu the same conception was expressed in the form of *liṅga-worship*. . . . But the time came in India, when this same worship became widespread even among the Brāhmans."[7] Griswold is also of the opinion that "the later philosophical and theological systems of India as well as her characteristic attitude of pessimism toward life may be regarded, not as pure Aryan, but as Ârya-Dravidian products. The significance of the Ṛigveda is that its hymns, with negligible exceptions, represent the Aryan as standing in stern antagonism to the Dasyu and all his ways. It is therefore the purest expression on the soil of India of the Aryan spirit."[8]

In order to try to understand the Vedic civilization let us consider for a moment a few aspects of the Indo-Europeans who were the antecedents of the Rigvedic age. Griswold has given us the following picture:

The pastoral and agricultural stage had been reached. . . . The outlines of the present family system were already in existence, the father being the head, and the son's wife being adopted into the clan of her husband. It was the joint family system, the primitive names indicating that the family consisted of a man and his wife and children, his brothers and their families, his sons and their families, besides the old people, grandfather and grandmother. . . . The authority of the head of the family was unlimited. He had the power of life and death. Sons were greatly

[6] Griswold, *The Religion of the Ṛigveda,* pp. 34, 37, 40. [7] *Ibid.,* p. 40.
[8] *Ibid.,* pp. 52–53.

desired as warriors, avengers of blood, performers of funeral rites, and as means for the continuation of the clan. There was, owing to the chronic warfare of the time, usually a dearth of men and a superfluity of women. Hence girl infants, as not needed, were often exposed. Old people, too, were frequently put out of the way, especially in time of need. The joint family coffer was controlled by the head of the family. Primitive Indo-European marriage was by purchase or capture. The lot of the wife was not easy. She was more or less a beast of burden. Her mother-in-law ruled her with an iron hand. Separate dining of the two sexes was . . . a primitive custom. There are traces also among the Scythians, Thracians, Slavs, Germans and Indo-Aryans of "satī," the custom of a wife voluntarily accompanying her husband in death; also of a distinct prejudice against the second marriage of widows. The brother was the guardian of the honour of his sister; and after the death of the father an unmarried sister came under his authority. Indo-European antiquity was dominated by the idea of the necessity of marriage. So indispensable was it considered that, according to the evidence, the unmarried dead were sometimes even married ritually to the living, that they might be thus provided for in the life to come. The future comfort of the dead husband was the primitive idea of "satī." The patriarchal family may have been preceded by the so-called "matriarchate," according to which descent was reckoned from the mother. The so-called "mutterrecht" was clearly found among the pre-Aryan Etruscans, Picts, and Iberians. While the change to the patriarchal system would diminish the independence of women, it would greatly increase the dignity and purity of family life. Whether there was a totemistic stage, is disputed.[9]

Griswold continues his picture of the pre-Vedic period by saying that

Monogamy was the rule, polygamy the exception. As between different clans, probably exogamy was the custom. There is evidence to indicate joint land possession on the part of the members of a clan. The wife as purchased was the property of her lord and master. Hence marriage was later called the lordship (*patitva*) of the husband over the wife. Accordingly there was a double standard of morality.[10]

With regard to religion, Griswold points out that

There were two lines of development . . . the worship of ancestors and the worship of "Heavenly Ones." . . . The service and worship of an-

[9] Griswold, RRV, pp. 7, 9, 10.

[10] *Ibid.*, p. 10.

cestors was one of the foundations of primitive social organization. Relatives were united in ancestor-worship, in the right of inheritance, and in the duty of blood-revenge. A son was necessary to perform the funeral rites of his father. The patriarchal head of a family or clan, while alive, was the human father, but on his death became a divine father. He was the guardian genius of the clan, charged especially with the duty of promoting its fertility. Rites connected with ancestral worship involved expert guidance, in other words, priestly functions. In all primitive societies the head of the family, as the one standing, because of age and experience, in closest communication with the ancestors, is usually priest, shaman or medicine man. Old women as priestesses doubtless shared in similar functions. There were no priests in the technical sense, but there may have been families in which propitiatory and magic rites were handed down from father to son.

In addition to the awe and reverence felt toward dead ancestors there was a keen sense of the potency and mystery of natural phenomena. Here again we have the working of analogy. Children and people in the childhood stage find it natural to ascribe to inanimate objects the same powers of will and effort which they themselves are conscious of possessing. Accordingly, from a very primitive period, the whole of nature was regarded as an aggregate of animated entities. Each object or phenomenon of nature, such as heaven, earth, sun, wind, lightning, etc., could be named, isolated from the rest, and made into a special object of awe and wonder. Thus to name things was to fixate attention upon them, make them objects of reflection and imagination, and so proceed in the direction of full personification. . . . What can be assumed . . . with practical certainty to be prehistoric is, in the words of Schrader, "the mere capacity and the tendency to form into a divinity every conception in nature or in culture which was of significance for primitive man." . . . Father Sky and his children, the Devas, constituted "the real kernel of the primitive Aryan religion." Such an interpretation of the sky represents the beginning at once of Indo-European myth-making and Indo-European science. . . . In fire, dawn, lightning, etc., the primitive Indo-European peoples adored the mysterious powers, the divine *animae,* which manifested themselves in the phenomena of the sky, but possibly not as yet any god who was regarded as a person. . . . The primitive tendency to regard all nature as animate was the first step towards a spiritual interpretation of the universe. This reading of the world in terms of human life was the beginning of anthropomorphism, every external object as well as man being regarded as possessing an *anima.* It was only a question of time for the human figure to be added to the human *anima* present in each phenomenon.[11]

Another period, the Indo-Iranian, should be considered for a moment. Before the Indian group separated from the Iranian there was a close connection of the "Vedic and Avestan religion as well as of language." [12] The worship of ancestors and the worship of "Heavenly Ones" continued. The conception of "order" became more explicit. Also, as Griswold points out, "a movement in the direction of ethical monotheism preceded the Indo-Iranian dispersion." [13] Griswold says that "scholars practically agree that Varuṇa equals Ahura Mazda, that is to say, the ethical god of the Ṛik is regarded as the same in origin as the ethical and supreme god of the Avesta." [14] The Rig-Veda often mentions ancient priestly families. In this connection Griswold points out that

> Mixed up though they be with mythical and legendary material, there are nevertheless quite likely in many of them historical reminiscences of priestly families reaching back into the dim past, possibly to the time before the separation of the Indo-Iranian clans. Such specialization of function led to great results in India. Priestly technique demanded considerable knowledge—knowledge that could be gained only through division of labour—for its proper exercise. In this way the tradition was naturally set of a learned priestly class made up of different orders of priests. As a result, the religious literature of India, so far as it has been aryanized, is the work of the priesthood, and its fundamental conceptions represent largely the thinking of the same dominant community.[15]

In considering the influence of this religious literature upon India's women it is important to note that the early worshippers addressed many female deities. Griswold tells us that

> The whole "clan of the devas" is conceived anthropomorphically after the analogy of human society. They wear ornaments of gold, ride in cars drawn by horses, and have houses. They fight against demons, as Aryans fight against the Dasyus. They are glorified Kṣatriyas. Some gods are male, others female. Indra, god of the lightning-flash and thunder-roll, is suitably represented as a man; Uṣas, the many-coloured dawn, as a fair and richly dressed woman.[16]

---

[11] Griswold, RRV, pp. 11, 12–13, 14, 15. [12] *Ibid.*, p. 21. [13] *Ibid.*, p. 25.
[14] *Ibid.*, pp. 24–25. [15] *Ibid.*, p. 27. [16] *Ibid.*, p. 105.

The gods and goddesses are represented as members of families; some are parents, such as Heaven and Earth (Dyāus and Pṛithivī); others are sisters, brothers, wives, and husbands. For the most part they live together harmoniously. The Devas are helpful to one another. The god Indra, however, is an exception to this mutual helpfulness; but as he is the weather god, ever changing in character, perhaps the discord he causes is excusable. Among the gods of the Vedas there exists a division of labor. Each deity directs some part of life.

In this matter of anthropomorphism, however, we must be careful not to overemphasize what is just a certain poetical conception in terms of what we individually may consider the divine and the human. We must not indiscriminately ascribe human characteristics as we conceive them today to poetic creations that may have been considered more emphatically divine in the conception of another age. In the Hindu sacred scriptures sometimes we find a goddess called a father or a son (A.V.7.6.1); likewise, a masculine divinity may have the appellation "mother." Even though a goddess is called "mother," it does not follow that this female divinity shall possess the exact traits of character humanity has come to consider desirable and even necessary in an ideal earthly mother.

Griswold tells us that the Hindu goddesses may be divided into

> . . . three groups: (*a*) those having a natural basis, as Uṣas "Dawn," Sarasvatī the deified "Sarasvatī" river, Pṛithivī Earth, Rātrī "Night," Pṛiṣṇi the "mottled" storm-cloud, and Vāc "Speech"; (*b*) abstract feminine nouns personified as goddesses, e.g., Puraṁdhi "Plenty," Iḷā "Nourishment," Dhiṣaṇā "abundance"; (*c*) goddesses as wives of the great gods, as Indrāṇī, Varuṇānī and Agnāyī. The great gods are furnished with wives in order to make the parallel between the human race and the divine race complete.[17]

Sometimes these gods and goddesses are joined as dual divinities. This union of man and woman follows the primeval conception of the marriage of Heaven and Earth, Dyāus-Pṛithivī. Sometimes the names of two female deities are joined, such as "Naktā-Uṣasā, 'night and dawn.' " [18]

[17] Griswold, RRV, p. 103.

[18] *Ibid.*, p. 104.

In presenting some of the actual texts of Hinduism which bear upon the status of the "feminine," space permits only relatively few references despite the wealth of material. An endeavor has been made in this study to present a fair choice of passages of outstanding and typical character. At best we must realize that the meaning of some of this ancient literature must be conjectured. Portions of the material are so obscure that a uniform rendering of their meaning often is difficult and debatable. A single passage may be presented in different ways by various translators. Professor Louis H. Gray, of Columbia University, says that the Rig-Veda has been interpreted by

> . . . an elaborate commentary by Sāyaṇa, a South Indian scholar (latter half of 14th cent., A.D.), and in the earliest stage of European study of the Veda it was believed that it would be sufficient to translate the text according to this commentary—a process which is actually exhibited in the version by H. H. Wilson (London, 1866–88). There is, however, an earlier source in the *Nirukta* of Yāska, who was eighteen centuries prior to Sāyaṇa, and who not merely diverges from him, but declares that his own predecessors, whose works are no longer extant, differed both from himself and from each other. In other words, the meaning of a large number of Vedic words and passages was lost in India. This fact, together with the many contradictions found in Sāyaṇa's commentary, led R. Roth to urge that the Rigveda must be explained from itself, together with the assistance furnished by comparative philology and the closely cognate language of the Avesta. The results of this method are admirably presented in the translation by H. Grassmann (Leipzig, 1876–77). Yet, if the "traditional" school inclined to one extreme, the "linguistic" school inclined to the other. The result was a growing conviction that the golden mean should be followed, and on this basis A. Ludwig retranslated the Rigveda (Prague, 1876–88), not disregarding the native commentaries of Yāska and Sāyaṇa, and at the same time taking into account the data afforded by comparative philology, etc. Some scholars, however, have not been satisfied with this general principle, and have sought to interpret the Rigveda along other lines. Thus A. Bergaigne explained practically the entire text allegorically (cf. his *Religion védique,* Paris, 1878–83), and his pupil, P. Regnaud (*Le Rig-Véda,* Paris, 1892), endeavoured to prove that the whole Rigveda was composed for the sacrificial ritual. On the other hand, an "Indian" school arose, headed by R. Pischel and

K. Geldner, who, in their *Vedische Studien* (Stuttgart, 1889–1901), maintain that the Veda is to be interpreted from the India of the classical period, a round millennium later. Both the "ritual" and the "Indian" schools have a certain justification: some Vedic verses may well have been composed for the liturgy, and, even where this is not the case, the ritual use of Vedic passages may assist in casting light upon the meaning attributed to them (whether rightly or wrongly). . . . Curiously enough comparative religion has thus far played little part in Vedic interpretation, though its importance has been recognized by H. Oldenberg (*Religion des Veda,* Berlin, 1894, pp. 33–38), and has been sanely applied by L. von Schroeder in his *Mysterium und Mimus in Rigveda* (Leipzig, 1908).[19]

H. D. Griswold points out that

Dayānand Sarasvatī built upon the theistic element in the Ṛv. . . . Brunnhofer . . . lays hold of the fact that the roots of the Ṛv. run deep into the Indo-Iranian period. It is for him almost as much an Indo-Iranian as an Indian book. Hillebrandt . . . stresses the importance of the later Vedic ritual for understanding the Ṛv. Macdonell and Keith cherish well-balanced views on Vedic topics.[20]

Thus we note the various points of view that Rigvedic exegesis has taken. Griswold points out the fact that the tendency of the best modern Vedic scholarship is "to emphasize the largeness of the context in which the Ṛigveda is to be set and studied." [21]

Thus it happens that sometimes translators will use an allegorical method of interpretation; at other times a mystical suggestion; or again a more literal rendering. The reader also must remember that in attempting to convey Vedic thought in a foreign language often adequate words are lacking to express a particular idea. So even at best it must be borne in mind that many a stanza of this early literature is problematical—one paraphrase being perhaps as likely as another. As much critical examination as possible must be used upon the translations. The very Hindu scriptures warn of the difficulties in interpretation of religious books. In discussing metaphysical doctrine with Hari, who is called "the lord and spiritual guide of the wise," [22] Siva says: "People differ in com-

[19] Gray, article "Interpretation (Vedic and Avesta)," in Hastings, *Encyclopaedia of Religion and Ethics,* VII, 395–96.

[20] Griswold, RRV, pp. 77, 78.

[21] *Ibid.,* p. 79.

[22] Sen, tr., *Brahma-Vaivarta Purāṇa* (Kṛiṣṇa Janma-Khaṇḍa, 43.34–45), II, 292.

mentaries or interpretations of all religious books." (Brahma-Vaivarta Purāṇa, Kṛiṣṇa Janma-Khaṇḍa, 43.79–90; Sen, II, 295).

Let us consider now some of the Vedic feminine divinities. First let us take Aditi. This goddess expresses the personified conception of boundless freedom.[23] She is supposed to free those who worship her from sin and suffering. She is the mother of the world, or of common nature. The Ādityas are her sons.

> She is asked for light (R.V.4.25.3); her imperishable light is celebrated (R.V.7.82.10); and Dawn is called "the face of Aditi" (R.V.1.113.19). This is the aspect of Aditi which Hillebrandt makes central—Aditi as the light of day in its boundlessness and imperishability. . . . Max Müller thought of Aditi as the unlimited expanse of space visible to the eye, and Roth as the boundlessness of the sky as opposed to the finite earth. [24]

Aditi also seems to be identified with the earth. Pischel thinks of Aditi as "the inexhaustibly creative and generous one." [25] Aditi also stands "for universal nature in a Pantheistic sense." [26] A. A. Macdonell says that "the goddess Aditi is identified with all the deities, with men, with all that has been and shall be born, with air, and heaven (R.V.1.89)." [27] All the Vedic references to Aditi are filled with praise and show no slander upon this feminine divinity. The poetic imagination of the Vedic poets describes Aditi in words such as the following:

> May Aditi welcome, even as a mother, her dear heart-gladdening son, my song that lauds her. R.V.5.42.2.[28]

> . . . Aditi, good to all men. R.V.7.10.4.

> May Goddess Aditi assign us riches. R.V.7.40.2.

> Divine and foeless Aditi quickly listens. R.V.7.40.4.

> Aditi, guard our herd by day, by night; Aditi, free from guile!
> Aditi, ever strengthening, save us from grief!

---

[23] See Oldenberg, *Die Religion des Veda,* pp. 203–7; Macdonell, *Vedic Mythology,* p. 122; Schroeder, *Arische Religion,* I, 295–407.

[24] Griswold, RRV, p. 145.

[25] *Ibid.*

[26] *Ibid.*

[27] Macdonell, HSL, p. 70.

[28] Unless otherwise stated, the translations of the Vedas are by R. T. H. Griffith, a former principal of Benares College in India: *The Hymns of the Rigveda; The Texts of the White Yajurveda; The Hymns of the Sāmaveda;* and *The Hymns of the Atharva-veda.*

And in the day our hymn is this: May Aditi come nigh to help!
With loving-kindness bring us weal, and chase our foes!

R.V.8.18.6,7.

And thee too, O Great Aditi, thee also, Goddess, I address,
Thee very gracious to assist!
Save us in depth and shallow from the foe, thou Mother of Strong Sons!
Let no one of our seed be harmed!
Far-spread, wide-ruling, grant that we, unharmed by envy, may expand!
Grant that our progeny may live!

R.V.8.56.10–12.

In Book 4, Hymn 18, Griffith states that Indra, Aditi, and Vāmadeva are said to be the *ṛishis* or seers as well as the deities of the hymn, since it consists of conversation in which all bear part. In Book 6 Aditi is referred to as the "mother of Indra" (R.V.6.20.8).

The White Yajur-Veda likewise praises Aditi:

We call to succour us the mighty Mother of those whose sway is just, the the Queen of Order,
Strong ruler, far-expanding, ne'er decaying, Aditi, gracious guide, and good protectress.

W.Y.V.21.5.

The Black Yajur-Veda says:

Then may we, O Āditya, in thy rule,
Be guiltless before Aditi.[29]

B.Y.V.1.5.11.k; Keith, HOS, XVIII, 82.

The tone of the Atharva-Veda likewise is reverent toward Aditi and indeed shows the importance of this goddess. We find verses such as the following:

Aditi is the sky and air's mid-region. Aditi is the father, son and mother;
Aditi, all the Gods and the Five Nations.

We call for help the Queen of Law and Order, great mother of all those whose ways are righteous,
Far-spread, unwasting, strong in her dominion,—Aditi, wisely leading, well protecting!

29 Keith, tr., *The Veda of the Black Yajus School, entitled Taittiriya Sanhita,* "Harvard Oriental Series," Vols. XVIII, XIX.

Let us bring hither, in pursuit of riches, Aditi with our word, the Mighty Mother,
Her in whose lap the spacious air is lying. May she afford us triply-guarding shelter!

A.V.7.6.1,2,4.

Pṛithivī, the earth, is highly lauded in the Rig-Veda. A. A. Macdonell states: "She quickens the soil, for she scatters rain, and the showers of heaven are shed from the lightning of her cloud. She is great (*mahī*), firm (*dṛḷhā*) and shining (*arjunī*). . . . Pṛithivī is spoken of as 'kindly Mother Earth' (10.18.10)." [30] The Atharva-Veda contains sixty-three passages in praise of this goddess. The following will give an idea of the temper of these lines:

May she whose heart is in the highest heaven, compassed about with truth, and everlasting,—
May she, this Earth, bestow upon us lustre, and grant us power in loftiest dominion! . . .

Kind, ever gracious be the Earth we tread on,—the firm Earth, Pṛithivī, borne up by Order, mother of plants and herbs, the all-producer.

May that Earth grant us breath and vital power! Pṛithivī, give me life of long duration! . . .

Be gracious unto us, O Earth! Let not the robbers find us! Keep the deadly weapon far away! . . .

Earth! may thy summer and thy rains and autumn, thy winter and thy dewy frosts and springtime,—
May thy years, Pṛithivī! and ordered seasons and day and night pour out for us abundance! . . .

May she, the Earth, assign to us the opulence for which we yearn! . . .

O Earth, my Mother! set thou me happily in a place secure! A.V.12.1.8, 17,22,32,36,40,63.

Griswold points out that in the Rig-Veda

Dyāus "Heaven" is celebrated in six hymns in conjunction with Pṛithivī "Earth," the two appearing in the dual compound *Dyāvāpṛithivī* "Heaven and Earth." Dyāus apart from Pṛithivī has not a single hymn in his

[30] Macdonell, VM, p. 88.

honour, in this respect falling behind the lady Earth, who is celebrated alone in one hymn. . . . In their majesty . . . they are like two proud fair women. As parents, they protect all creatures and bestow treasures, fame and dominion.[31]

Griswold further states that "the conception of the parenthood of Heaven and Earth is very ancient and widespread, being found in the mythology of many peoples. . . . As in Hebrew thought heaven and earth embrace the universe, so in Vedic thought they are the two world-halves that comprehend everything." [32]

Another deity frequently mentioned in the Vedas is Sarasvatī. In the minds of the poets of the Vedas, Macdonell tells us that Sarasvatī is associated always with the river. "She is the best of Mothers, of rivers, and of goddesses (R.V.2.41.16). . . . She is invoked to descend from the sky, from the great mountain, to the sacrifice (R.V.5.43.11). . . . She is called *asuryā* or divine (R.V. 7.96.1). . . . She herself is a purifier [R.V.vii.45.2]. . . . She stimulates, directs and prospers the devotions of her worshippers (R.V.1.3.10,11; 2.3.8; 6.61.4). . . . To her worshippers she affords protection, and conquers their enemies (R.V.7.95.4,5; 2.30. 8; 6.49.7)." [33] Anyone who has lived in India can understand readily the praise and devotion which the early dwellers of this land might feel toward the life-giving power of a river, for upon the supply of water depended their very existence.

Wealthy in spoil, enriched with hymns, may bright Sarasvatī desire,
With eager love, our sacrifice!
Inciter of all pleasant songs, inspirer of all gracious thought,
Sarasvatī accept our rite!
Sarasvatī, the mighty flood,—she with her light illuminates,
She brightens every pious thought.

R.V.1.3.10–12.

May Sarasvatī, auspicious, grant felicity! R.V.1.89.3.

Best Mother, best of Rivers, best of Goddesses, Sarasvatī,
We are, as 'twere, of no repute. Dear Mother, give thou us renown!
In thee, Sarasvatī, divine, all generations have their stay.

R.V.2.41.16.

---

[31] Griswold, RRV, pp. 98, 99.
[32] *Ibid.,* pp. 99, 102.
[33] Macdonell, VM, pp. 86, 87.

Sarasvatī with speech was a Physician. W.Y.V.19.12.

Vāc, the goddess of speech and eloquence, and symbol of the potency of the magic word, later was identified with Sarasvatī. In the Atharva-Veda (4.1.2), we find:

Let this Queen come in front, her Father's daughter, found in the worlds for earliest generations. [Griffith note: "*This Queen:* Vāk, Speech personified, the Word, the first creation and representative of Spirit, and the means of communication between men and Gods. *For earliest generation:* in Rigveda 10.125.7,8, Vāk is represented as saying that she brings forth the Father, that is, Heaven the father of all things, and that she holds together all existence. Similarly, the Logos, the Word 'was in the beginning' and 'all things were made by him' (St. John 1.1)." I, 129.]

The Waters are thought of as young women, celestial daughters, wives, and mothers. They are beseeched for their precious fluid, as they are supposed to bring ghee, milk, and honey. They are called "wealth giving," because they fertilize the earth and cause plentiful harvests. They are represented as delighting the gods and thus causing them to grant favors. Also the Waters have the power to grant boons.

I call the Waters, Goddesses, wherein our cattle quench their thirst!
Oblations to the Streams be given.

Amrit is in the Waters. In the Waters there is healing balm.
Be swift, ye Gods, to give them praise.

Within the Waters—Soma thus hath told me—dwell all balms that heal,
And Agni, he who blesseth all. The Waters hold all medicines.

O Waters, teem with medicine to keep my body safe from harm,
So that I long may see the Sun!

Whatever sin is found in me, whatever evil I have wrought,
If I have lied or falsely sworn, Waters, remove it far from me.

R.V.1.23.18–22.

Kind be the Goddesses to lend us help! . . .
May their streams bring us health and wealth!

S.V.1.1.3.13.

With regard to these goddesses, Macdonell says that "the divine Waters bear away defilement, and are even invoked to cleanse from moral guilt, the sins of violence, cursing and lying. They bestow remedies, healing, long life, and immortality." [34]

Another important goddess in the Vedas is Uṣas, the dawn, a "personification of one of the most radiant phenomena." [35] She is characterized as a charming lady. Uṣas appears in the eastern sky in delicate beauty. She is transparent. Uṣas has many lovers—Agni, Sūrya, Pūṣan, and the Aśvins. Griswold points out that "Uṣas is the daughter of Dyāus, the sister of Bhaga, the kinswoman of Varuṇa, and the wife (or mistress) of Sūrya." [36] Indra has been characterized as a Kshatriya lord; in like manner Uṣas has been considered as representing a Kshatriya lady. Uṣas also is supposed to dispose of night and to make evil spirits disappear. It is she who prepares an entrance to heaven. She is the goddess Bounty, who lights the sky so that treasures may be found. Uṣas is believed to be immortal. She is associated with the duration and measurement of time, that is, with the notion of past, present, and future. Griswold states that

> Uṣas as regularly appearing in the east is an expression of *ṛita* in the sense of "cosmic order." . . . She is an expression also of "ritualistic order." As preceding the gods of light, Agni, Sūrya, Savitar, etc., Uṣas is called "the mother of the gods" (R.V.1.113.19).[37]

From this point of view, she is also said to have generated Sun, sacrifice, and Agni (R.V.7.78.3). Grace and attractiveness belong to Uṣas. Certainly in the representation of this goddess the early poets have given us imagery of unsurpassed natural beauty. Professor R. E. Hume states that "the most beautiful odes to the dawn in any literature are those in the Sanskrit language, now to be found in the Rig Veda." [38]

> This Lady, giver of delight, after her Sister shining forth, Daughter of
> Heaven, hath shown herself. . . .
> O Dawn, thou rulest over wealth.
> Thinking of thee, O Joyous One, as her who driveth hate away,
> We woke to meet thee with our lauds.

---

[34] Macdonell, HSL, p. 92.
[35] Griswold, RRV, p. 244.
[36] *Ibid.*, p. 105.
[37] *Ibid.*, pp. 252, 253.
[38] Hume, chairman's address at the World Congress of Faiths, Cambridge, 1938, in *The Renascence of Religion*, p. 136.

Our eyes behold thy blessed rays, like troops of cattle loosed to feed.
Dawn hath filled full the wide expanse.
When thou hast filled it, Fulgent One! thou layest bare the gloom with light.
After thy nature aid us, Dawn!
Thou overspreadest heaven with rays, the dear wide region of mid-air
With thy bright shining lustre, Dawn.

R.V.4.52.1–7.

In addition to the goddesses so far mentioned, there are numerous others in the Vedic pantheon. For instance, there are verses to goddesses having a natural basis such as Rodasī, lightning personified as the wife of Rudra or the Maruts; Sūryā, the sun-maiden; the Apsarases or river goddesses, including Urvaśī; Sītā, furrow or husbandry personified; and Aranyāṇī, the spirit of the woodland. There are goddesses designated as wives of the gods, such as Aśvinī, the consort of the Aśvins; Śacī, might personified, consort of Indra; and Saraṇyū, the daughter of Tvaṣṭar, wife of Vivasvat. There are found also many abstract feminine nouns personified as goddesses, such as Aramati, the genius of devotion; Bhāratī, a goddess of prayer and worship; Rākā, the giver, a goddess of bounty; Svastī, goddess of welfare or prosperity; Ṣunritā, goddess of pleasantness and gladness; Hotrā, invocation personified; Varūtṛī, guardian goddess; Ṣansa, prayer or wish personified; Diti, plenty; Bṛihad Divā, the great goddess; and Śraddhā, faith. Sinīvālī, the goddess of Procreation, is said to be Indra's equal.

In the Vedic hymns goddesses are spoken of as most thoughtful, first of those who merit worship, the first creation and representative of Spirit, those who hold together all existence. Goddesses are prayed to as exalted heavenly ladies, as Heaven's mighty daughters, as blessed dames, and skillful goddesses. The Vedic Hindus called upon feminine deities to give strength, blessings, good gifts, lengthened days, wide pastures free from dangers, wealth in kine and horses, health, enjoyments, children, food, welfare for the people, wealth that makes for happiness—in short, all that the Vedic Hindus longed to possess. Goddesses were designated as teachers of the sons of men, eloquent, holy ones, immortal, heroic, pure, auspicious, those who must be honored, kind, lofty, fair, radiant, benevolent, lovely, opulent, queens of all that strengthens, divine, givers of power and life, the Logos, the Law's protectresses, and the mothers of the great gods.

Not only is Mother Earth spoken of as a goddess, but likewise Heaven, as in R.V. (3.54.7; and 5.19.4). In the A.V. (5.2.9) Heaven and Earth are referred to as two sisters. This appears to be the reference also in R.V. (3.54.7; 5.19.4; and 10.120.9). Heaven also is referred to as a mother in the A.V. (20.107.10) and possibly in the W.Y.V. (33.28). Similar references appear in R.V. (3.1.7; 3.2.2; 3.5.7; and 10.120.9). Hindus very definitely recognize the importance of the mother in the conception of deity.

In regard to the status of women in the earliest Vedas, there are many instances which would seem to suggest that monogamy was practiced. For instance, we find verses such as the following:

A wife is home and dwelling. R.V.3.53.4.

. . . like a loving matron for her husband. R.V.1.124.7.

Perfect, O Gods, the union of the wife and husband. R.V.10.85.23.

This shrine have we made ready for thy coming, as the fond dame attires her for her husband. R.V.4.3.2.

They anoint thee, (Agni), like a welcome friend with milk and butter, when thou makest husband and wife of one mind. Macdonald, R.V. 1.131.3; and also 5.3.2.[39]

The gambler's wife is left forlorn and wretched. The mother mourns the son who wanders homeless. R.V.10.34.10.

Sad is the gambler when he sees a matron, another's wife, and his well-ordered dwelling. R.V.10.34.11.

She never vexed me, nor was angry with me, but to my friends and me was ever gracious.
For the die's sake, whose single point is final, mine own devoted wife I alienated.
My wife holds me aloof. Her mother hates me. The wretched man finds none to give him comfort.
R.V.10.34.2,3. [Griffith note: "*Whose single point is final:* the speaker has apparently lost all by throwing aces." II, 429.]

---

[39] Macdonald, *The Vedic Religion,* p. 157.

"Play not with dice. No! Cultivate thy corn-land. Enjoy the gain; and deem that wealth sufficient.
There are thy cattle, there thy wife, O gambler." So this good Savitar himself hath told me.

R.V.10.34.13.

First have the liberal gained a fragrant dwelling, and got themselves a bride in fair apparel. R.V.10.107.9.

Agni hath given the bride again with splendour and with ample life.
Long-lived be he who is her lord. A hundred autumns let him live.
R.V.10.85.39.

Who shall divide the accordant wife and husband? R.V.10.95.12.

J. J. Meyer states that "the Veda knows nothing of any hetaerism," [40] and that "the Indo-Europeans evidently already had a well-ordered family life before their dispersal." [41] The *Vedic Index* states that although there is "abundant evidence that the standard of ordinary sexual morality was not high," [42] still the marriage tie was not lightly regarded. Griswold says that "monogamy was the rule." [43]

Despite verses which would seem to point toward monogamy, it is evident also that a Hindu could have more than one wife. The following lines from the Vedic scriptures substantiate this fact.

Like a King among his wives thou dwellest. R.V.7.18.2.

. . . as yearning wives cleave to their yearning husband. R.V.1.62.11.

. . . as wives embrace their lord. R.V.10.43.1.

. . . both wives of Kuyava. R.V.1.104.3.

Like rival wives on every side, enclosing ribs oppress me sore. R.V.1.105.8.

Indra hath taken and possessed all castles, like as one common husband doth his spouses. R.V.7.26.3.

Between both poles the car-horse goes pressed closely, as in his dwelling moves the doubly-wedded. R.V.10.101.11.

. . . the favourite wife neglected.
. . . the favourite wife most dearly loved.
A.V.20.128.10,11.

---

[40] Meyer, *Sexual Life in Ancient India,* I, 124.
[41] *Ibid.*
[42] Macdonell and Keith, V.I., I, 480.
[43] Griswold, RRV, p. 10.

A spell to rid a jealous wife of a rival is quoted below.

From out the earth I dig this plant, an herb of most effectual power,
Wherewith one quells the rival wife and gains the husband for oneself.

Auspicious, with expanded leaves, sent by the Gods, victorious plant,
Blow thou the rival wife away, and make my husband only mine!

Stronger am I, O stronger One, yea, mightier than the mightier;
And she who is my rival wife is lower than the lowest dame.

Her very name I utter not. She takes no pleasure in this man.
Far into distance most remote drive we the rival wife away!

R.V.10.145.1–4.

Nevertheless, despite these verses relating to polygamy, which lowered the status of women, on the whole it would seem as though the normal Vedic household had one husband and one wife. The *Vedic Index* says that "a Vedic Indian could have more than one wife . . . but the evidence points to the wife first wedded alone being a wife in the fullest sense." [44]

It is important also for us to note that a wife was on "a level of equality, at the hearth, which was the altar of sacrifice." [45] It was the wife's duty to prepare the sacred vessels. The piety and happiness of a married couple is noticeable in the lines from the Rig-Veda (8.31.5–9) quoted below.

O Gods, with constant draught of milk, husband and wife with one accord
Press out and wash the Soma juice.

They gain sufficient food. They come united to the sacred grass,
And never do they fail in strength.

Never do they deny or seek to hide the favour of the Gods.
They win high glory for themselves.

With sons and daughters by their side they reach their full extent of life,
Both decked with ornaments of gold.

Serving the Immortal One with gifts of sacrificial meal and wealth,
They satisfy the claims of love, and pay due honour to the Gods.

R.V.8.31.5–9.

Nigh they approached, one-minded, with their spouses, kneeling to him adorable, paid worship. R.V.1.72.5.

---

[44] Macdonell and Keith, V.I., I, 478.

[45] Macdonald, VR, p. 158.

Praiseworthy blessing hast thou laid upon the pair who with uplifted ladle serve thee, man and wife. R.V.1.83.3.

Couples desirous of thine aid are storming thee, pouring their presents forth to win a stall of kine, pouring gifts, Indra, seeking thee. R.V.1.131.3. [Griffith note: "*Couples:* sacrificers and their wives who are associated with them in offering oblations." I, 182.]

From olden time the matron goes to feast and general sacrifice. R.V. 10.86.10.

To this mine utterance, O ye men, give credence, what good the man and wife obtain by praying:
A manly son is born and gathers riches, and thrives forever sinless in the dwelling.

W.Y.V.8.5.

I cook the offering. I present oblation. Only my wife attends the holy service. A.V.12.3.47.

Rise to the altar. Bless this dame with offspring.
Promote this woman. Drive away the demons. . . .
Approach this woman here with store of cattle.
Together with the deities come to meet her. . . .
Fashioned at first by Right, set by the Spirit, this altar of Brahmaudana was appointed.
Place the pure boiler on it, woman! Set thou therein the rice-mess of Celestial Beings.

A.V.11.1.21,22,23.

According to Griffith's note, this prayer from the White Yajur-Veda was spoken by a woman:

Thou art our Father, Father-like regard us. Obeisance be to thee. Do not thou harm us.
May we, accompanied by Tvashṭar, win thee. Vouchsafe me sons and cattle. Grant us offspring. Safe may I be together with my husband. W.Y.V.37.20. [Griffith note: "*Accompanied by Tvashṭar:* favoured by the God who presides over procreation and the bestowing of children." Page 296.]

The Black Yajur-Veda contains another example of a prayer in which during the religious service the woman actually speaks.

I yoke thee with milk, with ghee;
I yoke thee with water, and plants;
I yoke thee with offspring;
Today being consecrated, do thou win strength for us,
Let the lady of holy power advance,
Let her sit on the altar with fair colour;
Then may I, full of desire,
Enter my own place, here.
With fair offspring, with noble husbands,
We are come to thee,
O Agni, to thee that deceivest the foe,
The undeceivable, we that are not deceived.
I loosen this bond of Varuṇa
Which Savitṛ, the kindly, hath bound,
And in the birthplace of the creator, in the place of good action,
I make it pleasant for me with my husband.

B.Y.V.iii.5.6.a–e; Keith, HOS, XVIII, 283.

The Atharva-Veda, Book 12, Hymn 3, is a prayer accompaniment during the preparation and presentation of sacrificial offerings to the gods by a householder and his wife, with prayer for prosperity and happiness on earth and in heaven. In this hymn we find passages such as the following:

Whate'er thy wife, away from thee, makes ready, or what, O wife, apart from thee, thy husband,
Combine it all! Let it be yours in common, while ye produce one world with joint endeavour.
All these now dwelling on the earth, mine offspring, these whom this woman here, my wife, hath borne me,—
Invite them all unto the vessel. Knowing their kinship the children have met together.

A.V.12.3.39,40.

Although women seem to have been on a level of equality at the hearth, it will be noted that while sons are prayed for, daughters are not. It is stated in the Black Yajur-Veda (i.i.6.4) that the birth of a daughter may be avoided by not spreading a bunch of sacrificial grass in all directions.[46] There is no intercession made for daughters.

[46] Keith, tr., B.Y.V., HOS, XVIII, 211.

There are passages in the Vedas which show that the Aryans did not have always the highest opinion of woman. The following is

. . . the highest praise which the *Ṛishi* Ṣyāvāṣwa could give to a queen, his greatest benefactor, who had not only treated him with reverence, but had given him a herd of cattle, and costly ornaments, and put him in the way of obtaining the woman on whom he had set his heart.[47]

Ṣasīyasī, though a female, is more excellent than a man who reverences not the gods, nor bestows wealth. R.V.5.61.6; Wilson, III, 344, 345.

Verse 17 of Rig-Veda 8.33, says:

The mind of woman brooks not discipline,

Her intellect hath little weight.

R.V.8.33.17.

We also find the following statement in the Rig-Veda.

With women there can be no lasting friendship; hearts of hyenas are the hearts of women. R.V.10.95.15.

To a person who has observed Indian life closely it is apparent that probably there is no other land where marriage so completely occupies the activities of the people. The Hindu parents plan for the marriage of their child even from its birth. It is important, then, that we note the earliest references to marriage in the scriptures. On the whole, in Vedic days there seems to have been

. . . considerable freedom on the part of both man and woman in selecting a wife or a husband. At any rate, it is not clear that either the father or the mother controlled the marriage of son or daughter of mature age, though no doubt the parents or parent often arranged a suitable match. The marriage was frequently arranged through an intermediary, the "wooer" (*vara*) presumably after those concerned had in effect come to an agreement.[48] (R.V.10.78,4; 10.85.15,23).

With forelock loosened o'er his brow, here comes the wooer of the bride,
Seeking a husband for this maid, a wife for this unmarried man.
Wooer! This girl hath toiled in vain, going to others' marriages.
Now to her wedding, verily, wooer! another maid shall come.

[47] Macdonald, VR, p. 165.
[48] Macdonell and Keith, V.I., I, 482; see also II, 244.

Dhātar upholds the spacious earth, upholds the sky, upholds the sun.
Dhātar bestow upon this maid a husband suited to her wish.

A.V.6.60.1–3.

In the following references we see that sometimes dowries were given. Especially it was certain that dowries would be given when girls "suffered from bodily defects," as the Vedic Index states.

How many a maid is pleasing to the suitor who fain would marry for her splendid riches? R.V.10.27.12.

No lovely wife who brings her dower in hundreds rests upon his bed. A.V.5.17.12.

. . . like a bride dowered by her sire. R.V.9.46.2.

The sale of a daughter was not unknown. In the Rig-Veda there is a passage which possibly refers to a brother's giving a dowry in order to get a husband for his sister. However, discredit seems to have been attached to such a practice.

For I have heard that ye give wealth more freely than worthless son-in-law or spouse's brother. R.V.1.109.2.

From the *Vedic Index* we learn: "Occasionally marriages by capture may have taken place, but only as knightly feats, as when Vimada carried off Purumitra's daughter against her father's wish, but very possibly with her own consent." [49]

Ye, mounted on your chariot, brought to Vimada the comely maid of Purumitra as a bride. R.V.10.39.7.

Marriage celebrations are very happily described in the Vedas.

Tvashṭar prepares the bridal of his daughter. All the world hears the tidings and assembles. R.V.10.17.1.

Here it was that the bridegroom with his relatives and friends appeared to meet those of the bride.

As maidens deck themselves with gay adornment to join the bridal feast, I now behold them. R.V.4.58.9.

Agni hath given the bride with splendour and with ample life. R.V. 10.85.39.

---

[49] Macdonell and Keith, V.I., I, 482–83.

We see that the bridegroom grasps the bride's hand and leads her in expectation of long and happy unity.

I take thy hand in mine for happy fortune, that thou mayst reach old age with me thy husband.
Gods, Aryaman, Bhaga, Savitar, Purandhi, have given thee to be my household's mistress.

R.V.10.85.36.

I place upon the lap of Earth the Goddess, a firm auspicious stone to bring thee children.
Stand on it, thou, greeted with joy, resplendent! A long, long life may Savitar vouchsafe thee!

As Agni in the olden time took the right hand of this our Earth,
Even so, I take and hold thy hand.

A.V.14.1.47,48.

Sweet are the glances of our eyes! Our faces are as smooth as balm!
Within thy bosom harbour me. One spirit dwell in both of us!
A.V.7.36. [Griffith note: "A charm to be pronounced by bride and bridegroom." I, 343.]

When the festivities are over, bride and bridegroom go to the latter's home in an elaborate marriage procession.

Thought was the pillow of her couch. Sight was the unguent for her eyes.
Her treasury was earth and heaven, when Sūryā went unto her Lord.

Hymns were the cross-bars of the pole. Kurīra-metre decked the car.
The bridesmen were the Aśvin Pair. Agni was leader of the train.
R.V.10.85.7,8.

Her spirit was the bridal car. The covering thereof was heaven.
Bright were both steers that drew it, when Sūryā approached her husband's home.

R.V.10.85.10.[50]

Certainly the new wife's position within the joint-family system was secure. The marriage ceremony presents the high status of the bride.

[50] For a more detailed account of the early Vedic wedding, see Zimmer, *Altindisches Leben,* pp. 310–14. Also see Hillebrandt, *Ritual-Litteratur, Vedische Opfer und Zauber, Hochzeit,* pp. 63–68; Das, *Ṛgvedic Culture, Wedding Rites,* pp. 370–84.

Over thy husband's father and thy husband's mother bear full sway.
Over the sister of thy lord, over his brothers rule supreme.
R.V.10.85.46.

The same verse recurs with slight verbal variations in A.V. (14. 1.44). Thus it is evident that the wife was not an object of subjection in the new home, but was afforded an equal status, indeed, one of high importance. In his summary of the Vedic ideal of marriage, the former curator of the Government Oriental Library at Mysore, Pandit Mahadeva Sastri, a Sanskrit scholar of the highest order, has declared that "the marriage relation should be entered into by a man and a woman at a mature age, when they may be fully alive to the responsibilities of the householder's life, both of them having been duly educated for a proper discharge of their duties."[51]

In the Rig-Veda the happy results of marriage are frequently set forth. The joy of sons and grandsons is pictured. The Vedic Hindu speaks of his wife and sons as God-given.

Agni hath bestowed on me riches and sons and this my spouse.
Be ye not parted. Dwell ye here. Reach the full time of human life.
With sons and grandsons sport and play, rejoicing in your own abode.
R.V.10.85.41,42.

O Dawn, enriched with ample wealth, bestow on us the wondrous gift
Wherewith we may support children and children's sons.
R.V.1.92.13.

O Bounteous Indra, make this bride blest in her sons and fortunate!
Vouchsafe to her ten sons! And make her husband the eleventh man.
R.V.10.85.45.

The desire for sons was voiced in such words as the following:

Vouchsafe blessing upon the wombs that bring male children forth. R.V. 10.63.15.

Prepare accordantly the mother for the infant's birth.
On the right way bring forth the boy. Make him come hither. I am here.
The Amulet which Aditi wore when desirous of a son,
Tvashṭar hath bound upon this dame and said, "Be mother of a boy."
A.V.6.81.1–3.

---

[51] Sastri, *The Vedic Law of Marriage*, p. 18.

O Dhātar, Thou Disposer, lay within the body of this dame
A male germ with the noblest form, for her, in the tenth month, to bear.
A.V.5.25.10.

I with my thought have commerced with divine far-sighted Dakshiṇā.
Steal not my life; I will not thine. May I, O Goddess, in thy sight find for myself a hero son.
W.Y.V.4.23.

May he come forth alive, unharmed, yea, living from the living dame. R.V.5.78.9.

In the Atharva-Veda (6.17.2–4) we read how the Mother Earth conceived the germ of all the things that be, the stately forest trees, the mountains, and the hills. Even so, it is prayed that the germ of life shall be productive in a woman that she may bear a son.

On the failure to produce natural children, "adoption was possible." [52] However, that practice does not seem to have been always in favor. The following lines in the Rig-Veda appear to condemn the usage:

Agni, no son is he who springs from others. Lengthen not out the pathways of the foolish.

Unwelcome for adoption is the stranger, one to be thought of as another's offspring, R.V.7.4.7,8.

So important was it for a father to have a son that it was possible for the father who had a daughter, but no sons, to appoint the daughter's son to "perform his funeral rites." [53]

Wise, teaching, following the thought of Order, the sonless gained a grandson from his daughter. R.V.3.31.1.

This practice also seemed to account for the difficulty of the brotherless maiden in finding a husband. There was always the possibility that the maiden's father would desire her children to be his heirs.

Also it is recognized that a brother may beget children "with the wife of a dead man, or perhaps of a man who is childless (R.V. 10.40.2). . . . Sonlessness (*avīratā*) is placed on the same level

[52] Macdonell and Keith, V.I., I, 528; see also lengthy discussion in Zimmer, AIL, p. 318.

[53] Griffith, R.V., I, 347 *n*.

as lack of property (*amati*), and Agni is besought to protect from it." [54] "Give us not up to indigence, Agni, nor want of hero sons" (R.V.3.16.5). With regard to the complicated question of adopting a son, there is a lengthy discussion in Julius Jolly's *Recht und Sitte,* where it is suggested that the treasuring of the male descendants was in order to create a large class of workers. To the man, as the possessor of the wife, belonged the possession of the children, even though he was not their father. A man could adopt strange children and become their father protector. Authorities cannot agree as to just where each son should be placed in the line of inheritance. By all authorities, however, the first blood son is placed at the head. Jolly points out that to the Hindus adoption is a serious matter—a relationship not to be entered into lightly, but according to holy ceremonies. The son must be made as one of the family's own, resembling the real son.[55] The *Vedic Index* points out that adoption sometimes was resorted to not only "when natural children existed, but when it was desired to secure the presence in the family of a person of specially high qualifications." [56]

According to the following verses the birth of a daughter was not desired:

> Preserve the babe at birth! Make not the boy a female child. A.V.8.6.25.
>
> Elsewhere may he effect the birth of maids, but here prepare a boy. A.V. 6.11.3.

Heinrich Zimmer says that nowhere in the Vedic songs do we find a wish for a daughter.[57] It might be suggested that the literature of nearly all other peoples has shown lack of desire for female children. Before the advent of Mohammed the Arabs are reported to have buried female children alive.[58] It must be said in favor of the Vedic Hindu that there are no proofs that the exposure of female children was regularly practiced.

However, A. A. Macdonell points out that "the Yajur-Veda

[54] Macdonell and Keith, V.I., I, 487.
[55] Jolly, RS, p. 74.
[56] Macdonell and Keith, V.I., I, 528; see also Zimmer, AIL, p. 318.
[57] Zimmer, AIL, p. 319.
[58] Hauri, *Der Islam,* p. 8; see also list of references in Meyer, SLAI, I, 6.

speaks of girls being exposed when born." [59] Farquhar also reminds us that "since the father was supreme, and since every family wanted sons, there was a tendency to set less value on woman. In consequence, many girl babies were exposed or put to death in every race practising ancestor-worship." [60] In the creative period of the Vedas, Farquhar draws the conclusion, "Like most primitive peoples, they practised the exposure of girl children and old people." [61] We know also that this custom existed down to 1830, because from that date onward, "a steady persistent crusade was carried on against female infanticide by the Government of India." [62]

The Vedas disclose very little concerning the care of a child, despite the fact that progeny was so highly prized. No doubt, the mother took care of the children. Surely the fact that children grew up at all amid the hazards of primitive life suggests that the mother must have exercised wise care. One could wish that more descriptions of this plain living had been recorded. However, we do find a few verses such as the following, which show a mother's tender touch:

Savitar covers both all-fostering worlds with praises, even as a woman cherishes her children. R.V.3.38.8.

Even as a mother to her sons, be gracious. A.V.6.30.3.

Let Mitra guard him, as a kind mother guards the son she nurses. A.V. 2.28.1.

Let women and their sons be friendly-minded. A.V.3.4.3.

O Aśvins, give me your aid, as sire and mother aid their son. R.V.10.39.6; see also W.Y.V.20.77.

In the Atharva-Veda (6.140) is a homely prayer for the safe cutting of a child's first teeth:

Two tigers have grown up who long to eat the mother and the sire:
Soothe, Brahmaṇaspati, and thou, O Jātavedas, both these teeth.
Let rice and barley be your food, eat also beans and sesamum.
This is the share allotted you, to be your portion, ye two Teeth. Harm not your mother and your sire.

[59] Macdonell, HSL, p. 163.
[60] Farquhar, PH, p. 18.
[61] *Ibid.*, p. 22.
[62] *Ibid.*, p. 165.

Both fellow teeth have been invoked, gentle and bringing happiness.
Elsewhither let the fierceness of your nature turn away, O Teeth! Harm not your mother or your sire.

A.V.6.140.1–3.

The son is instructed not to harm his mother or father, as follows:

When grown in strength, let him not wound his father, nor disregard his mother. A.V.6.110.3.

The father in the Rig-Veda would seem to stand for all that is good and kind. Certainly there is no indication that a father exercised cruel subjection over his wife and daughters.

O Mighty Indra, with sweetest song I grasp thy garment's hem, as a child grasps his father's. R.V.3.53.2.

When at the coming of the rains, the water has poured upon them as they yearned and thirsted,
One seeks another as he talks and greets him with cries of pleasure, as a son his father.

R.V.7.103.3.

A father guards his son. W.Y.V.35.17.

. . . like a son cherished in his father's house. R.V.8.19.27.

In the early Aryan family the members were bound together in a strong relationship. The father (*pitṛ*) was the protector and supplied the food, while the mother was the meter-out (*mātṛ*) of daily nourishment. Many are the lines suggesting tender family feeling. Some of the Vedic deities are worshipped as mother and father.

With care and marvels the Ṛibhus had done proper service to assist their Parents. R.V.4.33.2.

They made their Parents, who were lying like posts that moulder, young again forever. R.V.4.33.3.

O Goddess Earth . . . Thou art a celestial design. W.Y.V.11.68,69.

Ye, Mothers, have a hundred homes; yea, and a thousand are your growths.
Do ye, who have a thousand powers, free this my patient from disease.
Be glad and joyful in the plants, both blossoming and bearing fruit,

Plants that will lead us to success, like mares who conquer in the race.
Plants, by this name I speak to you, Mothers, to you the Goddesses.
W.Y.V.12.76,77.

May the Wind waft to us that pleasant medicine. May Earth our Mother give it, and our Father Heaven. W.Y.V.25.17.

Heaven and Earth cling close. . . .
As sire and mother to their child.
W.Y.V.33.67.

Well be it with our mother and father! Well be it with our cows and beasts and people! A.V.1.31.4.

The Vedas give us a picture of a Hindu woman's house. Various parts of the house and its appurtenances are mentioned; for example: wickerwork (*akṣu*); fireplace (*āṣṭrī*); pillow (*upabarhana*); pillar (*upamit*); coverlet (*upavāsana*); fire tongs (*dhṛṣṭi*); side post (*pakṣa*); women's quarters (*patnīnāṃ sadas*); roof (*chandas*); grass thatch (*tṛṇa*); bed (*talpa*); door (*dur*); doorpost (*durya*); hall (*prācīnavaṃśa*); bench (*proṣṭha*); and couch (*śayana*). More important still, in constructing the picture of the Hindus of those days, we find many beautiful lines in praise of the spirit of the home.

The home on which the wanderer thinks, where cheerfulness and joy abound,—
We call the home to welcome us.
W.Y.V.3.42.

His home is like a lake with lotus-blossoms, like the Gods' palaces adorned and splendid. R.V.10.107.10.

Now Mitra, Varuṇa, Aryaman, vouchsafe us freedom and room for us and for our children! R.V.7.62.6.

To us who laud thee, Agni, bring fresh food and safe and happy homes. R.V.5.6.8.

May he prosper our home! R.V.4.53.7.

Also through their own right the heroes have grown strong, and dwell in safe and happy homes. R.V.7.74.6.

Safe may we be until we reach our homes, and rest us, and unyoke. R.V. 3.53.20.

He [Indra] is like home, like sweet and fair nutrition. R.V.4.16.15.

May he, Sūrya, the Sage, self-excellent, grant us a sheltering home, a house that wards the fierce heat off on every side. R.V.5.44.7.

Queen of the Home! Thou, sheltering, kindly goddess, wast stablished by the gods in the beginning.
Clad in thy robe of grass, be friendly-minded, and give us wealth with goodly men about us.
A.V.3.12.5. [Griffith note: "*Queen of the Home:* the female deity who presides over house-building, and who was originally commissioned by the Gods to instruct men in this art." I, 98.]

May all our hopes' fulfillment guard this dwelling. A.V.3.12.8.

Grass-covered, clad with straw, the house, like Night, gives rest to man and beast.
Thou standest, built upon the earth, like a she-elephant, borne on feet. A.V.9.3.17. [Griffith note: "*Borne on feet:* the four corner pillars representing the elephant's legs." I, 437.]

Freedom from hate I bring you, concord and unanimity.
Love one another, as the cow loveth the calf that she hath borne.
One-minded with his mother, let the son be loyal to his sire.
Let the wife, calm and gentle, speak words sweet as honey to her lord.
No brother hate his brother. No sister to sister be unkind.
Unanimous, with one intent, speak ye your speech in friendliness.
That spell through which Gods sever not, nor ever bear each other hate,—
That spell we lay upon your home, a bond of union for the men.
Intelligent, submissive, rest united, friendly and kind, bearing the yoke together.
Come, speaking sweetly each one to the other. I make you one-intentioned and one-minded.
Let what you drink, your share of food, be common. Together with one common bond I bind you.
Serve Agni, gathered round him like the spokes about the chariot nave.
With binding charm I make you all united, obeying one sole leader and one-minded.
Even as the gods who watch and guard the Amrit, at morn and eve may ye be kindly-hearted.
A.V.3.30.1–7. [Griffith note: "The hymn is a prayer or charm to secure love and concord in a family." I, 125–26.]

In a hymn which invokes a benediction upon the completion of a new house is found the following prayer for the fulfillment of all hopes:

We loose the bands of thy bamboos, of bolts, of fastening, of thatch,
We loose the ties of thy side-posts, O House that holdest all we prize.
We loosen here the ties and bands of straw in bundles, and of clamps,
Of all that compasses and binds the Lady Genius of the Home.
We loose the loops which men have bound within thee, loops to tie and hold.
Be gracious, when erected, to our bodies, Lady of the Home.
Store-house of Soma, Agni's hall, the ladies' bower, the residence,
The seat of Gods art thou, O Goddess House.

A.V.9.3.4–7.

The love of children is rooted deeply in the Hindu's nature, and it is gratifying to note that sometimes the Vedic Hindu actually prays for children rather than only for sons.

Vouchsafe us freedom and room for us and for our children. R.V.7.62.6.

In the following hymn protection is invoked for a man's wife and children:

Guard on all sides this woman! Guard my children, us, and all our wealth!
Let not malignity o'ercome, nor adversaries conquer us.

A.V.2.7.4.

There is no trace in the Rig-Veda that women were secluded as inferiors. The *Vedic Index* says that "the maiden may be assumed to have grown up in her father's house . . . sharing in the work of the house." [63] She is believed to have mingled freely with the youth of the village.

The *Vedic Index* also states that "women did not go to the Sabhā [assembly], for they were, of course, excluded from political activity." [64] In regard to the assembly, in a love charm in the Atharva-Veda the maiden addresses the man she loves as follows:

I am speaker here, not thou. Speak thou where the Assembly meets. A.V. 7.38.4.

---

[63] Macdonell and Keith, V.I., II, 485.

[64] *Ibid.*, p. 427.

Yet "Assembly" is personified as Prajāpati's daughter. Also in A.V. (8.10) the poet identifies Virāj with Vāc, the Word, and speaks of Virāj as entering the assembly. In this hymn the poet states that:

He who knows this becomes polite and courtly; and people come as guests to his assembly. A.V.8.10.5.

Our knowledge of the legal position of daughters is scant. Brotherless maidens seem to have had a hard time of it. They were likely to be ruined physically, although the Rig-Veda states that religious terrors would await the man who took advantage of such a woman R.V. (4.5.5).

Those maidens . . . must now stand . . . reft of power, like sisters who are brotherless. A.V.1.17.1. [Griffith note: "*Brotherless:* unsupported and helpless, when their father is dead, and they have no brother on whom the duty of protecting and finding husbands for them would naturally devolve." I, 21.]

Macdonell and Keith summarize the dependent state of women in the Vedic documents:

Women could not take an inheritance, and were not independent persons in the eyes of the law, whether married or not. Presumably before marriage they lived on their parents or brothers, and after that on their husbands, while in the event of their husbands predeceasing them, their relatives took the property, burdened with the necessity of maintaining the wife. Their earnings would be appropriated by their nearest relative—usually father or brother—in the few cases in which unmarried women could earn anything, as in the case of courtezans. . . . If the father was dead or feeble, the sister was dependent on her brother and on his wife.[65]

The following verse gives us a picture of a home occupation in which the daughters of a family were engaged: "Their little maidens are at home, at home they wait upon the cows" (A.V.20.127.5).

The inclusive and authoritative thesaurus of primary material of the contents of the Vedas, Macdonell and Keith's *Vedic Index,* says that "there is . . . no evidence to show whether a son, when grown up, normally continued to stay with his father, his wife becoming a member of the father's household, or whether he set up a house of his own: probably the custom varied." [66]

[65] Macdonell and Keith, V.I., II, 486, 496.

[66] *Ibid.,* I, 527.

Macdonell and Keith state also that "adultery was generally regarded among Āryan peoples as a serious offense against the husband of the woman affected." [67] On the other hand, there are commentators who differ from this view. Weber [68] thinks there was indifference to adultery in Vedic times. Julius Jolly speaks of the tolerance of prostitution in the Vedas, but he also points out that this did not hinder the development of strict marriage laws.[69]

Incest was proposed to the deity Yama by his sister Yamī, as indicated in the legend in R.V. (10.10.1–14). From this reference, however, we see that incest was not approved. Zimmer believes that incest was not the custom.[70] In R.V. (10.162.5) reference to incest also was made. The *Vedic Index* states,

> Mention is further made in R.V.10.61.5–7, to the wedlock of Prajāpati and his daughter, which is, however, interpreted mythologically in the Brāhmaṇas (Aitareya Brāhmaṇa 3.33; Śatapatha Brāhmaṇa 1.7.4.1), an interpretation which may be correct.[71]

With regard to the myth of Prajāpati and his daughter, however, Professor Max Müller tells us:

> When Kumārila is hard pressed by his opponents about the immoralities of his gods, he answers with all the freedom of a comparative mythologist: "It is fabled that Prajāpati, the Lord of Creation, did violence to his daughter. But what does it mean? Prajāpati, the Lord of Creation, is a name of the sun, and he is called so, because he protects all creatures. His daughter Ushas is the dawn. And when it is said that he was in love with her, this only means that, at sunrise, the sun runs after the dawn, the dawn being at the same time called the daughter of the sun, because she rises when he approaches." [72]

In Rig-Veda (2.29.1) we find reference to illegitimate love and the abandonment of the offspring of such a union. In at least three verses apparently brotherless girls were reduced to becoming prostitutes (R.V.1.124.7; 4.5.5; A.V.1.17.1). There is possible reference to prostitution in Rig-Veda (8.17.7; 1.167.4; 2.15.7;

[67] *Ibid.*, I, 396.

[68] Weber, *Indische Studien,* 10.83 *et seq.*

[69] Jolly, RS, p. 48.

[70] Zimmer, AIL, p. 321.

[71] Macdonell and Keith, V.I., I, 397.

[72] Max Müller, *History of Ancient Sanskrit Literature,* pp. 529, 530. See also Griffith, R.V., II, 611.

2.13.12) and in A.V. (5.5.8). On the other hand, in the following lines the deity Indra took pity upon an illegitimate son of a maiden:

Lord of Bay Steeds, thou broughtest from the ant-hill the unwedded damsel's son whom ants were eating. R.V.4.19.9.

> So Indra . . . caused the unwedded damsel's [*agru*] son,
> The castaway, to share in the lauds.
>
> R.V.4.30.16.

With regard to polyandry in the Vedas, there is a difference of opinion among able scholars. Macdonell and Keith make the definite statement that

. . . polyandry is not Vedic. There is no passage containing any clear reference to such a custom. The most that can be said is that in the Rig-Veda (10.85.37,38) and the Atharvaveda (14.1.44,52,61; 2.14.27) verses are . . . found in which husbands are mentioned in relation to a single wife.[73]

Griswold says that in the case where the Lady Dawn chose the two Horsemen to be her husbands, we have

a bit of mythological polyandry (R.V.4.43.6; 1.119.5). The situation is complicated by the fact that the Sun Maiden is represented also as the sister of the Aśvins (R.V.1.180.2) as well as their wife. . . . These embarrassing connections represent the mythological rendering of the phenomena of the morning sky, in terms of human relationships.[74]

Julius Jolly, in *Recht und Sitte,* gives an excellent account of the aboriginal peoples who dwelt in India, whose descendants sometimes even today practice polyandry.[75] On the other side, Meyer thinks that probably polyandry "was to be found among the primitive population in and about India," [76] and that "polyandry may have been found in isolated cases among the Aryan Indians." [77] However, Meyer thinks that on the whole polyandry probably must be called "non-Aryan." [78]

There is no evidence in the early Vedic texts for the practice of child-marriage. To the people of those days marriage was the union

[73] Macdonell and Keith, V.I., I, 479.
[74] Griswold, RRV, pp. 259, 260.
[75] Jolly, RS, p. 48.
[76] Meyer, SLAI, I, 115.
[77] *Ibid.,* pp. 115, 116.
[78] *Ibid.,* p. 108.

of two persons of full development. In the following verse there is reference to a woman who was old and still unmarried:

O Aśvins! to Ghoshā, stricken in years, living in her father's dwelling, ye gave a husband. R.V.1.117.7.

In the Vedas are to be found many love poems, yearnings of youths for maidens, and vice versa, and there are even spells and potions to endeavor to compel the love of man and woman. The following is a charm to win and secure a girl's love:

From honey sprang this plant to life. With honey now we dig thee up.
Make us as sweet as honey, for from honey hast thou been produced.
My tongue hath honey at the tip, and sweetest honey at the root:
Thou yieldest to my wish and will, and shalt be mine and only mine.
My coming in is honey-sweet; and honey-sweet my going forth.
My voice and words are sweet. I fain would be like honey in my look.
Sweeter am I than honey, yet more full of sweets than licorice:
So mayst thou love me as a branch full of sweets, and only me.
Around thee have I girt a zone of sugar-cane to banish hate,
That thou mayst be in love with me, my darling, never to depart.

A.V.1.34.1–5. [Griffith note: "*My coming in . . . my going forth.* All my doings; my general conduct. *To banish hate:* and, of course, to inspire love. *My darling, never to depart:* more literally, 'that thou mayst never go away,' or become alienated from me." I, 39.]

The latter part of the following hymn definitely shows that sometimes the man was prepared to use strenuous means to gain the woman of whom he was enamored:

Let the Impeller [Kāma, the god of love,] goad thee on. Rest not in peace upon thy bed.
Terrible is the shaft of Love. Therewith I pierce thee to the heart.
That arrow winged with longing thought, its stem Desire, its neck Resolve,
Let Kāma, having truly aimed, shoot forth and pierce thee in the heart.
The shaft of Kāma, pointed well, that withers and consumes the spleen,
With hasty feathers, all aglow, therewith I pierce thee to the heart.
Pierced through with fiercely-burning heat, steal to me with thy parching lips,
Gentle and humble, all mine own, devoted, with sweet words of love,
Away from mother and from sire I drive thee hither with a whip,

That thou mayst be at my command and yield to every wish of mine.
Mitra and Varuṇa, expel all thought and purpose from her heart.
Deprive her of her own free-will, and make her subject unto me.
A.V.3.25.1–6.

The following is the lullaby, or sleep charm, of a lover who is secretly visiting his love:

The Bull who hath a thousand horns, who rises up from out the sea,—
By him, the strong and mighty one, we lull the folk to rest and sleep.
Over the surface of the earth there breathes no wind, there looks no eye.
Lull all the women, lull the dogs to sleep, with Indra as thy friend!
The women sleeping in the court, lying without, or stretched on beds,
The matrons with their odorous sweets—these, one and all, we lull to sleep.
Each moving thing have I secured, have held and hold the eye and breath.
Each limb and member have I seized in the deep darkness of the night.
The man who sits, the man who walks, whoever stands and clearly sees—
Of these we closely shut the eyes, even as we closely shut this house.
Sleep, mother! let the father sleep! sleep, dog, and master of the home!
Let all her kinsmen sleep. Sleep, all the people who are round about.
With soporific charm, O sleep, lull thou to slumber all the folk.
Let the rest sleep till break of day. I will remain awake till dawn, like Indra free from scath and harm.

A.V.4.5.1–7. [Griffith note: "*The Bull who hath a thousand horns:* the sun with his countless rays of light, whose setting brings the time of rest and sleep; or perhaps the starry heaven, as Grassmann translates, is intended." I, 135.]

The following is a maiden's love charm:

I dig this healing herb that makes my lover look on me and weep;
That bids the parting friend return and kindly greets him as he comes.
This herb wherewith the Āsurī drew Indra downward from the Gods,
With this same herb I draw thee close that I may be most dear to thee.
Thou art the peer of Soma, yea, thou art the equal of the Sun,
The peer of all the Gods art thou! Therefore we call thee hitherward.
I am speaker here, not thou. Speak thou where the assembly meets.
Thou shalt be mine and only mine, and never mention other dames.
If thou art far away beyond the rivers, far away from men,
This herb shall seem to bind thee fast and bring thee back my prisoner
A.V.7.38.1–5.

The following woman's charm is addressed to a sacred plant:

Thou hast grown up, a source of joy, to bless me with prosperity.
A hundred are thy tendrils; three-and-thirty, thy descending shoots.
With this that bears a thousand leaves I dry thy heart, and wither it.
Let thy heart wither for my love; and let thy mouth be dry for me.
Parch, and dry up with longing. Go with lips that love of me hath dried.
Drive us together, tawny! fair! a go-between who wakens love.
Drive us together, him and me, and give us both one heart and mind.
Even as his mouth is parched who finds no water for his burning thirst,
So parch and burn with longing, go with lips that love of me hath dried.
Even as the mongoose bites and rends and then restores the wounded snake.
So do thou, mighty one, restore the fracture of our severed love.

A.V.6.139.1–5.

Other love charms of women are:

This is the Apsarases' love-spell, the conquering resistless ones'.
Send the spell forth, ye deities! Let him consume with love of me.
I pray, may he remember me, think of me, loving and beloved.
Send forth the spell, ye deities! Let him consume with love of me.
That he may think of me, that I may never, never think of him.
Send forth the spell, ye deities! Let him consume with love of me.
Madden him, Maruts, madden him. Madden him, madden him, O Air.
Madden him, Agni; madden him. Let him consume with love of me.

A.V.6.130.1–4.

If thou shouldst run three leagues away, five leagues, a horse's daily stage,
Thence thou shalt come to me again, and be the father of our sons.

A.V.6.131.3.

The following is a charm against jealousy:

Brought hitherward from Sindhu, from a folk of every mingled race,
Fetched from afar, thou art I deem, a balm that cureth jealousy.
As one with water quencheth fire, so calm this lover's jealousy,
Like heat of fire that burneth here, or flame that rageth through the wood.

A.V.7.45.1–2.

In the Atharva-Veda (2.36.1–8) we find a charm supposed to be used by a matchmaker, or intermediary, for securing a husband for a marriageable girl.

To please us may the suitor come, O Agni, seeking this maid. . . .
May she be soon made happy with a husband.
As bliss beloved by Soma, dear to Prayer, and stored by Aryaman,
With the God Dhātar's truthfulness I work the bridal oracle.
O Agni, may this woman find a husband. Then verily King Soma makes her happy.
May she bear sons, chief lady of the household. Blessed and bearing, rule beside her consort.
As this lair, Maghavan! that is fair to look on was dear to wild things as a pleasant dwelling,
So may this woman here be Bhaga's darling, loved by her lord and prizing his affection.
Mount up! Embark on Bhaga's ship, the full, the inexhaustible,
Thereon bring hitherward to us the lover whom thou fain wouldst wed.
Call out to him, O Lord of Wealth! Make thou the lover well-inclined.
Set each on thy right hand who is a lover worthy of her choice.
Here is the Bdellium and the gold, the Auksha and the bliss are here:
These bring thee to the husbands, so to find the man whom thou wouldst have.
May Savitar lead and bring to thee the husband whom thy heart desires.
O Plant, be this thy gift to her!

A.V.2.36.1,3–8. [Griffith note: "*The suitor:* the interceder or match-maker whose business is to find a suitable wife for his friend or employer. *O Agni:* addressed as especially connected with marriage, regulating, as the Sun, the proper season for its celebration, and, as the sacrificial fire, the consecrator of the rite. *Beloved by Soma:* as Sūryā, the typical bride, was married to Soma, the young maid is regarded as originally belonging to him. *Chief lady of the household: mahishī,* the technical term for the first married wife; the principal consort of a king. *Bhaga:* the Dispenser, who brings wealth and happiness, and blesses conjugal love. *Bdellium:* a costly fragrant gum . . . It may have formed part of the girl's dowry; or she may have been anointed and perfumed with it. *The gold:* as dowry or personal ornaments." I, 78–79.]

In regard to the love of youths and maidens the Vedas also say:

Like as a young man followeth a maiden, so doth the Sun the Dawn, refulgent Goddess. R.V.1.115.2.

. . . speeding like lover to his love. R.V.9.38.4.

So maidens bow before the youthful gallant who comes with love to them who yearn to meet him. R.V.10.30.6.

Soma joys and is delighted, as a young man with fair and pleasant damsels. R.V.10.30.5.

Accept our praise song, as a youth accepts a maid. R.V.8.35.5.

The young maid repelleth not her lover. R.V.10.178.3.

There is a remarkable instance of a woman, Apālā, whose cutaneous disease was cured by having been drawn through the hole of a car, a wagon, and a yoke by the deity Indra (R.V.8.80.7, repeated in A.V.14.1.41). Such a cure, however, is to be found reported, not only in Hindu scriptures, but similar charms are found in various other parts of the world. In commenting upon the passage Griffith states that according to Simrock (*Handbuch der deutschen Mythologie,* p. 538) and Kelly (*Folk-Lore,* pp. 154–57),

. . . the custom of creeping through a gap in a wall, or a hole in a rock or tree, for the cure of certain diseases, was formerly, and is still, well known in various parts of Europe. . . . In English villages, children were sometimes drawn through the arch made by a strong blackberry shoot in order to free them from whooping-cough. The process was, it seems, supposed to symbolize the regeneration or new birth of the patient.[79]

It appears from the following verse that a daughter-in-law felt timidity in the presence of her father-in-law:

They creep away from the sun, as a daughter-in-law away from her father-in-law. A.V.8.6.24. Whitney and Lanman, *Atharva-Veda Saṃhitā,* HOS, VIII, 498.

The distress of women in war is evidenced by Atharva-Veda (5.20.5).

Hearing the drum's far-reaching voice resounding, let the foe's dame, waked by the roar, afflicted,
Grasping her son, run forward in her terror amid the conflict of the deadly weapons.

A.V.5.20.5.

The following lines give us a varied picture of woman in Vedic days:

[79] Griffith, A.V., II, 167.

. . . a woman who splits cane . . . a woman who works in thorns . . . a woman who embroiders . . . a washerwoman . . . a woman who deals in love-charms . . . a female dyer . . . a female ointment-maker . . . a female scabbard maker. W.Y.V.30.8,9,12,13,14.

. . . holding aloft the water, as a water-bearer in her jar. A.V.10.8.14.

. . . the plant which Jamadagni dug to make his daughter's locks grow long. A.V.6.137.1.

Women love one who sings. B.Y.V.6.1.6.6. Keith, HOS, XIX, 493.

Glory dwelleth in a maid. A.V.10.3.20.

A weary woman seeks her couch. A.V.4.20.3.

O maiden! it truly is not as thou fanciest. A.V.20.133.1.

In no country of the world is feminine attire more beautiful and graceful than in India. Even as in their picturesque modern saris, so also one can well picture the lovely appearance of the garments of the Vedic ladies from the following words:

Like women-folk, the floods that bring prosperity have caught his [Varuṇa's] hue and colour, as they gleamed and shone. R.V.10.124.7.

. . . like women at a gathering, fair to look on, and gently smiling. W.Y.V.17.96.

. . . as maidens deck themselves with gay adornment to join the bridal feast. W.Y.V.17.97.

Although radiant goddesses have been created by the ancient Hindu poets, yet the very same documents present menacing, bloody, feminine forces of destruction. She-fiends are encountered abundantly; and prayers are uttered for their destruction.

Agni, with thy glowing face burn fierce against the female fiends. R.V.10.118.8.

Sprung from the Snowy Mountain's [*Himavat*] side, this ointment of the
three-peaked hill
Crushes . . . every witch and sorceress.

A.V.4.9.9.

Ill dream and wretchedness of life, . . . stingy hags,
All the she-fiends of evil name and voice, we drive away from us.

Death caused by famine, caused by thirst, failure of children, loss of kine,—
With thee, O Apāmārga, all this ill we cleanse and wipe away.
A.V.4.17.5–6. [Note: *Apāmārga*—A plant believed to possess magical powers.]

She too who wanders like an owl at night-time, hiding her body in her guile and malice,—
May she fall downward into endless caverns.

R.V.7.104.17.

The word *"Dāsī"* occurs both in the Rig-Veda and in the Atharva-Veda, meaning "female slave."

Seek thou a wanton *Dāsī* girl, and strike her with thy thunderbolt. A.V.5.22.6.

The slave-girl, wet-handed, smearing the pestle and the mortar, hath cleansed the waters. A.V.12.3.13.

Macdonell and Keith state that "aboriginal women were, no doubt, the usual slaves, for, on their husbands being slain in battle, they would naturally have been taken as servants. They would sometimes also become concubines." [80]

A gift of fifty female slaves hath Trasadasyu given me. R.V.8.19.36.

In the Atharva-Veda we find women mentioned among the mourners at a funeral:

Quickly around his funeral fire, dance women with dishevelled locks,
Striking the hand upon the breast, and uttering their evil shriek.

A.V.12.5.48.

In this same document we find the following funeral hymn:

Choosing her husband's world, O man, this woman lays herself down beside thy lifeless body,
Preserving faithfully the ancient custom. Bestow upon her here both wealth and offspring.
Rise, come unto the world of life, O woman! Come, he is lifeless by whose side thou liest.

A.V.18.3.1,2.

[80] Macdonell and Keith, V.I., I, 357.

In a note at the end of this passage, Griffith explains the phrase "Choosing her husband's world" as meaning that "the widow is, or is supposed to be, ready to follow her husband, but is dissuaded by her friends." [81] Griffith believes that "The ancient custom [*dharma purāṇa*]" means that the custom had been followed by "the Aryan immigrants in earliest times, but not generally observed when these funeral hymns were composed." [82] Griffith states that

> Old Northern poetry contains many instances of the observance of this "ancient custom." Nanna was burnt with Baldr; Brynhild gave orders that she should be burnt with Sigurd; Gunnhild slew herself when Asmund died; and Gudrun was reproached with having survived her husband.[83]

Griffith explains the word "here" as meaning that "the widow is to remain in the world of life and be rewarded for her show of affection." [84]

The Atharva-Veda continues the funeral hymn:

> I looked, and saw the youthful dame escorted, the living to the dead. I saw them bear her,
> When she with blinding darkness was enveloped, then did I turn her back, and lead her homeward.
>
> A.V.18.3.3.

The Rig-Veda also contains:

> Let these unwidowed dames with noble husbands adorn themselves with fragrant balm and unguent.
> Decked with fair jewels, tearless, free from sorrow. First let the dames go up to where he lieth.
>
> Rise, come unto the world of life, O woman! Come, he is lifeless by whose side thou liest.
> Wifehood with this thy husband was thy portion, who took thy hand and wooed thee as a lover.
>
> R.V.10.18.7,8.

From the above passages it would appear that during the Vedic age the custom of *Satī* was "in abeyance, at least as a general

[81] Griffith, A.V., II, 236.
[82] *Ibid.*
[83] *Ibid.;* also see Zimmer, AIL, pp. 329–31.
[84] *Ibid.*

rule."[85] To judge from the other Indo-Germanic parallels, at all times the practice seems to have been used mainly among families of the warrior class. In his historical and philosophical enquiry (*Suttee*) Edward Thompson declares that "widow-sacrifice was once almost universal."[86] Yet the *Oxford History of India* states that the rite was never regarded "as obligatory on all widows."[87] More will be said of *Satī* in relation to the Purāṇas. In the funeral ceremonies of the Aryans, as presented in the Rig-Veda, Thompson declares there are "only one or two lines that may, on a dubious twisting and loosening of their natural meaning, glance at Suttee."[88] Professor H. H. Wilson[89] points out that the one instance which may seem to enjoin it was a line deliberately changed. Max Müller agrees with this point of view, for he calls this line "mangled, mistranslated and misapplied."[90] R. W. Frazer speaks of "a slight misreading" of the line.[91] In the original text the line in question runs:

Ā-rohantu janayo yonim agre. R.V.10.18.7. (Let the mothers advance to the altar first.)

By a very slight verbal change in the ending of one word, the line became:

Ā-rohantu janayo yonim agneḥ. (Let the mothers go into the womb of fire.)

Thompson believes that widow-burning "cannot have been established by this change of text, but only encouraged."[92] From the following passage we do know that in Vedic days there were widows who could be remarried. The Atharva-Veda states:

> When she who hath been wedded finds a second husband afterward,
> The Twain shall not be parted, if they give the goat Pañcaudana.
> A.V.9.5.27. [Griffith note: "*A second husband:* after the death of the first." I, 446.]

---

[85] Macdonell and Keith, V.I., I, 488, 489.
[86] Thompson, *Suttee,* p. 24.
[87] Smith, *Oxford History of India,* p. 665.
[88] Thompson, *Suttee,* p. 16.
[89] *Essays and Lectures on the Religion of the Hindus,* II, 270–92.
[90] *Selected Essays on Language, Mythology and Religion,* I, 335.
[91] Frazer, *Indian Thought, Past and Present,* p. 279.
[92] Thompson, *Suttee,* p. 18.

Her later husband comes to have the same world with his remarried spouse. A.V.9.5.28; Whitney, HOS, VIII, 537.

Zimmer feels that we can say very little about widows from our Vedic sources of knowledge. He, too, points out that there were second husbands in the Atharva-Veda; and yet he reminds us that we cannot prove that widow-burning never occurred among the early Aryans. He is of the opinion that it was in use among Indo-Europeans.[93] Macdonell and Keith think Zimmer stressed the universality of the custom too much. They state that "the Rig-Veda already reveals a state of society in which the actual burning of the wife was avoided by a semblance of it in the funeral ritual." [94] They point out, however, that "on the death of her husband, in some cases the widow burned herself or was burned by his relations." [95] Macdonell and Keith state that "this is clearly implied in the reference to this ancient custom in the Atharvaveda (18. 3.1). On the other hand, the Rigveda does not contemplate the custom anywhere; but on the contrary, considers the widow as married apparently to the brother of the dead man (10.18.7,8)." [96] Macdonell and Keith show that "another passage of the Rigveda (10.40.2) clearly refers to the marriage of the widow and the husband's brother,[97] which constitutes what the Indians later knew as *Niyoga*." [98] The *Vedic Index* says that "this custom was probably not followed except in cases where no son was already born. This custom was hardly remarriage in the strict sense, since the brother might—so far as appears—be already married himself." [99]

If one reads the Vedas carefully, many variations in their philosophy are apparent. Often they are repetitious and far-fetched. Some verses are degrading. Hatred and jealousy appear in certain hymns. K. S. Macdonald points out that labors of love are rare and likewise "acts of charity toward the poor, the widow, or the

[93] Zimmer, AIL, p. 331.
[94] Macdonell and Keith, V.I., I, 489.
[95] *Ibid.*, p. 488.
[96] *Ibid.*
[97] *Niyoga:* "The appointing a brother or any near kinsman to raise up issue to a deceased husband by marrying his widow." Monier-Williams, *Sanskrit-English Dictionary*, p. 552, col. 3.
[98] *Ibid.*, p. 477. For further discussion on the history of *Niyoga* marriage, see Frazer, ITPP, pp. 319–21.
[99] Macdonell and Keith, V.I., I, 477.

orphan." [100] It would seem as though seekers wished boons only for themselves. Yet in the early Vedas there are many evidences of a high sense of morality.

It is essential that we view the Vedas historically. Also we must guard against too much enthusiasm on their behalf, even as Max Müller has said:

> Looking at many of the books that have lately been published on the religions of the ancient world, I do not wonder that such a belief [as to their being "full of primeval wisdom and religious enthusiasm, or at least of sound and simple moral teaching"] should have been raised; but I have felt that it was high time to dispel such illusions, and to place the study of the ancient religions of the world on a more real and sound, on a more truly historical basis.[101]

This famous Oriental scholar states:

> Whether I am myself one of the guilty or not, I cannot help calling attention to the real mischief that has been done, and is still being done, by the enthusiasm of those pioneers who have opened the first avenues through the bewildering forest of the sacred literature of the East. . . . What we want here, as everywhere, is the truth and the whole truth; and if the whole truth must be told, it is that, however radiant the dawn of religious thought, it is not without its dark clouds, its noxious vapours. . . . I confess it has been for many years a problem to me . . . how the Sacred Books of the East should, by the side of so much that is fresh, natural, simple, beautiful, and true, contain so much that is not only unmeaning, artificial, and silly, but even hideous and repellent.[102]

Clearly the Vedas are important historical documents which tell us of the early Aryans who had reached the pastoral and agricultural stage. We learn about all types of people, good and bad. If we find the coarse and crude amid the fair and beautiful, it is perhaps but a realistic interpretation of life as the *ṛishis* saw it or divined that it ought to be. It is a vivid, captivating portrait of an ancient people, their poetry and their faith. In this picture we note a joy in life which is healthy.

Although the four Vedas are unquestionably the earliest extant group of Hindu writings, yet there may have been earlier writings which now are lost. Martin Haug warns us:

[100] Macdonald, VR, p. 233. [101] SBE, I, ix. [102] *Ibid.*, x–xii.

If we look at the history of poetry with other nations, we nowhere find profane songs precede religious poetry. The latter owes its origin entirely to the practical worship of beings of a higher order, and must, as every art does, go through many phases before it can arrive at any state of perfection and refinement. Now in the collection of the hymns of the Rigveda, we find the religious poetry already so highly developed, the language so polished, the metres already so artificially composed, as to justify the assumption, that the songs which have reached our time, are not the earliest productions of the poetical genius and the devout mind of the ancient Indians. Generations of poets and many family schools in which sacred poetry was regularly taught, just as the art of the bards and scalds with Celtic and Scandinavian nations, must have preceded that period to which we owe the Vedas. If an old song was replaced by a new one, which appeared more beautiful and finished, in most cases the former was irrecoverably lost. Old and new poets are frequently mentioned in the hymns of the Rigveda; but the more modern *ṛishis* of the Vedic period appear not to have regarded the productions of their predecessors with any particular reverence which might have induced them to keep their early relics. . . . The first sacrifices were no doubt simple offerings performed without much ceremonial.[103]

Griswold presents the unmistakable fact that the Rig-Veda is "the fountain-head of Hindu religion, philosophy, law, art and social institutions." [104] From an ethical point of view the conceptions of the Rig-Veda are mostly tribal, depicting an early stage of society. Farquhar reminds us that "the early peoples did not possess the conception of a lofty moral law by which all customs and all men are judged." [105] However, there are some suggestions of a high sense of honor.

If we have sinned against the man who loves us, have ever wronged a
brother, friend or comrade,
The neighbor ever with us, or a stranger, O Varuṇa, remove from us the
trespass.
If we as gamesters cheat at play, have cheated, done wrong unwittingly or
sinned of purpose,
Cast all these sins away like loosened fetters; and, Varuṇa, let us be thine
own beloved.

R.V.5.85.7,8.

[103] Haug, tr., *The Aitareya Brāhmaṇam of the Rigveda,* Introduction, I, 29, 30.
[104] Griswold, RRV, p. 328.
[105] Farquhar, PH, p. 192.

It might be remindful to note here a remark of Griswold's, namely, that perhaps "even up to the present time the world has hardly transcended the stage of tribal morality!" [106]

Griswold has pointed out that

> The Ṛigveda is as frankly polytheistic as Homer's *Iliad* or Vergil's *Aeneid.* Animism, or polytheistic nature worship, lies at the foundation of all of the Indo-European mythologies, Indian and Iranian as well as Greek, Roman and Teutonic. [p. 342] . . . During the latter part of the Ṛigvedic period there was a steady movement toward unity. This movement assumed two forms, one looking toward monotheism and the other toward pantheism. [p. 344] . . . Varuṇa represented the nearest approach in Vedic India to the doctrine of monotheism. [p. 347] . . . In the Ṛigveda, polytheism, pantheism and monotheism, exist side by side in unstable equilibrium, a condition of things which is reproduced through the whole history of Hinduism. [p. 350] . . . While certain aspects and teachings of the Ṛigveda, such as its dominant polytheism, its incipient pantheism and its increasing tendency toward an abstract and non-ethical intellectualism find their fulfilment in the later Hinduism, there are other aspects of Ṛigvedic teaching which point rather in the direction of Christianity, such as the monotheistic and ethical Varuṇa, the high-priestly and mediatory Agni, the emphasis on the forgiveness of sin in connection with Varuṇa and the Ādityas, and the doctrine of the last things—heavenly home, luminous body, beatific vision, etc.—so different from the later doctrine of transmigration [pp. 370–71].[107]

Farquhar feels that "the religion of Christ is the spiritual crown of the religion of the Ṛigveda." [108]

If the authors of the Vedas were to return to the modern world, we may wonder what they would say of the condition of many Indian women. Those ancient sacred writers knew nothing of child-marriages. If they could view some unhappy and unfair present-day marriages, they well might wonder what had become of the lofty attitude often expressed in descriptions of Vedic weddings. They certainly would not advocate widow-burning or the pathetic, heart-rending sorrow that attends so many present-day Hindu

[106] Griswold, RRV, p. 341.
[107] *Ibid.*, pp. 342, 344, 347, 350, 370–71.
[108] Farquhar, *The Crown of Hinduism,* p. 77.

widows. Certainly they would be unaware of what is meant by "purdah," the seclusion of women, with its attendant ravages of disease. If something had not happened to the application of these sacred writings, it is reasonable to suppose that today the position of many Hindu women would not be so handicapped.

The change which took place in the estimate of woman would appear to be like another relapse in the Rig-Veda. Griswold describes this tragedy well. He says,

Every student recognizes that the noblest element in the Ṛik is Varuṇa: creator, sovereign, all-knowing, all-seeing mind, source of order both cosmic and moral, from whose holy will spring the ordinances that govern all the powers of nature and also the moral and religious life of men, God of righteousness, mercy and grace, who punishes the stubborn sinner, releases the sinner who repents and seeks a nobler life, and holds happy and loving communion in personal friendship, with the righteous man. . . . Yet before the end of the Vedic period, Varuṇa had become a petty godling, lord of the waters; and all the priceless promise of that early faith had been completely lost to India. . . . Every serious mind must recognize that we have here a religious tragedy of the utmost gloom and disaster.[109]

Now, of course there is much to be condemned with regard to the position of women in the Vedas. On the whole, however, considering the primitive age in which these people lived and the fact that polygamy, prostitution, and even incest are recognized to have existed, it seems a remarkable fact that a high moral strain in family organization did run through the early Aryan civilization, an influence that gave to woman generally a status of some dignified consideration. With reference to the early migration R. W. Frazer declares:

It may be that during the long journey towards India the women became few in number, so that they received a consideration which would not otherwise be granted them. There is evidence from the Rig Vēda that women in Vedic times occupied a far higher position than they did in their ancestral homes, or even in later days in India.[110]

---

[109] Griswold, RRV, p. 373.

[110] Frazer, ITPP, pp. 278–79.

Whether this be unexceptionable or not, it is certain that the Vedic poets visioned, and set down, verses of high praise for the feminine. It is our task in the present study to see what happened to this Vedic vision of womanhood.

CHAPTER II: THE BRĀHMAṆAS

IN CONSIDERING the set of literary documents subsequent to the four Vedas, namely, the Brāhmaṇas, we shall deal with "the earliest Indo-European prose writings now extant."[1] They are extremely valuable, as they are a source of one of the most important periods in the development of India. In them we learn of the social life of the period between the Vedas and the Upanishads. The Brāhmaṇas represent the ideology of a sacerdotal caste which played upon the natural religious instincts of the Hindus. The priests succeeded in changing the early Nature-Worship of the Hindus into a code of intricate artificial ceremonies of sacrifice which has brought about to the present day endless wasteful expenditures of spiritual energy as well as material substance. These religious leaders unceasingly strove to gain control over the minds of the people. They encouraged a divine halo to be placed upon the priesthood. As Julius Eggeling, the Regius Professor of Sanskrit at Edinburgh University, has suggested, "A complicated ceremonial, requiring for its proper observance and consequent efficacy the ministrations of a highly trained priestly caste, has ever been one of the effective means of promoting hierarchical aspirations."[2]

It is amazing to note the naïve frankness with which the Brahmans set forth their ambitious desires. One wonders how they succeeded in overcoming the powerful Kshatriya caste. Remarkable perseverance helped the Brahmans to gain their desired end. No doubt, they even persuaded kings to further the cause of the priesthood.

In the five-volume translation of the *Śatapatha-Brāhamaṇa* Julius Eggeling tells us:

[1] Hume, WLR, p. 22.

[2] SBE, XII, ix–x.

The more complicated the ceremonial, the greater the dependence of the lay worshipper on the professional skill of the priests, and the greater the number of priests required for the proper performance of these ceremonies, the larger the gains derived by the priesthood generally from this kind of occupation. What more natural, therefore, than that the highest importance should have been ascribed to these performances, and an ever-increasing attention bestowed on the ceremonial.[3]

In regard to the Brāhmaṇas this author further speaks of the "wearisome prolixity of exposition, characterized by dogmatic assertion and a flimsy symbolism rather than by serious reasoning." [4]

There is a decided difference in the primitive worship of the Rig-Veda and the highly complicated ceremonial of the Brāhmaṇas. In many instances the Brāhmaṇas resorted to a fantastic interpretation of the early Vedas in order to make them justify ceremonies in which priests of various classes could officiate. The early, simple, prayerful religion of the Vedic Aryans became in the Brāhmaṇas a strict system of highly elaborated ceremonials. That ardent friend of India, the late Professor Max Müller, in *A History of Ancient Sanskrit Literature,* has stated:

No one would have supposed that at so early a period, and in so primitive a state of society, there could have risen up a literature which for pedantry and downright absurdity can hardly be matched anywhere. . . . The general character of these works is marked by shallow and insipid grandiloquence, by priestly conceit, and antiquarian pedantry. It is most important to the historian that he should know how soon the fresh and healthy growth of a nation can be blighted by priestcraft and superstition. It is most important that we should know that nations are liable to these epidemics in their youth as well as in their dotage. These works deserve to be studied as the physician studies the twaddle of idiots, and the raving of madmen. They will disclose to a thoughtful eye the ruins of faded grandeur, the memories of noble aspirations.[5]

Max Müller continued, "Never was dogmatism more successfully veiled under the mask of free discussion than in the Mīmānsā or discussion of the Brāhmaṇas." [6] Nevertheless, despite such adverse

[3] Eggeling, tr., SBE, XII, xv.
[4] *Ibid.,* p. ix.
[5] Page 389.
[6] *Ibid.,* p. 428.

criticism, it must be recognized that there are some passages in the Brāhmaṇas that contain deep thought and uplifted feeling. Max Müller himself declared, "In spite of their general dreariness, the Brāhmaṇas well deserve to be preserved from destruction." [7]

In the Brāhmaṇas we see that the Aryan invaders have conquered the aborigines. The word *"varṇa"* now means "class" as well as "color." In an article in the *American Journal of Theology* Professor R. E. Hume states:

Both in the long history of Hinduism and at the present time the system of caste has been the main stronghold of Hinduism. With few exceptions, namely, among the progressive modern social reformers, the breaking of caste is the crucial practical test of ceasing to be a Hindu. This characteristic system of caste arose after a successful period of warfare in India had added a despised helotic element to the pre-existent threefold social organization which the Indo-Aryans had shared with the Iranians. In Persia no such religiously obligated caste system arose as in India. . . . In India the complex military, economic, and social enslaving of one people by another more powerful body of invaders was sanctioned religiously; and therewith the entire organization of society became fairly rigidly fixed on what was professed to be a divinely ordained basis.[8]

In the Brāhmaṇas we find that deities are lowered in character. For instance, Vishṇu, one of the high gods of the Rig-Veda, is presented as a dwarf in the Brāhmaṇas. The priests and sacrifices are now more important than the gods. Professor R. E. Hume tells us that:

The first great war of the Hindus at the original invasion into India had been accompanied by much prayer and personal sacrifice. The continuance of these processes was stressed, but in a formal perfunctory manner. The particular interpretation which was put upon the early military and religious success resulted in a distinct hardening of religion. The relatively simple Vedic religion was transformed in this period of Hinduism into a system of strict domination, elaborate ceremonies, various material offerings, and even bloody animal sacrifices, all under the control of the Brahman priests. . . . No other sacred scriptures of the world can parallel the claim made in these "Priestlies" of Hinduism, that a person's salvation depends upon paying fees to officiating priests.[9]

[7] *Ibid.*, p. 427.
[8] Hume, *Hinduism and War*, p. 35.
[9] Hume, WLR, pp. 22, 23.

Continuously from this period sacerdotalism has been a very important part of the Hindu religion. Salvation, according to the Brāhmaṇas, is to be obtained chiefly through sacrifice performed by the Brahman priests who receive material gifts. In contrast to all the other religions of the world, the Brāhmaṇas of Hinduism make the unparalleled claim for their priests to be classified along with the gods.

Verily, there are two kinds of gods: for, indeed the gods are the gods; and the Brahmans, who have studied and teach sacred lore, are the human gods. The sacrifice of these is divided into two kinds: oblations constitute the sacrifice to the gods; and gifts to the priests, that to the human gods, the Brahmans who have studied and teach sacred lore. With oblations one gratifies the gods; and with gifts to the priests, the human gods, the Brahmans who have studied and teach sacred lore. Both these kinds of gods, when gratified, place him in a state of bliss [sudhā]. Śatapatha 2.2.2.6; SBE, XII, 309–10. Also in Śatapatha 4.3.4.4; SBE, XXVI, 341.

Quite specific is the teaching that the gods effectualize the sacrifices which are accompanied by gifts to the Hindu priests.

By means of dakshiṇās (gifts to the priests) the gods again invigorated it [the sacrifice]. . . . Whatever, therefore, fails in this sacrifice when slain, that he now again invigorates by means of gifts to the priests; whereupon the sacrifice becomes successful. For this reason, he makes gifts to the priests. Śatapatha 2.2.2.2; SBE, XII, 308, 309.

In all fairness it must be noted that there are elements of religious strength in the Brāhmaṇas. There is, for instance, a certain perception of the need of divine sacrifice in religion and life, of the desirability of some religious experts in society, of the necessity of systematizing, even standardizing, some aspects of religious worship and ceremony. Unwholesome as have been many Brahmanical edicts and influences, nevertheless, many priests have contributed much of value to the intellectual and ethical development of Hinduism. On the other hand, there are many weaknesses in the Brāhmaṇas. There is still no genuine unity in nature or in a divine realm to be noted in the Brāhmaṇas, which name many gods, although Prajāpati is lauded as the highest deity. The low moral character of several of the deities, such as Prajāpati, Vishṇu, and Indra, is noticeable. The interpretation of sacrifice is a conception too materialistic, rather than a moral or spiritual conception. The aristocracy of the priesthood is too ceremonial and exclusive, involuntarily recruited by birth only. The religion in the Brāhmaṇas is too self-benefiting. The gods are chiefly to be used for the worshipper's benefit. There is no idea of social service. Certainly in the Brāhmaṇas the spontaneous worship of Vedic days is lost.

So it was that the clever Brahmans managed to control the people. Even the Kshatriyas seemed to endure the edicts of the Brahmans. Primarily the priests realized they must control women. In this respect they had much to overcome. There was the early worship of goddesses with which to reckon. Likewise woman's sex-nature, giving her the power of motherhood, had to be reckoned with. Her freedom was a hindrance to the power and domination of the priests. The Brahmans felt that this must be conquered; so with verbal agitation they succeeded in lowering the position of woman. She must be considered an inferior creature without a mind. With a heartless cruelty they decided that gradually even religious rights must be taken away from woman.

The priests saw to it that their directions for worship contained a tremendous overemphasis on the physical aspect of womanhood. The Brāhmaṇas are filled with passages of explanation regarding sexual matters. Also the necessity of male offspring for salvation was stressed emphatically. The Brahmans emphasized the natural desire for a son, now not alone for the idea of ethical and personal immortality, but for transmigration of souls. A son begotten became involved in the idea of salvation. Such desire was one factor which increasingly helped to bring about unfortunate child-marriages, with all the accompanying misery.

> Since now men desire a son,
> Both those that have and those that have not knowledge,
> What doth a man gain by a son?
> Tell me that, O Nārada.
>
> "A debt he payeth in him,
> And immortality he attaineth,—
> That father who seeth the face
> Of a son born living.
> The delights in the earth,

The delights in the fire,
The delights in the waters of living beings,—
Greater than these is that of a father in a son.
By means of a son have fathers ever
Passed over the deep darkness;
The self is born from the self.
The (son) is (a ship), well-found, to ferry over. . . .
Seek a son, O Brahmans,
This is the world's advice.
Food is breath; clothing a protection;
Gold, an ornament. Cattle lead to marriage.
A wife is a comrade, a daughter, a misery (*kṛipaṇam*);
And a son, a light in the highest heaven.
A sonless one cannot attain heaven."

Aitareya Brāhmaṇa 7.13; HOS, XXV, 299, 300.[10]

With regard to the phrase describing a daughter as a "misery," the two eminent English translators of the Aitareya Brāhmaṇa, A. B. Keith and Martin Haug, differ as to the interpretation of the word *"kṛipaṇam."* Haug in his translation published at the Government Central Depot in Bombay interprets with the idea of appreciativeness, by rendering the word *"kṛipaṇam"* as "object of compassion." On the other hand, in the "Harvard Oriental Series" translation Keith gives the word the meaning "a misery." In his General Index he interprets the word quite explicitly when he says "daughter not desired." This is typical of the diversity in the actual treatment of womankind throughout Hinduism. Thus not only in the original Sanskrit texts is there praise and condemnation, but the various translations have resulted in different inferences that have been associated with unfortunate social conditions among the women of India. Here is an example of the ease with which followers of a religion deduce whatever meaning they wish from a passage. As Max Müller called the change of the word *"agre"* to *"agneḥ"* in the famous funeral hymn "mangled, mistranslated, and misapplied" so also an early diversity of meaning possibly is to be found in the word *"kṛipaṇam."* As modern translations can show an antithesis in meaning, so the *ṛishis* as far back as 800 B.C., in

[10] Keith, tr., HOS, XXV, 299, 300.

the period of the Brāhmaṇas, may at times have thought of a daughter as an object of tenderness and compassion and again as undesirable and miserable. From the latter implication could have grown up some of the unfortunate conditions that so desperately have affected the status of many Hindu daughters. It is not difficult to deduce the emphasis which a scheming priest might wish to put upon such a phrase.

It is reasonable to suppose that due to the intricacies of the psychology of personality complete subjection of woman by the Brahmans did not take place at once. Even during the period of the Brāhmaṇas there were evidences of respect for woman. The views of all men with regard to all women could not be dominated by the priests. Some men insisted upon worshipping the power of motherhood.

In the course of a religious ceremony in the Brāhmaṇas is the statement that the wife should have a resting place in the house. "The house being the wife's resting-place, he thereby establishes her in that safe resting-place, the house" (Śatapatha 3.3.1.10; SBE, XXVI, 61). Here again a difference in interpretation may have taken place. The "resting-place" originally may have meant to the *ṛishis* a place where a wife should enjoy security. The Brahmans stated that in the Hindu's house "a sister, though of the same womb, lives as inferior to a wife, though of a different womb" (Aitareya 3.37; HOS, XXV, 188). At first glance such words would seem to suggest security. However, as one reads on, it would appear that even in her own home, a wife was not likely to speak for herself. The priests were careful to state that "in his house his wife is not likely to answer back" (Aitareya 3.24; HOS, XXV, 180). The implication might be that however cruelly a wife might be treated in the house she would not dare to answer back. Thus a sense of healthful and happy security hardly could be deduced from the phrase "safe resting-place." From assigning the house as "the resting-place" of the wife, two conclusions might have been drawn —one to the advantage and the other to the disadvantage of the Hindu woman. Either the house could be the place in which to rest when rest is needed, or under the dominance of unscrupulous enforcers of religious doctrine it could become a prison in which there was no escape from enforced, continuous rest. Because of the very nature of the human constitution such so-called "rest" or "inaction" becomes idleness and unhappy uselessness.

Further, in "The Priestlies," or the Brāhmaṇas, we find that the Hindu woman could not eat with her husband in her own home. The Śatapatha Brāhmaṇa states:

> Whenever human women here eat, (they do so) apart from men. Śatapatha 1.9.2–12; SBE, XII, 259.

> He (the husband) should not eat food in the presence of his wife; for from him (who does not do so) a vigorous son is born, and she in whose presence (the husband) does not eat food bears a vigorous (son). Such, indeed, is the divine ordinance. Śatapatha 10.5.2.9,10; SBE, XLIII, 369–70.

At the close of the period of the Brāhmaṇas there appeared a new religious order. Some men became hermits, or forest dwellers (*vānaprasthas*). They believed that by worshipping their gods with fire and prayer, and by practicing the old tapas, material blessings might be won. By such austerity the man might be "purified and elevated morally and spiritually." [11] The wife of such a hermit was permitted to go with him to his forest hut. Also we must note Meyer's remark that "in the Brāhmaṇa literature the women speculate and argue with the men, just as Draupadī does in the Epic. Of course, very much of this in the Brāhmaṇas may go back to the Kshattriya influence." [12] In the Brāhmaṇas women were not altogether excluded from religious sacrifices. The Śatapatha Brāhmaṇa says:

> He girds her with a cord (*yoktra*); for, with a cord they yoke the draught-animal (*yogya*). Impure is that part of woman which is below the navel; and therewith she will be facing the sacrificial butter. That part of her he thereby conceals with the cord, and only with the pure upper part of her body she then faces the sacrificial butter. Śatapatha 1.3.1.13; SBE, XII, 72.

The following religious observance, which was allowed to maidens, was primarily for the purpose of securing a husband:

> Let the maidens then also walk round, thinking, "May we enjoy pros-

[11] Farquhar, PH, pp. 167–68.

[12] Meyer, SLAI, II, 440.

perity!" That sister of Rudra, named Ambikā, indeed is the dispenser of happiness. Hence the maidens also should walk round, thinking, "May we enjoy prosperity." The text (W.Y.V.3.60b) (prescribed) for them is "We worship Tryambaka, the fragrant bestower of husbands. Even as a gourd (is severed) from its stem, so may I be severed from this (world), not from thence (yonder world)!" By saying "from this," she means to say "from my relatives." And by saying, "not from thence," she means to say, "not from husbands." Husbands, doubtless, are the support of woman; hence she says "not from thence." Śatapatha 2.6.2.13–14; SBE, XII, 441.

If by dwelling upon the securing of a husband through a religious ceremony the Brahmans had meant the acquisition of a real partner in marriage which would represent the mutual respect and comradeship of one man and one woman, then such a religious exercise might well have been sanctioned by their followers. But this evidently was not always their design. We do find the following noble appreciation of wedlock:

The wife is faith; the sacrificer, truth. Faith and truth are the highest pair. By faith and truth as a pair he conquers the worlds of heaven. Aitareya 7.10; HOS, XXV, 297.

But on the other hand, the following quotation from the Brāhmaṇas should be adduced:

They—to wit, (many) wives—are a form of prosperity (or social eminence). Śatapatha 13.2.6.7; SBE, XLIV, 313.

Further evidences of polygamy are found in the literary endeavors of the Brahman priests.

She who is first taken to wife is the consecrated consort. Śatapatha 6.5.3.1; SBE, XLI, 238.

Even if there are many wives as it were, one husband is a pair with them. Aitareya 3.47; HOS, XXV, 195.

One man has many wives; but one wife has not many husbands. Aitareya 3.23; Haug, II, 197.

The Brāhmaṇas contain evidence that a wife who did not bear a son could be discarded.

. . . a discarded wife. Śatapatha 13.2.6.6; SBE, XLIV, 313. [Note:] *A discarded wife,* "that is, a former favourite, but now neglected; or, according to others, one who has borne no son."

On the following day he goes to the house of a discarded (wife), and prepares a pap for Nirṛti; a discarded wife is one who has no son. He cooks the pap for Nirṛti of black rice, after splitting the grains with his nails. He offers it with "This, O Nirṛti, is thy share. Accept it graciously. Hail!" For, a wife that is without a son, is possessed with Nirṛti (destruction, calamity); and whatever of Nirṛti's nature there is in her, that he thereby propitiates. Thus Nirṛti does not take possession of him while he is consecrated. The fee for this (oblation) consists of a black decrepit, diseased cow; for, such a one also is possessed with Nirṛti. He says to her (the wife), "Let her not dwell this day in my dominion!" Thus he removes evil from himself. Śatapatha 5.3.1.13; SBE, XLI, 65. [Note: "According to the commentary on Kātyāyana Śrauta Sūtra 15.3.35, she has to betake herself to a Brahman's house, where the king has no power."]

The Śatapatha Brāhmaṇa states that a daughter who has been given in marriage by her father must remain faithful to her husband. When Sukanyā is reminded of her decrepit, ghostlike husband and she is urged to leave him, she replies:

To whom my father has given me, him will I not abandon, as long as he lives. Śatapatha 4.1.5.9; SBE, XXVI, 274.

Despite a lowered estimate of woman in the Brāhmaṇas, it will be noted that in many passages of those same sacerdotal documents reverence for goddesses persisted.

To Aditi, hail! To Aditi, the mighty, hail! To Aditi, the most merciful, hail! . . .

To Sarasvatī, hail! To Sarasvatī, the pure, hail! To Sarasvatī, the great, hail! Śatapatha 13.1.8.4.5; SBE, XLIV, 293.

Aditi is this earth. Thus, "Sinless may we belong to thee and to her (the earth)!" Śatapatha 6.7.3.8; SBE, XLI, 280.

. . . the divine protectresses, dear to all the gods. Śatapatha 6.5.4.6; SBE, XLI, 243.

O Iḍā, blithesome, adorable, lovable, bright, shining, Aditi (inviolable), Sarasvatī (sapful), mighty, glorious. Śatapatha 4.5.8.10; SBE, XXVI, 415–16.

. . . the divine wives of the gods. Śatapatha 6.5.4.4; SBE, XLI, 242.

Aditi by name, we praise with speech. Śatapatha 5.1.4.4; SBE, XLI, 18.

O divine waters. Śatapatha 5.1.4.6; SBE, XLI, 19.

O Mother Earth, injure me not, nor I thee! Śatapatha 5.4.3.20; SBE, XLI, 103.

. . . the divine Aditi. Śatapatha 6.5.4.3; SBE, XLI, 242.

Another Brāhmaṇa makes an extensive laudation of the goddess Aditi:

Aditi is the heaven. Aditi is the atmosphere; verily she is the heaven, she is the atmosphere. Aditi is the mother. She is the father. She is the son. . . . Aditi is all the gods, the five races: the gods who were before the Asuras; five races, yonder person which is in the sun, in the moon, in the lightning, in the water, within the eye here. That is they. That is she. Aditi is what is born. Aditi is what is to be born. Jaiminīya, or Talavakāra Upaniṣad Brāhmaṇa 1.41.5–8; Oertel, p. 119.[13]

This (earth) is She, the Great One (Mahī). Jaiminīya, or Talavakāra, Upaniṣad Brāhmaṇa 3.4.7; Oertel, p. 163.

Despite high praise for goddesses, and the implication that both gods and goddesses were necessary and important, the following verse in the Śatapatha Brāhmaṇa shows that great care was taken to try to establish the preëminence of the male among gods and men.

To the male (deity) he makes offering first, then to the females. He thereby endows the male pre-eminently with power. To a single male he makes offering, and to many females; whence even a single man has many wives. To the male (deity) he makes offering both with the *Vashaṭ*-call and the *Svāhā*-call, to the female (deities) only with the *Svāhā*. He thereby endows the male preëminently with power. Śatapatha 9.4.1.6; SBE, XLIII, 230.

In emphasizing the position of women as inferiors to masculine masters the priests declare:

Other libations he completes by mixing, but this one he diminishes; for, ghee is a thunderbolt, and by that thunderbolt, the ghee, the gods smote the wives and unmanned them. Thus smitten and unmanned, they neither

---

[13] Oertel, tr., *The Jaiminīya, or Talavakāra, Upaniṣad Brāhmaṇa.* Reprinted from *Journal of the American Oriental Society,* XVI, 79–260.

owned any self, nor did they own any heritage. In like manner does he now, by that thunderbolt, the ghee, smite the wives, and unman them. Thus smitten and unmanned, they neither own any self, nor do they own any heritage. Śatapatha 4.4.2.13; SBE, XXVI, 366, 367.

He makes women to be dependent; whence women are sure to be attendant upon man. Śatapatha 13.2.2.4; SBE, XLIV, 300.

. . . my wife becoming obedient to me. Jaiminīya, or Talavakāra, Upaniṣad Brāhmaṇa 1.54.6; Oertel, p. 132.

Concerning female slaves the Brāhmaṇas contain such characteristic passages as the following:

Thou art the son of a female slave; we will not eat with you. Kauṣītaki 12.3; HOS, XXV, 414.

The son of Atri presented ten thousand girls, well endowed with ornaments on their necks, who had been gathered from all quarters. Aitareya 8.22.3; Haug, II, 525.

At times it would seem as though the Brahmans did note delicacy in tender marital relationships.

Whence, if any one goes to his mate, he cultivates sweet scent and a beautiful appearance. Śatapatha 9.4.1.4; SBE, XLIII, 230.

The Brahmans repeated the declaration in the Rig-Veda (10.95.15).

Truly there is no friendship with women, and theirs are the hearts of hyenas. Śatapatha 11.5.1.9; SBE, XLIV, 71–72.

The most important of the priestly documents reëmphasizes the low estimate of woman.

Women are given to vain things. . . . It is to him who dances and sings that they most readily take a fancy. Śatapatha 3.2.4.6; SBE, XXVI, 53.

Perhaps these Brahmanical writings did not report the full story of the life of those days insofar as the wishes of the majority of people were concerned regarding the "feminine." It is likely that many women did not realize at the time that some religious leaders were trying to subjugate womanhood. Much of the spiritual freedom which Hindu women had formerly possessed was wrested from them in the Brāhmaṇas.

CHAPTER III: THE UPANISHADS

IN A LECTURE delivered before the Indian Institute at Oxford University, on May 17, 1938, Professor R. E. Hume stated that

> in the long history of human thought in all countries, the Upanishads of ancient India stand preëminent as the very earliest and most vigorous attempts to attain unto absolute truth. Within the system of Hinduism itself, as elsewhere, we find commendations of truth-seeking and truth-speaking. For example, there is a magnificent verse in the Rig-Veda (10.85.1), repeated in the Atharva-Veda (14.1.1), which says "Truth is the base that bears the earth." But, in contrast with such isolated verses, and particularly in contrast with the natural enjoyments of things and other persons, the Upanishads have the high honor of antedating all other efforts of the human mind to commend the higher satisfaction which is to be derived from a systematic persistent knowledge of the eternal nature of the Reality in the midst of which we humans are located.

Thus the Hindus' love of philosophic speculation is "dominant in the third set of sacred scriptures, the Upanishads, 'Séances,' where youths and even women display interest in philosophic discussion." [1] In the Upanishads

> All the Vedic deities, indeed all things and all events, are to be regarded as manifestations of one Power at the heart of the world. In the language of traditional religion, that "It" may be called the power of prayer (*brahma*). But philosophically Brahma is to be interpreted as the absolute, infinite, eternal, omnipresent, impersonal, indescribable, neuter Being. It may also be designated as Spirit (*Ātman*), a world-soul, into which the individual human spirit also is to be merged. . . . In contrast with the one infinite abiding Reality, the manifold world with all its changing finite phenomena must be regarded as a dream or an illusion

[1] Hume, WLR, p. 24.

(*māyā*). . . . Theoretically, then, salvation is simply a quiet unstriving realization of one's real self as free from all changes, even from transmigration, and as completely absorbed in *Brahma-Ātman*. Practically, however, the way of knowledge may be supplemented by the *Yoga* method of inducing trance-consciousness or trans-consciousness. Quiet suppression of all sense-activity, even of breathing, may be made to promote breathless contemplation on the ineffable, eternal, absolutely inactive, indescribably blissful Brahma, which is already immanent within one's own heart. Ethically there are no distinctions whatsoever, either of right or of wrong, either of good or evil, because this religion puts the individual immediately into oneness with the serene, supernatural, almost incomprehensible, impersonal Supreme Being. . . . Hinduism in the Upanishads still retains the four-fold caste system as aboriginally created, though now from Brahma. But according to the Upanishads salvation is to be obtained chiefly through one's own philosophic speculation upon a pantheistic Supreme Being.[2]

In that early period some Hindu women were notable for their learning, as is evidenced by the philosophic disputations reported in the Upanishads. In the Kena Upanishad the unknown character of the "newly discovered Being and the idea that only by Its will do even the gods perform their functions" [3] is indicated in the following legend.

Brahma appeared to the gods, but they did not understand who it was. They deputed Agni, the god of fire, to ascertain its identity. He, vaunting of his power to burn, was challenged to burn a straw, but was baffled. Upon his unsuccessful return to the gods, Vāyu, the god of wind, was sent on the same mission. He, boasting of his power to blow anything away, was likewise challenged to blow a straw away, and was likewise baffled. To Indra, the next emissary, a beautiful woman, allegorized by the commentator as Wisdom, explained that the incognito was Brahma, through whose power the gods were exalted and enjoyed greatness.[4]

In that very space he came upon a woman exceeding beautiful, Umā, daughter of the Snowy Mountain (*Himavat*). [Note: "Com. allegorizes her as 'Knowledge,' who dispels Indra's ignorance. In later mythology Umā is an epithet, along with Durgā, Kālī and Pārvatī, for the wife of Śiva; and she is represented as living with him in the Himālayas."]

---

[2] Hume, WLR, pp. 24, 25, 26. [3] Hume, tr., TPU, p. 15. [4] *Ibid.*

To her he said: "What is this wonderful being?" Kena, 3.25.(12); TPU, p. 338.[5]

"It is Brahma," she said. "In that victory of Brahma, verily, exult ye." Thereupon he knew it was Brahma. Kena, 4.26.(1); TPU, p. 339.

Gārgī is another woman in the Upanishads who takes part in philosophical discussions. Indeed, it would appear that this woman Gārgī out-questioned and out-wearied the chief philosopher of the Upanishads!

Then Gārgī Vācaknavī questioned him. "Yājñavalkya," said she, "since all this world is woven, warp and woof, on water, on what, pray, is the water woven, warp and woof?"

"On wind, O Gārgī." Bṛihad-Āraṇyaka 3.6; TPU, p. 113.

Not satisfied with this reply, Gārgī puts the philosopher hard to it to answer her persistent interrogations. "On what then, pray," she continues, "is the wind woven?" To this question Yājñavalkya responds, "On the atmosphere-worlds." So Gārgī pursues her inquiries from the atmosphere-worlds to the worlds of the Gandharvas, to those of the sun, the moon, the stars, the gods, Indra, Prajāpati, and the worlds of Brahma. Then Yājñavalkya cautions: "Gārgī, do not question too much, lest your head fall off! In truth, you are questioning too much about a divinity about which further questions cannot be asked. Gārgī, do not over-question!" Thereupon Gārgī Vācaknavī held her peace.[6]

Later the same woman continues her questioning. The Bṛihad-Āraṇyaka Upanishad treats of the ultimate warp of the world—the unqualified Imperishable.

1. Then Gārgī Vācaknavī said: "Venerable Brahmans! Lo, I will ask him [i.e. Yajñavalkya] two questions. If he will answer me these, not one of you will surpass him in discussions about Brahma."

"Ask, Gārgī."

2. She said: "As a noble youth of the Kāśīs or of the Videhas might rise up against you, having strung his unstrung bow, and taken two foe-piercing arrows in his hand,—even so, O Yājñavalkya, have I risen up against you with two questions. Answer me these."

[5] The selections from the Upanishads are presented from Professor R. E. Hume's translation, *The Thirteen Principal Upanishads*.

[6] Hume, tr., TPU, pp. 113, 114.

Yājñavalkya said: "Ask, Gārgī."

3. She said: "That, O Yājñavalkya, which is above the sky, that which is beneath the earth, that which is between these two, sky and earth, that which people call the past and the present and the future,—across what is that woven, warp and woof?"

4. He said: "That, O Gārgī, which is above the sky, that which is beneath the earth, that which is between these two, sky and earth, that which people call the past and the present and the future,—across space is that woven, warp and woof."

5. She said: "Adoration to you, Yājñavalkya, in that you have solved this question for me. Prepare yourself for the other."

"Ask, Gārgī." . . .

7. "Across what then, pray, is space woven, warp and woof?"

8. He said: "That, O Gārgī, Brahmans call the Imperishable (*akṣara*). It is not coarse, not fine, not short, not long, not glowing like fire, not adhesive like water, without shadow and without darkness, without air and without space, without stickiness, odorless, tasteless, without eye, without ear, without voice, without wind, without energy, without breath, without mouth, (without personal or family name, unaging, undying, without fear, immortal, stainless, not uncovered, not covered), without measure, without inside and without outside. It consumes nothing soever. No one soever consumes it.

9. "Verily, O Gārgī, at the command of that Imperishable the sun and the moon stand apart. Verily, O Gārgī, at the command of that Imperishable the earth and the sky stand apart. Verily, O Gārgī, at the command of that Imperishable the moments, the hours, the days, the nights, the fortnights, the months, the seasons, and the years stand apart. Verily, O Gārgī, at the command of that Imperishable some rivers flow from the snowy mountains to the east, others to the west, in whatever direction each flows. Verily, O Gārgī, at the command of that Imperishable men praise those who give, the gods are desirous of a sacrificer, and the fathers are desirous of the Manes-sacrifice.

10. "Verily, O Gārgī, if one performs sacrifices and worship and undergoes austerity in this world for many thousands of years, but without knowing that Imperishable, limited indeed is that work of his. Verily, O Gārgī, he who departs from this world without knowing that Imperishable is pitiable. But, O Gārgī, he who departs from this world knowing that Imperishable is a Brahman.

11. "Verily, O Gārgī, that Imperishable is the unseen Seer, the unheard Hearer, the unthought Thinker, the ununderstood Understander. Other

than It there is naught that sees. Other than It there is naught that hears. Other than It there is naught that thinks. Other than It there is naught that understands. Across this Imperishable, O Gārgī, is space woven, warp and woof."

12. She said: "Venerable Brahmans, you may think it a great thing if you escape from this man with merely making a bow. Not one of you will surpass him in discussions about Brahma."

Thereupon Gārgī Vācaknavī held her peace. Bṛihad-Āraṇyaka 3.8.1–5, 7–12; TPU, pp. 117–19.

In the same "Great Forest Treatise" metaphysical instruction concerning the pantheistic Soul is given to a woman.

1. Now then, Yājñavalkya had two wives, Maitreyī and Kātyāyanī. Of the two, Maitreyī was a discourser on sacred knowledge (*brahmavādinī*); Kātyāyanī had just (*eva*) a woman's knowledge in that matter (*tarhi*). Now then, Yājñavalkya was about to commence another mode of life.

2. "Maitreyī!" said Yājñavalkya, "lo, verily, I am about to wander forth from this state. Behold! Let me make a final settlement for you and that Kātyāyanī."

3. Then spake Maitreyī: "If now, sir, this whole earth filled with wealth were mine, would I now thereby be immortal?"

"No, no!" said Yājñavalkya. "As the life of the rich, even so would your life be. Of immortality, however, there is no hope through wealth."

4. Then spake Maitreyī: "What should I do with that through which I may not be immortal? What you know, sir,—that, indeed, explain to me."

5. Then spake Yājñavalkya: "Though, verily, you, my lady, were dear to us, you have increased your dearness. Behold, then, lady! I will explain it to you. But, while I am expounding, do you seek to ponder thereon."

Then Yājñavalkya declares that not for love of husband is a husband dear, but for love of the Soul (*Ātman*) a husband is dear. Likewise, it is for love of the Soul that a wife, sons, wealth, cattle, Brahmanhood, Kshatrahood, the worlds, the gods, the Vedas, and beings are dear. He declares:

6. . . . "Lo, verily, it is the Soul (*Ātman*) that should be seen, that should be hearkened to, that should be thought on, that should be pondered on, O Maitreyī.

"Lo, verily, in the Soul's being seen, hearkened to, thought on, understood, this world-all is known.

7. "Brahmanhood deserts him who knows Brahmanhood in aught else than the Soul."

Yājñavalkya assures Maitreyī that Kshatrahood likewise, as well as the worlds, the gods, the Vedas, and beings, desert him who knows them in aught else than the Soul. He states:

8. "It is—as, when a drum is being beaten, one would not be able to grasp the external sounds, but by grasping the drum or the beater of the drum the sound is grasped. . . .

11. "It is—as, from a fire laid with damp fuel, clouds of smoke separately issue forth, so, lo, verily, from this great Being (*bhūta*) has been breathed forth that which is Rig-Veda, Yajur-Veda, Sāma-Veda, [Hymns] of the Atharvans and Aṅgirases, Legend (*itihāsa*), Ancient Lore (*purāṇa*), Sciences (*vidyā*), Mystic Doctrines (*upaniṣad*), Verses (*śloka*), Aphorisms (*sūtra*), Explanations (*anuvyākhyāna*), Commentaries (*vyākhyāna*), sacrifice, oblation, food, drink, this world and the other, and all beings. From It, indeed, have all these been breathed forth."

Yājñavalkya further describes the Soul to the woman Maitreyī:

13. "It is,—as a mass of salt, without inside, without outside, entirely a mass of taste, even so, verily, is this Soul, without inside, without outside, entirely a mass of knowledge.

"Arising out of these elements, into them also one vanishes away. After death there is no consciousness. Thus, lo, say I." Thus spake Yājñavalkya.

14. Then said Maitreyī: "Herein, indeed, you have caused me, sir, to arrive at the extreme of bewilderment. Verily, I understand It (i.e., this *Ātman*) not."

Then said he: "Lo verily, I speak not bewilderment. Imperishable, lo, verily, is this Soul, and of indestructible quality.

15. "For where there is a duality, as it were, there one sees another; there one smells another; there one tastes another; there one speaks to another; there one hears another; there one thinks of another; there one touches another; there one understands another. But where everything has become just one's own self, then whereby and whom would one see? then whereby and whom would one smell? then whereby and whom would one taste? then whereby and to whom would one speak? then whereby and whom would one hear? then whereby and of whom would one think? then whereby and whom would one touch? then whereby and whom would

one understand? whereby would one understand him by means of whom one understands this All?

"That Soul (*Ātman*) is not this, it is not that. It is unseizable, for it cannot be seized; indestructible, for it cannot be destroyed; unattached, for it does not attach itself; is unbound, does not tremble, is not injured.

"Lo, whereby would one understand the understander?

"Thus you have the instruction told to you, Maitreyī. Such lo, indeed, is immortality." Bṛihad-Āraṇyaka 4.5.1–8,11,13–15; TPU, pp. 144, 145, 146, 147.

In the Upanishads woman is referred to as having been created by the Primeval Being.

3. Verily, he had no delight. Therefore one alone has no delight. He desired a second. He was, indeed, as large as a woman and a man closely embraced. He caused that self to fall (*pat*) into two pieces. Therefrom arose a husband (*pati*) and a wife (*patnī*). Therefore this is true: "Oneself (*sva*) is like a half-fragment," as Yājñavalkya used to say. Therefore this space is filled by a wife. Bṛihad-Āraṇyaka 1.4.3; TPU, p. 81.

Remarkable is the statement that a man's wife is his voice.

His mind truly is his self (*Ātman*): his voice is his wife. Bṛihad-Āraṇyaka 1.4.17; TPU, p. 86.

As in the Brāhmaṇas, so also in the Upanishads there are instructions regarding sexual matters. Very striking is the explicit justification of forcible sex-violation of a woman by a man.

If she should not grant him his desire, he should bribe her. If she still does not grant him his desire, he should hit her with a stick or with his hand, and overcome her, saying: "With power, with glory I take away your glory!" Thus she becomes inglorious. Bṛihad-Āraṇyaka 6.4.7; TPU, p. 169.

On the other hand, in the following verse it is noteworthy that a daughter was desired and that the parents went through a religious ceremony for the fulfillment of that desire.

17. Now, in case one wishes, "That a learned (*paṇḍita*) daughter be born to me! that she attain the full length of life!"—they two should have rice boiled with sesame, and should eat it prepared with ghee.—They are likely to beget her. Bṛihad-Āraṇyaka 6.4.17; TPU, p. 171.

A daughter, however, does not help a father to attain the sense of security which a son is able to provide.

By his son a father stands firm in this world. Bṛihad-Āraṇyaka 1.5.17; TPU, p. 90.

The condemnation of a barren woman is continued throughout the centuries from the Vedas into the Upanishads. False teaching is likened to a barren woman.

It [false teaching] is false. It is like a barren woman. Maitri Upanishad 7.9; TPU, p. 456.

It is to be observed that a mother is classified not only with a father, teacher, and guest, but also with a deity.

Be one to whom a mother is as a god.
Be one to whom a father is as a god.
Be one to whom a teacher is as a god.
Be one to whom a guest is as a god.
Taittirīya 1.11.2; TPU, pp. 281–82.

The custom of female slaves was still prevalent in the Upanishads, as well as in the earlier Vedas and Brāhmaṇas.

. . . a female slave. Chāndogya 5.13.1; TPU, p. 235.

Then he said: "It is well known that I have a full share of gold, of cows and horses, of female slaves, of rugs, of apparel." Bṛihad-Āraṇyaka 6.2.7; TPU, p. 161.

The Chāndogya Upanishad also says that a man who knows certain mystic lore ". . . should never abstain from any woman. That is his rule" (Chāndogya 2.13.2; TPU, p. 196). Promiscuity was practiced, as evidenced by the following story depicting a young man who wished to study religion:

Once upon a time Satyakāma Jābāla addressed his mother Jabālā: "Madam! I desire to live the life of a student of sacred knowledge. Of what family, pray, am I?"

Then she said to him: "I do not know this, my dear—of what family you are. In my youth, when I went about a great deal serving as a maid, I got you. So I do not know of what family you are. However, I am Jabālā by name; you are Satyakāma by name. So you may speak of yourself as Satyakāma Jābāla." Chāndogya 4.4.1–2; TPU, p. 218.

Harsh speech is forbidden to a mother as well as to a father, to a sister as well as to a brother.

If one answers harshly, as it were (*iva*), a father, or a mother, or a brother, or a sister, or a teacher, or a Brahman, people say to him: "Shame on you! Verily, you are a slayer of your father! Verily, you are a slayer of your mother! Verily, you are a slayer of your brother! Verily, you are a slayer of your sister! Verily, you are a slayer of your teacher! Verily, you are a slayer of a Brahman! Chāndogya 7.15.2; TPU, p. 258.

Praiseworthy also is the injunction that a mother who has given nourishment should herself be nourished.

The woman bears him as an embryo. She, being a nourisher, should be nourished. Aitareya 2.4.3; TPU, p. 299.

The goddess of boundlessness, Aditi, who is referred to so many times in the Vedas and in the Brāhmaṇas, continues to receive reverence in the Upanishads.

. . . the *aditi*–nature of Aditi (the Infinite). Bṛihad-Āraṇyaka 1.2.5; TPU, p. 75.

She who arises with life (*prāṇa*), Aditi (Infinity), maker of divinity . . . Katha 4.7; TPU, p. 354.

The universal, unitary reality, which constitutes the central concept of the Upanishads, is identified with various powers, both human and divine. It is identified with "a woman and the maiden too."

> That surely is Agni (fire). That is Āditya (the sun).
> That is Vāyu (the wind), and That is the moon.
> That surely is the pure. That is Brahma.
> That is the waters. That is Prajāpati (Lord of Creation).
>
> Thou art woman. Thou art man.
> Thou art the youth and the maiden too.
>
> Śvetāśvatara 4.2–3; TPU, p. 403.

CHAPTER IV: THE LAWS OF MANU

BEFORE the late centuries B.C. the Brahmans had become eminently powerful. Through their elaborate ceremonials they regulated every aspect of religious life. Law in India always has been connected closely with religion. Most influential among several books of law were those of Manu (*Mānava Dharma-Śāstra*), which probably is a compilation of many sources and contains elements of very varying values. The late Bodin Professor of Sanskrit at Oxford University ventured the characterization that this document is "perhaps one of the most remarkable books that the literature of the whole world can offer, and some of its moral precepts are worthy of Christianity itself." [1] Yet on the other hand, a very low estimate has been put on the same, as follows:

> It is Manu's code that has had the most negative effects, forging unbreakable shackles on Indian women for countless succeeding generations. Even today, it is his laws which keep millions helpless in the prison of Hindu orthodoxy. Manu for the first time legally assigned to woman her definite place in the scale of society. But his laws reflect a conflict even within himself between his valuation of woman as a spiritual entity on the one side, and as a unit in society on the other. He averred that a mother is more to be revered than a thousand fathers, yet his laws place woman socially on a level with the lowest of all groups in Aryan society, the Śūdra.[2]

Along with passages showing depreciation of woman, there will be quoted in this study many verses of praise. Manu made a curious combination of giving praise to woman and yet degrading her to the lowest point of Hindu society. Hindus of those days seemed

[1] Monier-Williams, *Hinduism*, p. 54. This estimate of Manu is repeated verbatim in his *Indian Wisdom*, p. 204.

[2] Das, *Purdah: the Status of Indian Women*, pp. 27–28.

not to have awakened to the realization of some of the Brahmans' greed for absolute power, even at the expense of the welfare of precious human lives. Upon sober analysis it seems amazing that tyrannical religious edicts should have gained such sway over reason and the appreciation of womanhood.

Polygamy was fostered by the Laws of Manu. Intrigue often resulted and brought deep sadness into many a zenana.

If after one damsel has been shown, another be given to the bridegroom, he may marry them both for the same price.[3] 8.204.

If there be four wives of a Brāhmaṇa in the direct order of the castes, the rule for the division (of the estate) among the sons born of them is as follows:

The (slave) who tills (the field), the bull kept for impregnating cows, the vehicle, the ornaments, and the house shall be given as an additional portion to the Brāhmaṇa (son), and one most excellent share.

Let the son of the Brāhmaṇī (wife) take three shares of the (remainder of the) estate; the son of the Kshatriyā, two; the son of the Vaiśyā a share and a half, and the son of the Śūdrā may take one share. 9.149–51.

The wives of the teacher, who belong to the same caste, must be treated as respectfully as the teacher; but those who belong to a different caste, must be honoured by rising and salutation. 2.210.

Despite these verses relating to polygamy, there are many verses which apparently indicate happy monogamous marriage.

In that family, where the husband is pleased with his wife and the wife with her husband, happiness will assuredly be lasting. 3.60.

If the wife is radiant with beauty, the whole house is bright. But if she is destitute of beauty, all will appear dismal. 3.62.

The husband who wedded her with sacred texts, always gives happiness to his wife. 5.153.

The husband receives his wife from the gods, (he does not wed her) according to his own will; doing what is agreeable to the gods, he must always support her (while she is) faithful. 9.95.

Neither a mother, nor a father, nor a wife, nor a son shall be cast off. He

[3] Unless otherwise stated, the Laws of Manu quoted are from G. Bühler's translation in the *Sacred Books of the East,* Vol. XXV.

who casts them off, unless guilty of a crime causing loss of caste, shall be fined by the king six hundred (*paṇas*). 8.389.

Neither by sale nor by repudiation is a wife released from her husband. 9.46.

He who carefully guards his wife, preserves (the purity of) his offspring, virtuous conduct, his family, himself, and his (means of acquiring) merit. 9.7.

"Let mutual fidelity continue until death." This may be considered as the summary of the highest law for husband and wife. 9.101.

Let man and woman united in marriage, constantly exert themselves, that (they may not be) disunited, (and) may not violate their mutual fidelity. 9.102.

The husband is declared to be one with the wife. 9.45.

In the Laws of Manu a barren wife is not altogether condemned. Indeed, in a polygamous family a barren wife is to be regarded as the mother of a son, if it happens that any other wife of her husband has borne a son.

If among all the wives of one husband one have a son, Manu declares them all (to be) mothers of male children through that son. 9.183.

The practice, which has been widely prevalent for more than twenty centuries among Hindu families, that the men folk and the women folk in the same family should eat apart, has been the explicit result of a prohibition which stands in the Laws of Manu and which occurs twice in the earlier Śatapatha Brāhmaṇa (1.9.2.12 and 10.5.2.9,10).

Let him not eat in the company of his wife, nor look at her, while she eats, sneezes, yawns, or sits at her ease. 4.43.

Also with regard to the eating of food Manu assigns a low position to woman.

A Brāhmaṇa must never eat (a dinner given) at a sacrifice that is offered by . . . a woman. 4.205.

[Let him never eat] (food) given . . . by a female who has no male (relatives). 4.213.

[Let him never eat] (food given) . . . by those who in all matters are ruled by women. 4.217.

He who has eaten the food of men whose food must not be eaten, or the leavings of women and Śūdras, or forbidden flesh, shall drink barley (gruel) during seven (days and) nights. 11.153.

Having washed his hands and sipped water, let him prepare (food) for his paternal relations, and, after giving it to them with due respect, let him feed his maternal relatives also. 3.264.

In certain situations, however, it is prescribed that food should be given to women—even before it is given to guests.

Without hesitation he may give food, even before his guests, to the following persons, (viz.) to newly-married women, to infants, to the sick, and to pregnant women. 3.114.

Concerning the question of food we learn from the Laws of Manu that receiving a gift of food from a woman is very important for a religious student starting his initiation ceremonies.

(The student) should beg alms according to the prescribed rule. . . .
Let him first beg food of his mother, or of his sister, or of his own maternal aunt, or of (some other) female who will not disgrace him (by a refusal). 2.48, 50.

Eight marriage rites are described in the Laws of Manu, and their virtues and faults are listed. It is indicated which rite is lawful for each caste. Results to offspring of these various types of marriage also are described intricately (3.20–44). Caste must be considered, as well as degrees of relationship (3.4). In (3.150,157) he who contracts an alliance with outcasts cannot be invited to a *Śrāddha,* which is a ceremony in honor of a deceased forefather. Although caste is important, yet the Laws of Manu declare that the spiritual process of faith can transcend customary caste distinction and can enable a man to obtain an excellent wife even from a lower social stratum.

He who possesses faith may receive pure learning even from a man of lower caste, the highest law even from the lowest, and an excellent wife even from a base family. 2.238.

Excellent wives . . . may be acquired from anybody. 2.240.

In addition to stating a general universal principle concerning woman and marriage, this Hindu document cites an actual historic instance when a woman of the lowest birth became worthy of honor through marriage with the sage Vasishṭha.

Akshamālā, a woman of the lowest birth, being united to Vasishṭha, and Sārangī, being united to Mandapāla, became worthy of honour. 9.23.

Indeed, Manu said there were many such instances.

These and other females of low birth have attained eminence in this world by the respective good qualities of their husbands. 9.24.

In planning a marriage, one is to avoid families that neglect sacred rites, as well as those in which no male children have been born, and families subject to disease (3.7). A prospective bride must not have reddish hair, red eyes, or be named after a constellation, tree, river, mountain, bird, or snake (3.8,9). Manu says that the names of women should be easy to pronounce, should not imply anything dreadful, should possess a plain meaning, be pleasing and auspicious, and should end in long vowels and contain a word of benediction (2.33). Among the regulations regarding marriage we find verses such as the following:

The elder brother who marries after the younger, the younger brother who marries before the elder, the female with whom such a marriage is contracted, he who gives her away, and the sacrificing priest, as the fifth, all fall into hell. 3.172.

For the sake of procuring good fortune to (brides), the recitation of benedictory texts (*svastyayana*), and the sacrifice to the Lord of creatures (Prajāpati) are used at weddings; (but) the betrothal (by the father or guardian) is the cause of (the husband's) dominion (over his wife). 5.152.

Once is the partition (of the inheritance) made; (once is) a maiden given in marriage; (and) once does (a man) say, "I will give." Each of those three (acts is done) once only. 9.47. [Note: "The object of the verse is to show that a marriage is indissoluble, because a girl can be given once only." SBE, XXV, 335, 336; see also 9.71.]

Incest is forbidden by the Laws of Manu (11.55,59,60,62,67). Certain other marriage relationships are debarred. For instance, a man must not marry the daughter of his father's sister, who is almost equal to a sister, or the daughter of his mother's sister or of his mother's full brother (11.172,173).

Manu states that the expenses of a first marriage may be obtained by begging (11.1). The nuptial ceremony is considered the Vedic sacrament for women and is equal to the initiation; serving the husband is equivalent to the residence in the house of the teacher; and the household duties are the same as the daily worship of the sacred fire (2.67). Manu enumerates many laws directing a wife's conduct. The temper of these laws is illustrated by verses of the following character:

Until death let her be patient (of hardships), self-controlled and chaste, and strive (to fulfil) that most excellent duty which (is prescribed) for wives who have one husband only. 5.158.

She must always be cheerful, clever in (the management of her) household affairs, careful in cleaning her utensils, and economical in expenditures. 5.150.

A wife must show to her husband such utter devotion that he must be treated like a god, even when he is conspicuously lacking in virtue.

Though destitute of virtue, or seeking pleasure (elsewhere), or devoid of good qualities, (yet) a husband must be constantly worshipped as a god by a faithful wife (*strī sādhvī*). 5.154.

Whatever be the qualities of the man with whom a woman is united according to the law, such qualities even she assumes, like a river (united) with the ocean. 9.22.

No sacrifice, no vow, no fast must be performed by women apart (from their husbands). If a wife obeys her husband, she will for that (reason alone) be exalted in heaven. 5.155.

She must not seek to separate herself from her father, husband, or sons. By leaving them she would make both (her own and her husband's) families contemptible. 5.149.

A wife who, being superseded, in anger departs from (her husband's) house, must either be instantly confined or cast off in the presence of the family. 9.83.

In childhood a female must be subject to her father; in youth, to her husband; when her lord is dead, to her sons. A woman must never be independent. 5.148.

Entrance into the second quarter of a man's existence, that of a householder, is said by Manu to require as preparation, study of the Vedas (3.2). Thus it is evident that life with his wife and family is considered sufficiently important to need spiritual prerequisites. Manu states that because men of the three other orders are daily supported by the householder with gifts of sacred knowledge and food, the order of the householder is the most excellent (3.78). The emphasis is clearly on man's attainment of domestic life in a thoroughly honorable manner. He must not follow the ways of the world, but is to live a pure, straightforward, honest life (4.11). The householder who desires happiness must strive after a perfectly contented disposition and must control himself (4.12). The husband is required to guard his wife carefully in order to keep his offspring pure (9.9). Manu admits that men cannot guard women completely by force, but he suggests that only by the employment of certain expedients can women be guarded (9.10). The Laws of Manu declare that servants alone, even though trustworthy and obedient, are not sufficient for the protection of wives. Only those women who of their own accord keep guard over themselves, are well guarded (9.12). According to the laws the husband should employ his wife in the collection and expenditure of his wealth, in keeping everything clean, in the fulfillment of religious duties, in the preparation of his food, and in looking after the household utensils (9.11). The perfect householder is described as the man who consists of three united persons, namely, his wife, himself, and his offspring (9.45).

The Laws of Manu state that women were created to be mothers and that they may perform religious rites along with their husbands.

> To be mothers were women created; and to be fathers, men. Religious rites, therefore, are ordained in the Vedas to be performed (by the husband) together with the wife. 9.96.

Yet we find other passages which deny to women the privilege of offering sacrifices.

> Neither a girl, nor a (married) young woman, nor a man of little learn-

ing, nor a fool, nor a man in great suffering, nor one uninitiated, shall offer an *Agnihotra*.[4]

For, such (persons) offering a burnt-oblation sink into hell. 11.36,37.

Furthermore, Manu declares that ceremonies must be performed for females in order to sanctify the body, but without recitation of sacred texts (2.66). In the performance of the many daily and domestic rites prescribed for a householder, Manu says, sacred fires must be kindled, many sacrifices must be made to the gods, to Brāhmaṇas, and to the manes, and guests must be received hospitably. Vedas must be recited. Then Manu adds that the wife is to take part in the evening oblation (3.67–121).

We must note that Manu recorded some tender appreciations of womanhood. Concerning the mother Manu says:

The teacher is ten times more venerable than a sub-teacher, the father a hundred times more than the teacher, but the mother a thousand times more than the father. 2.145.

Let him never offend the teacher who initiated him, nor him who explained the Veda, nor his father and mother, nor (any other) Guru, nor cows, nor Brāhmaṇas, nor any men performing austerities. 4.162.

The teacher, the father, the mother, and an elder brother must not be treated with disrespect, especially by a Brāhmaṇa, though he be grievously offended (by them). 2.225.

Towards a sister of one's father, and of one's mother, and towards one's elder sister, one must behave as toward one's mother; (but) the mother is more venerable than they. 2.133.

He who forsakes his mother, his father, or teacher without a (sufficient) reason . . . must be avoided. 3.157,161.

Neither a mother, nor a father, nor a wife, nor a son shall be cast off. He who casts them off, unless guilty of a crime causing loss of caste, shall be fined by the king. 8.389.

---

[4] *Agnihotra:* "After the performance of the ceremony of *Agnyādhāna,* which marks . . . initiation into the Fire-cult, it is incumbent on the initiated householder, called *Āhitagni,* and his wife to perform twice daily the *Yāga* known as *Agnihotra.* From the *Gārhapatya Agni* which is kept constantly burning, a portion of the Fire is taken by them to the *Āhavanīya* and *Dakṣiṇāgni* enclosures respectively, and kindled morning and evening, upon which libations are poured." Das, *Ṛgvedic Culture,* p. 492.

He who defames his mother . . . [or] his wife . . . shall be compelled to pay one hundred paṇas. *8.275.*

That trouble (and pain) which the parents undergo on the birth of (their) children, cannot be compensated even in a hundred years.

Let him always do what is agreeable to those (two) and always (what may please) his teacher. When those three are pleased, he obtains all (those rewards which) austerities (yield). *2.227–28.*

Obedience towards those three [mother, father, teacher], is declared to be the best (form of) austerity. *2.229.*

They [mother, father, teacher], are declared to be the three worlds; they, the three (principal) orders; they, the three Vedas; and they, the three sacred fires. *2.230.*

A woman who has been pregnant two months or more . . . shall not be made to pay toll at a ferry. 8.407.

He who neglects not those three [mother, father, teacher], (even after he has become) a householder, will conquer the three worlds; and, radiant in body like a god, he will enjoy bliss in heaven.

By honouring his mother he gains this (nether) world; by honouring his father, the middle sphere, but by obedience to his teacher, the world of Brahman.

All duties have been fulfilled by him who honours those three; but to him who honours them not, all rites remain fruitless.

As long as those three live . . . let him always serve them, rejoicing (to do what is) agreeable and beneficial (to them).

By (honouring) these three all that ought to be done by man, is accomplished. That is clearly the highest duty. Every other (act) is a subordinate duty. *2.232–34, 235, 237.*

With his father and his mother, with female relatives, with a brother, with his son and his wife, with his daughter, and with his slaves, let him not have quarrels.

If he avoids quarrels with these persons, he will be freed from all sins. 4.180–81.

Although women are excluded from participation in the very important religious ceremony of *Śrāddha* for the deceased forefathers, yet the male relatives who are acquired through the female line of the house are included in that important religious ceremony.

One may . . . entertain [at a *Śrāddha*] one's maternal grandfather, a maternal uncle, a sister's son, a father-in-law, one's teacher, a daughter's son, a daughter's husband. 3.148.

A very high status is assigned to woman in the following lines:

The production of children, the nurture of those born, and the daily life of men,—(of these matters) woman is visibly the cause.

Offspring, (the due performance of) religious rites, faithful service, highest conjugal happiness, and heavenly bliss for the ancestors and oneself, depend on one's wife alone. 9.27–28.

However, we also should note that the begetting and birth of a child is said to bring impurity to both the father and the mother (5.62–63). Woman is said (4.212 and 5.85) to be impure at the time of the birth of her child. Oblations are described (2.27) to remove the taint.

With regard to the status of daughters Manu says that if they are blemished, diseased, or deflowered, a bridegroom may annul a marriage, provided he had not known of such defects at the time of marriage (9.72,73). When a father gives his daughter to a man, she must not show disrespect to her husband, even though he is addicted to some evil passion, is a drunkard, or is diseased. In case she should show disrespect, she may be deserted by that husband for three months and be deprived of her ornaments and furniture (9.78).

Him to whom her father may give her, or her brother with the father's permission, she shall obey as long as he lives. And when he is dead, she must not insult (his memory). 5.151.

The sale of a daughter is forbidden by Manu (9.93).

No father who knows (the law) must take even the smallest gratuity for his daughter; for, a man who through avarice takes a gratuity, is a seller of his offspring. 3.51.

Manu states that even a Śūdra ought not to take a nuptial fee for his daughter (9.98).

With regard to the inheritance of daughters and granddaughters Manu provides quite explicitly. A daughter inherits from her mother (9.192,194). A daughter of a Brāhmaṇī wife inherits from co-wives (9.198). A daughter's daughter inherits from the maternal grandmother (9.193). If unmarried, a daughter inherits a fourth of her father's estate (9.118), as well as the separate property of her mother.

Concerning betrothal regulations Manu says that having promised a daughter to one man, a father must not give her to another (9.71). Manu calls a father reprehensible who does not give his daughter in marriage at the proper time (9.4). The Law of Manu (9.88) says that a father should give his daughter to a distinguished, handsome suitor of equal caste, even though she has not attained the proper age. But Manu declares (9.89) that though marriageable, the maiden should rather stop in her father's house until death than to be given to a man destitute of good qualities. According to Manu (9.90) a damsel should wait three years, though she be marriageable; but after that time she should choose a bridegroom of equal caste and rank for herself. In such a case she incurs no guilt, nor does he whom she weds (9.91). If a maiden chooses for herself, she shall not take away any ornaments given by her father or her mother or her brothers. If she does, this is considered theft (9.92).

Failing a son of his own, a father may appoint a daughter's son to perform funeral rites.

> He who has no son may make his daughter in the following manner an appointed daughter (*putrikā,* saying to her husband), "The (male) child, born of her, shall perform my funeral rites." 9.127.

An appointed daughter is equal to a son, and is entitled to an inheritance (9.130). If an appointed daughter dies by accident without leaving a son, the husband of the appointed daughter may without hesitation take that estate (9.135). The son of an appointed daughter shall take the whole estate of his maternal grandfather who leaves no son (9.131). The son of an appointed daughter also shall take the estate of his own father who leaves no other son. He is entitled to present two funeral cakes to his own father and to his maternal grandfather (9.132). The son of an appointed daughter first presents a funeral cake to his mother, the second to her father, and the third to his father's father (9.140). With regard to the possible complications of this system of an appointed daughter Manu warns (3.11), however, that a prudent man should not marry a maiden who has no brother, or one whose father is not known, lest she be made an appointed daughter.

The linguistic problem which arose in the Aitareya Brāhmaṇa (7.13) concerning the exact meaning of the Sanskrit word *"kṛipaṇam"* recurs in the Laws of Manu. In the *Sacred Books of the East* Bühler renders the translation as follows:

> One's wife and one's son must be considered as one's own body . . . one's daughter as the highest object of tenderness. Hence, if one is offended by (any one of) these, one must bear it without resentment. 4.184,185.

Burnell and Hopkins translate this passage of the Laws of Manu to mean that the daughter is "the chief miserable object." This interpretation might suggest "an object to be pitied" or a completely derogatory attitude toward a daughter. On the other hand, the word *"kṛipaṇam"* referring to daughter is translated as "the highest object of tenderness" in *Mānava-Dherma-Sāstra; or The Institutes of Menu,* by William Jones and G. C. Haughton. This translation was first published in 1825. Forty-four years later, in 1869, Standish Grove Grady, in his revised edition of that translation, still rendered the word as "the highest object of tenderness." Dutt, in *Manu Saṃhitā,* gives a favorable estimate of a daughter as "the receptacle of highest affection." In *Manu-Smṛti* Ganganath Jha presents a daughter as "the highest object of tenderness." Thus it is well for the student of religion to take note of linguistic difficulties and varied interpretations. In studying the history of religious laws that have become social customs many strange results sometimes occur even with regard to the exact meaning of a word.

Child-marriage is permitted for a girl even as early as the age of eight.

> A man, aged thirty years, shall marry a maiden of twelve who pleases him; or a man of twenty-four, a girl eight years of age. If (the performance of) his duties would (otherwise) be impeded, (he must marry) sooner. 9.94.

The duty of begetting sons is expressed in 2.28. The human body is made fit for union with Brahma by the performance of all duties, including the procreation of children.

Through a son he conquers the worlds. Through a son's son he obtains immortality. But through his son's grandson he gains the world of the sun. 9.137.

Exceedingly influential in all subsequent Hindu history has been the etymological explanation by Manu that the Sanskrit word *Put-tra* is derived from two Sanskrit words meaning savior from the hell called *Put*.

Because a son delivers (*trāyate*) his father from the hell called *Put*, therefore he was called *put-tra* (a deliverer from *Put*). 9.138.

The custom of adopting a son is quite clear in the Laws of Manu. An adopted son who possesses all good qualities may take the inheritance (9.141). However, there is specified a limitation in that an adopted son shall never take the family name and the estate of his natural father (9.142).

Despite the emphasis upon the necessity for sons, Manu provides other ways of going to heaven without having a son.

Many thousands of Brāhmaṇas who were chaste from their youth, have gone to heaven without continuing their race. 5.159.

Corporal punishment is prescribed for offenders, even women, according to the Laws of Manu.

On women, infants, men of distorted mind, the poor and the sick, the king shall inflict punishment with a whip, a cane, a rope and the like. 9.230.

A wife, a son, a slave, a pupil, and a (younger) brother of the full blood, who have committed faults, may be beaten with a rope or a split bamboo.

But on the back part of the body (only), never on a noble part. He who strikes them otherwise, will incur the same guilt as a thief. 8.299–300.

High-handed masculine authority is authorized further by passages such as the following:

A wife, a son and a slave, these three are declared to have no property.

The wealth which they earn is (acquired) for him to whom they belong. 8.416.

No crime causing loss of caste, is committed by swearing (falsely) to women, the objects of one's desire, at marriages, for the sake of fodder, a cow, or fuel, and in (order to show) favour to a Brāhmaṇa. 8.112.

Day and night women must be kept in dependence by the males (of) their (families); if they attach themselves to sensual enjoyments, they must be kept under one's control. 9.2.

The menial status of woman is expressly allowed in the following:

At the time of consultation let him (the King) cause to be removed idiots, the dumb, the blind, and the deaf, animals, very aged men, women, barbarians, the sick, and those deficient in limbs.

(Such) despicables . . . and particularly women, betray secret council; for that reason he must be careful with respect to them. 7.149–50.

The Laws of Manu declare that a wife may be superseded for various reasons.

A barren wife may be superseded in the eighth year; she whose children (all) die, in the tenth; she who bears only daughters, in the eleventh; but she who is quarrelsome, without delay.

But a sick wife who is kind (to her husband) and virtuous in her conduct, may be superseded (only) with her own consent and must never be disgraced. 9.81–82.

She who drinks spirituous liquor, is of bad conduct, rebellious, diseased, mischievous or wasteful, may at any time be superseded (by another wife). 9.80.

Manu gives a husband permission to confine an exceedingly corrupt wife to one apartment (11.177). A wife who when forbidden not to do so drinks spirituous liquor, even at festivals, or goes to public spectacles or assemblies shall be fined (9.84). Manu states (9.77) that for one year a husband shall bear with a wife who hates him; but after a year he shall deprive her of her property. Women who commit theft incur guilt (12.69). Six causes of the ruin of women are enumerated by Manu:

Drinking (spirituous liquor), associating with wicked people, separation from the husband, rambling abroad, sleeping (at unseasonable hours), and dwelling in other men's houses. 9.13.

Abortion is condemned by Manu. The Laws of Manu state that libations of water shall not be offered to women

> . . . who have joined a heretical sect, who through lust live (with many men), who have caused an abortion, have killed their husbands, or drink spirituous liquor. 5.89,90.

Penance is required for destroying the embryo of a Brāhmaṇa (11.88).

Prostitution is condemned. Manu states (8.226) that the nuptial texts are applied solely to virgins; nowhere to females who have lost their virginity; for, such females are excluded from religious ceremonies. The Laws of Manu say (4.209,211) that food given by a harlot must not be eaten. The eating of such food excludes one from the higher worlds (4.219). A king should consider a harlot as a thorn in the side of his people (9.259,260). He should banish dancers and singers from his town (9.225).

Adultery is forbidden (9.41). Penances must be performed by the men and women who commit adultery (11.62,177–79).

> Let no man converse with the wives of others after he has been forbidden (to do so). But he who converses (with them), in spite of a prohibition, shall be fined. . . .
>
> This rule does not apply to the wives of actors and singers, nor (of) those who live on (the intrigues of) their own (wives); for, such men send their wives (to others) or, concealing themselves, allow them to hold criminal intercourse.
>
> Yet he who secretly converses with such women, or with female slaves kept by one (master), and with female ascetics, shall be compelled to pay a small fine. 8.361–63.

A wife who violates the duty that she owes to her lord shall be devoured by dogs in a place frequented by many (8.371). By violating her duty toward her husband a wife is disgraced in this world; and after death she enters the womb of a jackal and is tormented by diseases as a punishment for her sin (5.164; 9.30). A man who is not a Brāhmaṇa ought to suffer death for adultery (8.359). A man who commits adultery is to be burned on a red-hot iron (8.372). Imprisonment, capital punishment, and heavy fines for adulterers are described in (8.373–79; 383–85). Adultery with the wife of a *Guru* is considered a sin (9.235,237; 11.49,55; 12.58). Such an act is to be punished in this world and in the next world. The king should inflict punishment upon men who commit adultery, and then banish them (8.352). The son and the husband of an adulteress are to be excluded from *Śrāddha* (3.151,155,156). No food may be eaten which is given by the son or the husband of an adulteress (3.158; 4.217). It is stated (4.133) that no particular attention must be shown to the wife of another man; in fact the Laws of Manu further state that in this world there is nothing so detrimental to long life as criminal conversation with another man's wife (4.134). Adultery is stated to cause a mixture of castes; and from this the Laws of Manu declare (8.353) that sin follows. It is prescribed that adultery, defiling a damsel, selling one's wife or child, practicing the arts of dancing and singing, and slaying women are offenses, causing loss of caste (11.60,62,66,67).

Slave girls are mentioned in the Laws of Manu (9.55). Manu states that he who secretly converses with female slaves shall be compelled to pay a fine (8.363). In one passage (9.178) we find that the son whom a Brāhmaṇa begets by a Śūdra female is called a *Pāraśava,* which means a living corpse. In another verse (9.179) we learn that a son who is begotten by a Śūdra on a female slave may, if permitted by his father, take a share of the inheritance.

Manu made it appear that even the sight of a woman would tempt a man beyond control. He said:

> It is the nature of women to seduce men in this (world). For that reason the wise are never unguarded in (the company of) females.
>
> For, women are able to lead astray in (this) world not only a fool, but even a learned man, and (to make) him a slave of desire and anger.
>
> One should not sit in a lonely place with one's mother, sister, or daughter; for, the senses are powerful, and master even a learned man [*vidvān*]. 2.213–15.

A husband must provide for his wife if he goes abroad.

> A man who has business (abroad) may depart after securing a maintenance for his wife; for, a wife, even though virtuous, may be corrupted, if she be distressed by want of subsistence.
>
> If (the husband) went on a journey after providing (for her), the wife

shall subject herself to restraints in her daily life. But if he departed without providing (for her), she may subsist by blameless manual work.

If the husband went abroad for some sacred duty, (she) must wait for him eight years; if (he went) to (acquire) learning or fame, six (years); if (he went) for pleasure, three years. 9.74–76.

Concerning widows Manu says:

Nor is a second husband anywhere prescribed for virtuous [*sādhvī*] women. 5.162.

The husband of a remarried woman must be carefully avoided. 3.166.

The son of a remarried woman must not be entertained at a *Śrāddha.* 3.155.

He who gives food destined for the gods or manes to a son begotten after the husband's death, causes the giver the loss (of the rewards), both in this life and after death. 3.169, 174–75.

A virtuous [*sādhvī*] wife who after the death of her husband constantly remains chaste, reaches heaven, though she have no son, just like those chaste men. 5.160.

A faithful wife, who desires to dwell (after death) with her husband, must never do anything that might displease him who took her hand, whether he be alive or dead.

At her pleasure let her emaciate her body by (living on) pure flowers, roots, and fruit; but she must never even mention the name of another man after her husband has died. 5.156–57.

Care must be taken of barren women, of those who have no sons, of those whose family is extinct, of wives and widows faithful to their lords, and of women afflicted with diseases. 8.28.

A woman who from desire to have offspring violates her duty towards her (deceased) husband, brings on herself disgrace in this world, and loses her place with her husband (in heaven). 5.161.

By twice-born [*dvi-jāta*] men a widow must not be appointed to (cohabit with) any other (than her husband); for they who appoint (her) to another (man), will violate the eternal law.

In the sacred texts [*mantra*] which refer to marriage the appointment (of widows) is nowhere mentioned, nor is the re-marriage of widows [*vidhavā-vedanam punar*] prescribed in the rules concerning marriage.

The virtuous [*sādhu*] censure that (man) who in his folly appoints a woman, whose husband died, to (bear) children (to another man). 9.64–65,68.

If the (future) husband of a maiden dies after troth verbally plighted, her brother-in-law shall wed her. 9.69.

(If the widow) of (a man) who died without leaving issue, raises up to him a son by a member of the family, she shall deliver to that (son) the whole property which belonged to the (deceased). 9.190.

The restriction against the remarriage of widows, which has been emphasized in India by numerous orthodox Hindus, has resulted in bringing about many unfortunate conditions. Too often widows, unable to remarry, have been forced to seek whatever type of living they could find. When many of these poor women have grown too old to be subservient to the pleasure of those priests who are unscrupulous and to religious pilgrims, they have been thrown upon society mercilessly. Changes come about slowly in any land; and although a certain amount of help is being given to unfortunate widows, great numbers will probably continue to be forced into lives of misery in India. It may take generations for the great mass of Hindus to be aware of the pitiful conditions of widows and especially of the needlessness of all this misery. Within the group of widows, especially among the numerous young widows of India, is a large class of women who might be used for social uplift in a country so sadly needing teachers, doctors, nurses, and social workers. Indeed, such adaptation is being undertaken and accomplished today among progressive patriotic reformers. Alas, for centuries the Hindu widow's spirit has been too often broken, and she has been obliged to make atonement for that for which she, in the name of reason, is not to blame. Through crushing centuries orthodox Hindu parents have sometimes allowed their daughters to be condemned for that which these maidens have been too young even to comprehend. A. R. Caton remarks that in the matter of widowhood "it is well known that Hindu Law forbade the remarriage of widows . . . but that injunction was never followed by many of the lower castes. And in 1856 legislation legalized remarriage for all Hindu widows." [5] Surely the time has come when ancient re-

[5] Caton, *The Key of Progress,* p. 91.

ligious pronouncements of this character should be understood, and where harmful to serviceable living they should be disposed of properly.

Concerning the wife who dies and also concerning a widower Manu says:

She who, controlling her thoughts, words and deeds, never slights her lord, resides (after death) with her husband (in heaven), and is called a virtuous [*sādhvī*] (wife).

In reward of such conduct, a female who controls her thoughts, speech and actions, gains in this (life) highest renown, and in the next (world) a place near her husband.

A twice-born man, versed in the sacred law, shall burn a wife of equal caste who conducts herself thus and dies before him, with (the sacred fires used for) the *Agnihotra,* and with the sacrificial implements.

Having thus, at the funeral, given the sacred fires to his wife who dies before him, he may marry again, and again kindle (the fires). 5.165–68.

A. R. Caton points out that "it has to be remembered that strict Hindu Law, the law of the sacred writings, is followed in its entirety only by the higher castes, and the higher castes constitute only a minority of all those who are classed as Hindus." [6] It would seem as though among the higher castes, where more privileges and security exist, there should be a speedy awakening to a realization of the need of more thorough examination of Hindu sacred writings in order that their direct effect upon modern social life may be understood. Hopeful signs of intelligent examination of sacred scriptures is evidenced, as Caton points out, in the attitude of progressive Indians such as Mr. H. B. Sarda. In his presidential address to the 42d Indian National Social Conference he said: "If marriage is a sacrament, and can be performed only once in life, why is a widower allowed to perform it a second, a third, or a fourth time when a widow is not so allowed?" [7]

More than once in the Laws of Manu women and low-caste Śūdras are bracketed together.

Let him who desires bodily purity, first sip water three times, and then twice wipe his mouth; but a woman and a Śūdra (shall perform each act) once (only). 5.139.

[6] Caton, KP, p. 91.

[7] *Ibid.*, p. 127.

Let him on no account talk to women, Śūdras, and outcasts [*patita*]. 11.224.

Despite this occasional grouping of women with the lowest Hindu caste, Manu expresses a notably high appreciation for worthy women, for in verse (9.26) he associates those wives who are truly admirable with goddesses.

Between wives (*striyaḥ*) who (are destined) to bear children, who secure many blessings, who are worthy of worship and irradiate (their) dwellings, and between the goddesses of fortune (*sriyaḥ,* who reside) in the houses (of men), there is no difference whatsoever. 9.26.

The exacting Laws of Manu considered goddesses important, for they described these deities as bringing men fortune even as do radiant and helpful wives.

Very explicit and noteworthy is the statement in this document that woman, equally with the male, is a direct emanation from the Divine Creator.

The Lord [*Prabhū*], dividing His own [*ātman*] body [*deha*], became half male and half female. 1.32.

With regard to sacramental rites, however, Manu again assigns a low status to women:

No religious ceremony for women should be (accompanied) by *mantras.* With these words, the rule of right is fixed; for, women, being weak creatures, and having no (share in the) *mantras,* are falsehood itself. 9.18. Burnell and Hopkins.[8]

There are instances of high appreciation of womanhood in the following Laws of Manu:

Women must be honoured and adorned by their fathers, brothers, husbands, and brothers-in-law, who desire (their own) welfare. 3.55.

Where women are honoured, there the gods are pleased. But where they are not honoured, no sacred rite yields rewards. 3.56.

Where the female relations live in grief, the family soon wholly perishes. But that family where they are not unhappy, ever prospers.

The houses on which female relations not being duly honoured, pronounce a curse, perish completely, as if destroyed by magic. 3.57–58.

---

[8] Burnell and Hopkins, tr., *The Ordinances of Manu,* p. 247.

The mouth of a woman is always pure [*śuci*]. 5.130.

She who shows aversion towards a mad or outcaste (husband), a eunuch, one destitute of manly strength, or one afflicted with such diseases as punish crimes, shall neither be cast off nor be deprived of her property. 9.79.

Men who seek (their own) welfare, should always honour women on holidays and festivals with (gifts of) ornaments, clothes, and (dainty) food. 3.59.

Way must be made . . . for one who is above ninety years old, for one diseased, for the carrier of a burden, for a woman. 2.138.

Some equally rigorous denunciations of womanhood are noticeable.

(When creating them), Manu allotted to women (a love of their) bed, (of their) seat and (of) ornament, impure desires, wrath, dishonesty, malice, and bad conduct. 9.17.

One man who is free from covetousness may be (accepted as) witness; but not even many pure women, because the understanding of females is apt to waver. 8.77.

Women must particularly be guarded against evil inclinations, however trifling (they may appear); for, if they are not guarded, they will bring sorrow on two families. 9.5.

Through their passion for men, through their mutable temper, through their natural heartlessness, they become disloyal towards their husbands, however carefully they may be guarded in this (world).

Knowing their disposition, which the Lord of creatures [Prajāpati] laid in them at the creation, to be such, (every) man should most strenuously exert himself to guard them. 9.15–16.

So the Laws of Manu, as do all the earlier documents of Hinduism, show various attitudes, both appreciative and depreciative, toward women. And the best of these ancient teachings are being discerningly discovered and applied in the progressive reform movements in India.

CHAPTER V: THE PURĀṆAS

THE Purāṇas, eighteen in number, are religious stories, or "ancient tales." They belong to what may be termed Popular Hinduism. In their present form they date from the early centuries A.D. Their importance as books of religious instruction is very great. Here again we find a similar combination of praise and blame for women. Persisting in spite of the prohibitions laid upon the feminine, however, we note the outstanding praise of goddesses, who in the Purāṇas occupy a position of great importance. The countenance of the goddess Kātyāyanī removes the grievances of the people. She is called the "Mother of the whole world" and is supposed to safeguard the universe.[1] Again and again goddesses are worshipped in order that they will protect and preserve the people from the fear of enemies. Earth is called "the nurse," the supporter and the nourisher of all creations.[2] The goddess Ambikā is revered by all the deities. The magnificent sages faithfully prostrate themselves to her.[3] The goddess Nārāyaṇī protects things in a spiritual and material form. She is the over-ruling power of the universe, the auspicious bestower of prosperity, happiness, and every desire. She has power to create, to preserve, and to destroy. She is intelligence and excellence.[4] Sarasvatī is very highly revered in the Purāṇas. In this goddess exists Brahmā in His one and in His many forms. Sarasvatī protects the universe; and in her are perceived all objects that are eternal. This lotus-eyed goddess is called the tongue of all.[5] The great goddess Gāyatrī gives enjoy-

[1] Pargiter, tr., *Mārkaṇḍeya Purāṇa,* 91.2; p. 512; compare Dutt, p. 371.
[2] Dutt, tr., *Vishṇu Purāṇa,* 1.13; p. 68.
[3] Dutt, tr., *Mārkaṇḍeya Purāṇa,* 84.2,4; p. 347; compare Pargiter, *op. cit.,* p. 482.
[4] *Ibid.,* 91.8,9,10,21; pp. 371, 372; compare Pargiter, *op. cit.,* pp. 513, 515.
[5] *Ibid.,* 23.30–37; pp. 111–13; compare Pargiter, *op. cit.,* pp. 127–28.

ment and emancipation.[6] Gāyatrī is represented as the better half of the Lord, and that is why she appeared from His body. Brahmā and Gāyatrī are reported to be inseparable.[7] The goddess Durgā is supposed to remove terror from every creature and to bestow a mind extremely bright. She dispels poverty and pain.[8] Sandhyā is the goddess of prayer.[9] Aditi is called the Mother of Gods.[10] By worshipping the goddesses Mahālaksmī, Gaurī, Maṅgala, and Sarasvatī a man is assured of becoming an inmate of the celestial abodes and a learned man in his next birth.[11] The mantra sacred to the goddess Gaurī should be deemed the fulfiller of all desires; and it is believed that the man who worships such a goddess and stands a suppliant at her feet is sure to enjoy a hundred summers on earth. This worship of the goddess Gaurī is recommended to help a man retain his intellectual faculties in perfect vigor even to the last day of his life and to free him from depredations by thieves and freebooters.[12] It is written that porridge should be offered especially to the goddess Kālarātrī.[13] Even when the sun was entirely covered with the massive folds of darkness, the goddess Kālī wandered about in the sky.[14] It is written that there are thirty-two Divine Mothers who have been created by Viṣṇu from His body. They are all prosperous and fortunate, and are powerful enough to create and to destroy the whole universe.[15] By means of worshipping the goddess Kuvjikā the gods conquered the demons and regained their lost kingdom of paradise with all its wealth and celestial weapons. Rohiṇī, the wife of Candra, should be worshipped.[16] Śrī is the goddess of fortune.[17] Satī is called the goddess who gives bliss, prosperity, and emancipation. The men and women who worship her with devotion are reported to obtain everything they desire.[18] By worshipping and making obeisance to the gods

[6] Dutt, tr., *Garuda Purāṇam,* 37; p. 89.

[7] A Taluqdar of Oudh (pseud.), tr., *Matsya Purāṇam,* 4.7–10; I, 13. "The Sacred Books of the Hindus," XVII.

[8] Pargiter, *Mārkaṇḍeya,* 84.16; p. 485.

[9] Dutt, tr., *Agni Purāṇam,* 116.1–26; I, 458.

[10] *Vishṇu,* 5.30; p. 395.

[11] *Agni,* 116.1–26; I, 460.

[12] *Ibid.,* 313.15–23, II, 1171.

[13] *Ibid.,* 132.27–32; I, 531.

[14] *Matsya,* 2.172.19; A Taluqdar of Oudh (pseud.), II, 139.

[15] *Ibid.,* 2.179.65,67; II, 156–157.

[16] *Agni,* 183.15–18; II, 688.

[17] *Ibid.,* 268.3–13; II, 989.

[18] *Matsya,* 1.60.10–12; A Taluqdar of Oudh (pseud.), I, 182.

and goddesses a man becomes the possessor of all wished-for objects in this life, and carries up the souls of his ancestors to the region of the god Brahmā.[19] In the Vishṇu Purāṇa, Śiva is represented as "the God who springs from the forehead of Brahmā who separates into male and female." [20]

The idea of a goddess being the *Śakti,* or energy, of her husband took definite form in Hinduism. Farquhar maintains that "the god is conceived as retired, absolute, inconceivable: the goddess is a sort of emanation from him, bringing his power down to man, and is a much more approachable being than her lord." [21] The two great sects, the Vishṇuite and the Śivaite, held supreme place in the religion of this period. A third sect also arose,

> . . . the *Śāktas,* or worshippers of Kālī, the wife of Śiva, as his *śakti.* They fall into two groups, the right-hand and the left-hand *Śāktas.* Both groups show many signs of aboriginal influence, notably animal sacrifice and magic rites; and the basis of the whole cult in both is phallic; but, while the right-hand group are respectable in their worship, the left-hand *Śāktas* are most immoral.[22]

Professors H. L. Friess and H. W. Schneider state that

> a wide-spread feature of popular religion from the earliest times among the natives of India is the worship of mother-goddesses. This phase of popular religion was rationalized in the Tantras, where the Devis, goddesses, were represented as the *Śaktis,* energies of the gods whose consorts they were. In the Tantras, too, a distinctive technique of worship was formulated making large use of quasi-mechanical means of inducing ecstasy. Thus interpreted and organized, Devi cults have become increasingly popular in modern times in certain parts of India, notably in Bengal.[23]

It has been pointed out that in the popular Devī cults, Umā, or Pārvatī, daughter of the mountain, as Śiva's consort "is mild and gracious, a heroic figure. . . . She is the mother of Skanda, the war-god, and of the elephant-headed Ganeśa. As Durga, the unapproachable, or Chandi, the wild one, or Kali, the black one, she

[19] *Agni,* 116.1–26; I, 460.
[20] Aiyar, *The Purāṇas in the Light of Modern Science,* p. 181.
[21] Farquhar, PH, p. 112.
[22] *Ibid.,* pp. 112–13.
[23] Friess and Schneider, RVC, pp. 85, 88.

is a deadly scourge; but she is worshipped more in some quarters than Śiva himself."[24] Sarasvatī is the consort and *Śakti* of Brahmā; Śrī, or Lakshmī, is the consort and *Śakti* of Vishṇu. The Tantras, which are manuals of the *Śākta* cult, resemble the literature of the Purāṇas.[25]

In order that the reader may catch the spirit of the abounding praise and respect accorded goddesses in the wealth of material on this subject in the Purāṇas, a few references will be given from the Mārkaṇḍeya, the Garuda, the Vishṇu, the Matsya, the Agni, the Bhāgavata, the Brahma-Vaivarta, and the Srimad Devī Bhāgavata Purāṇas.

Pushkara said:—"O King, repeat every day, for victory in war and success in life, the prayer with which the god Indra propitiated and secured the good graces of the goddess Lakshmī."

Indra said:—. . . "Salutations unto thee, O goddess, who dwellest in the bosom of thy beloved Vishṇu! Thou art success, the Svāhā, and the Svadhā with which libations are poured on the sacrificial fire, the embodied image of two of the holiest Mantras of the Vedas, the nectar or the ambrosia that keeps up and nourishes all sorts of life. I make obeisance to thee, O goddess, who dividest the day from the night and the night from the day, as the rosy dawn and the golden eve. I bow down to thee, who formest the holiest functions of human frame and minds, such as beauty, memory, faith, speech, the supreme knowledge, the occult light, the sacrificial knowledge and the knowledge of the soul, and who as an ushering light of beauty and faith, leads the souls of men to salvation and freedom. It is thy divine self, O thou goddess of matchless beauty, which has been hymnised in the verses of the Ṛik-, the Sāman-, and the Yajur-, Vedas, and which forms the immutable truths of the Science of Soul and the fundamental principles of Criminal Jurisprudence. The Universe but shines with thy reflected light; and all beauty is but a borrowed gleam of thy divine effulgence. Who can cover the universe with a shroud of beauty, save thy honoured self? O goddess, who art the embodied image of all religious sacrifices, and in whose body the heart of the mace-wielding Nārāyana has built its nest of happiness and peace,—Nārāyana whom the minds of the Yogins cannot comprehend in their meditations! Forsaken by thee, the primeval night once again enveloped the face of this happy creation; and it is only through thy

[24] *Ibid.*, p. 88.

[25] Farquhar, PH, pp. 113, 114.

favour, O goddess, that it has now been reinstated to light and joy. At thy gracious smile, wives nestle themselves round the neck of a man, children in the bloom and innocence of infancy sit smiling on his knees, friends flock at his gate, and plenty fills his stores and granaries. At thy blissful glance, the powerful antagonists of a man are scattered away like dry leaves before the winter wind; and health and prosperity become his portions in this life. What is there in this world which a man fails to acquire on whom your smile descends? O goddess, thou art the mother of all created beings, as the god Hari is their father; and thou fillest this universal space, O mother, with Vishṇu, thy consort. Never dost thou forsake, O thou who purifiest all things, my treasure, house, wearing apparel, wives, sons, friends, live stock and ornaments, O thou goddess of absolute purity, O thou who dwellest in the bosom of Vishṇu. Truth, fortitude, purity and good character leave a man, the moment thou forsakest such an unfortunate being; while in a single day, all those virtues again elevate him to godhead in life at thy gracious sight. The man on whom thy favour descends, is intelligent, erudite, brave, powerful and adorable, and is even honoured with the distinctions of high birth though born of a low parentage. O thou darling wife of Vishṇu, O thou who dost minister to the wants and woes of the universe, as a nurse doth to her infant ward, all these good virtues are counted as positive defects in a man on whom thou turnest thy back. Even the tongue of a Brahman cannot exhaust the countless boons and infinite virtues that constitute thy blessed self. Never forsake us, O thou goddess of lotus-like eyes."

Pushkara said:—"Thus hymnised by Indra, the goddess Lakshmī granted him the boons of perpetual sovereignty and victory in war. He who recites this psalm, or hears it recited by a Brāhmaṇa, becomes an emancipated spirit at the close of a prosperous career; and hence it becometh one to recite it constantly, or hear it recited by others." Agni 237.1–19; Dutt, II, 848–50.

The goddess adored in the three worlds, should be contemplated as possessed of a white complexion and seated on a full-blown lotus flower and carrying a rosary. The goddess should be invoked as follows:—"Om! Thou art the light, the sacrifice, the strength, the seventh sun, the abode of the gods. The universe is thy self; and thou fillest it with life and motion. Thou art the life of all and the duration of all lives. Om to the Earth! Come, O thou goddess, who grantest boon to thy votaries; and stay as long as I repeat thy holy name." Agni 215.31–34; Dutt, II, 773.

A picture of the goddess Bhadrakālī should be worshipped in the month of Āśhvina, with a view to achieve success in all departments of life. . . . And the goddess should be addressed as follows: "O thou goddess Bhadrakālī! O thou Supreme Durgā! O thou goddess Durgā who deliverest all beings from dangers and difficulties! O thou the invincible energy presiding over the three worlds! O thou dreadful, undaunted energy of the supreme Absolute! Grant me victory." Agni 268.14–15; Dutt, II, 989.

From the mouth of the Supreme Being sprang a goddess very fair in complexion, holding in her hand a lute and a book. Her beauty vied with ten millions of moons; and her eyes were like spring lotuses. She was ornamented with gems. Her raiment was resplendent like fire. This goddess is the fairest of the fair. . . . She is the supreme mother . . . of the learned folks. . . . She is the tutelary deity of the poets, the presiding goddess of speech, and known by the name of Saraswatī. Brahma-Vaivarta, Brahma Khaṇḍa 3.53–62; Sen, I, 8.

Some hold there is one Brahma, the emblem of eternal light. Others hold, Brahma is of two kinds, Prakriti and Puruṣa. Those who hold that Brahma is one, maintain that Brahma is the cause of all and transcends both Prakriti and Puruṣa, both of whom emanate from Him; or, they maintain that the same Brahma willfully divided Himself into two parts. . . . Puruṣa is eternal; and so is goddess Prakriti. . . . They are the parents of the world. Brahma Vaivarta, Kriṣṇa Janma Khaṇḍa, 43.56–67; Sen, II, 293, 294.

The varied excellences of the goddess Caṇḍikā are praised.

We prostrate ourselves to Caṇḍikā. . . . Thou, healing from all kinds of disorders, givest pleasure and strength to all people. Those that desire to follow thee, shall not feel distress, but will be restored. . . . Thou art supremely exalted in the sciences, in knowledge, in wisdom, in eloquence, in virtuous practice. Mārkaṇḍeya 91.26,27,29; Dutt, p. 373.

Along with various positive and negative characterizations, the Ultimate is also known as a motherly source.

That which is the unmanifested Cause, is called subtle Nature [*Pradhāna*] by the foremost saints,—external, and instinct with cause and effect. It is indestructible, supportless, immeasurable, undeteriorating, real, devoid of sound and touch, and without form, etc. It hath three several modes; and is the mother of the Universe, without beginning, and is the end of all. Vishṇu 1.2; Dutt, p. 6.

O Mother Universe! You are the refuge of all the Devas. Therefore, I salute you. You protect all the *Jīvas* [living beings]; therefore protect me. . . . Even the four-faced Lord Brahmā does not adequately know your limit. . . . O, one without any beginning or an end, guard me from the perils of this vast and fearful ocean of the world. You are with Viṣṇu in the form of Lakshmī, with Śiva in the form of Gaurī, with Brahmā in the form of Sāvitrī. You are the light of the sun and the moon, intellect in Brihaspati. . . . O Mother! You are fixed. You pervade all the universe. Matsya 1.284.11–18; A Taluqdar of Oudh (pseud.), II, 362.

The primeval masculine Creator is reported as having been unhappy in his solitude; and for that reason from his own self he created a beautiful woman, who is considered to be the equal of Brahmā.

Then Brahmā, in course of His practices, did not feel any comfort and happiness; for those (whom he had created), were single. He created a beautiful woman from His body. . . . She, by virtue of her austerities, equalled Brahmā, and was gifted with the faculty of the creation of the universe. Matsya 2.171.20–22; A Taluqdar of Oudh (pseud.), II, 136.

The Bhāgavata Purāṇa [26] includes the appellation "Mother" as an appropriate designation for the Creator of the universe.

The Creator of the universe! Thou art the means of our existence. Thou alone art our Mother, rather the friend, the ruler, the father, and the best (true) preceptor. Bhāgavata 1.11.7; Chatterjee, p. 344.

According to this teaching the feminine is a worthy part of the Hindu's conception of deity. Harendranath Maitra, in his idealistic interpretation of Hinduism, declares that "a religion that has no place for God as Mother will never take root in India." [27] This author continues with, "The Hindu thinks of God as Father, but the idea of Fatherhood is really absorbed in that of Mother as being deeper and tenderer. Mother is worshipped in India." [28] "The Hindus worship God in every relation, but most of all as Mother and Beloved." [29]

Not all goddesses in the Purāṇas are appealing in appearance and activity or benevolent. Some terrible goddesses are besought to inflict their wrath upon enemies.

[26] Chatterjee, *The Bhāgavata Purāṇa,* p. 35. [27] Maitra, HWI, p. 45.
[28] *Ibid.,* p. 43. [29] *Ibid.,* p. 42.

O thou goddess Cāmuṇḍā, who dwellest in the cremation-ground (of the universe), and who wieldest . . . a human skull in thy two hands. . . . O thou immense-mouthed goddess . . . whose laughter shakes the worlds in their orbits! . . . Advance, and advance, O thou goddess, whose jagged teeth cast down the gloom of night, and who art clad in an elephant-skin. Advance . . . with an extremely haggard and emaciated frame, and whose footsteps are followed by a concourse of many unearthly sounds. Advance . . . O thou supreme absolute monstress with a complexion like the flashes of heaven. Advance . . . with thy horrid teeth exposed in a demoniac laughter and thy bloody tongues protruding out of thy terrible mouth devouring fresh victims. . . . O thou goddess whose sullen look inspires terror in the breasts of all beings . . . and whose roar and battle-cry strikes terror into the breasts of all who hear them, show thy mettle. . . . Make thy weird laughter resound. . . . Accomplish this end of mine, O goddess, whose mouth vomits forth primal darkness through the interstices of thy horrible teeth, and who art the protectress from all banes and evils that beset our mundane existence. Soon and very soon accomplish this end. . . . Subjugate with thy mace all the forces of my enemy. Cut through . . . their ranks, O goddess. . . . Dance and sport in death. Shake and shake my enemies, and turn them topsyturvy. Kill and kill, O thou goddess, who dost fondly relish human flesh and blood. Trample down. . . . Pierce through. . . . Slay. . . . Chase, and pursue. . . . Fell to the ground the enemy, though bearing a charmed life, and possessed of a body hard as the bolt of heaven. . . . O thou goddess with eyes sunk in their sockets and a face resembling that of an owl, and a head rendered doubly ghastly by hairs standing erect on their roots! Burn . . . the enemy's forces. . . . Cook the armed hosts sent against me. . . . Overwhelm them. . . . Obstruct and impede the progress of the marching hosts; and break . . . their arms and weapons, O thou terrible looking goddess, with black serpents coiling round the body. . . . Break . . . their ranks, O thou who dost confound all order among the troops drawn up in circles and squares. And make all sorts of manoeuvres impossible. . . . Yell and yell, O thou goddess whose mouth vomits forth fatal fire. Undermine, tumble down and uplift the ground they stand upon. . . . Come, O thou goddess, whose thoroughfare is the heaven itself, cast thy noose and pierce with thy mace. Stop and enter (the line of the hostile armies). Paralyze their sense-organs such as the mouths, hands and feet. Cast a stupefying influence in all directions. . . . Stupefy all, either through ashes, drinking water, or through the subsoil. Agni 134.1–6; Dutt, I, 536, 537, 538, 539.

The association of womanhood with deification scarcely could be recognized in verses such as the following:

The fair sex is governed by desire. And women care much for pomp and pride. . . . Kings and persons ambitious of lofty stations in life, should not be excessively fond of female company. Agni 224.3–18; Dutt, II, 801.

A man should chastise his sons, brothers, cousins, wives and slaves with a strong string of thread or a rope made of the blades of Vena grass. Agni 227.46–50; Dutt, II, 815.

While his tender wife was exhausted with fatigue, . . . Viśwāmitra all of a sudden struck her with a chastising rod. Mārkaṇḍeya 7.59; Dutt, p. 30.

A king should never trust the ladies of the palace, especially those who are the mothers of children. Agni 224.33–42; Dutt, II, 803–4.

To the woman Tulsī, who is characterized as being beautiful but lustful, is credited the following condemnations:

No wise man believes a vile woman. Brahma-Vaivarta Prakriti-Khaṇḍa 16.41–51; Sen, I, 132.

The mouth of a woman rains honey; but her heart is like a jar full of poison. She uses sweet words; but her heart is keen like a razor. She has an eye constantly fixed on her own object on account of which she is submissive to her husband. Otherwise, she is disobedient. Her face is cheerful; but her mind is unclean. Brahma-Vaivarta, Prakriti-Khaṇḍa 16.41–51; Sen, I, 132.

A woman sows the seed of quarrel. Brahma-Vaivarta, Prakriti-Khaṇḍa 16.41–51; Sen, I, 132.

[A woman] is the embodiment of rashness and a mine of vices. She is hypocritical, recalcitrant and treacherous. . . . She is an obstacle to the path of devotion, a hindrance to emancipation. . . . She is practically a sorceress (a magician), and represents vile desire. Brahma-Vaivarta, Prakriti-Khaṇḍa 16.52–60; Sen, I, 132–33.

In the lines from the Mārkaṇḍeya and Garuda Purāṇas given below, vigorous condemnation rather than deification of the feminine is expressed:

He who is known through himself, is fortunate. He who is known through his father or grandfather is middling. But the worst of all is the man who gains renown through his mother or maternal relations. Mārkaṇḍeya 21.102; Dutt, p. 105.

No confidence should be reposed in . . . women. Garuda 109; Dutt, p. 320.

It is the absence of a nook of vantage, or the want of leisure, or of a person making love-overtures to her . . . that mainly accounts for the chastity of woman. Garuda 114; Dutt, p. 340.

The Devī Bhāgavata Purāṇa depreciates women in the following terms:

Falsehood, vain boldness, craftiness, stupidity, impatience, over-greediness, impurity, and harshness are the natural qualities of women. Devī Bhāgavata 1.5.83; Vijnanananda, p. 17.

On the other hand, the Brahma-Vaivarta Purāṇa teaches the need of a discerning estimate of women. Not all women folk are reprehensible. Some are praiseworthy, while others are condemnable.

God has divided the fair sex into two classes, viz., those who are chaste, and those who may be easily seduced. The chaste woman is praise-worthy; the unchaste one should be condemned. Brahma-Vaivarta, Prakriti-Khaṇḍa 16.61–72; Sen, I, 133.

The subservience of a woman to the wishes of a Brahman is commanded explicitly and unconditionally.

That Brāhmaṇa should be well fed and be devoutly looked upon as cupid . . . Each and every desire of that Brahman should be satisfied by the woman devotee. She should, with all heart and soul and with a smile on her face, yield herself up to him. Matsya 70.44,45; A Taluqdar of Oudh (pseud.), I, 212.

An actual historical case is recorded in which a certain Brāhmaṇa in the city of Prathishṭhāna demeaned his wife. In this record also is to be noted the utter fidelity of the wife in spite of her harsh treatment.

Kauśika . . . in consequence of his pristine sins, was assailed by leprosy. His wife served her diseased husband as if he were a deity, by shampooing his feet and limbs, bathing him, clothing him, feeding him . . . by serving him in solitude, and treating him with sweet words. Although always served by her with humility, that highly irascible and cruel (Brāhmaṇa) used to rebuke her angrily. Still the humble wife considered him as a deity, and regarded that horrible one as the best of men. Mārkaṇḍeya 16.14–18; Dutt, p. 79.

Adulterers are warned of dire punishment in several of the Purāṇas.

The man who would seduce the wife of a king, should be burnt alive in fire. Agni 227.58–66; Dutt, II, 818.

One who forcibly violates the modesty of an unwilling maid in the household, should be killed. Matsya 227.124; II, 246.

A man should not enter the female apartments, or treasure-rooms, of another man's house. Agni 154.13–31; Dutt, I, 596.

A man loses his caste by . . . adultery. Agni 168.28–38; Dutt, II, 644.

The souls of the crooked are cast into the hell of great conflagration (*Mahājvāla*); while those of persons who had visited the wives of their elders or superiors, or women who were in the forbidden degrees of consanguinity in life, are consigned to the torments of the saw-edged hell (*Krakacha*); while the begetters of hybrid children and the destroyers of other men's virtues, are punished in the hell of boiling treacle. Agni 203. 20–23; Dutt, II, 729.

A good man, if he sees a virtuous woman alone, does not talk to her. Brahma-Vaivarta, Prakriti-Khaṇḍa 16.41–51; Sen, I, 132.

Insult to women is indignity to Nature. Brahma-Vaivarta, Prakriti-Khaṇḍa 1.139–50; Sen, I, 88.

There is no sin more dreadful than the violation of the chastity of one's preceptor's wife. Brahma-Vaivarta, Brahma-Khaṇḍa 10.44–55; Sen, I, 32.

The wife of a preceptor, the queen, the step-mother, the mother, the daughter, the daughter-in-law, the mother-in-law, the pregnant wife, the sister, the brother's wife, the wife of the maternal uncle, the paternal or the maternal grandmother, the mother's sister, the brother's daughter, the female pupil, the pupil's wife, and the wife of the son of the sister or brother are prohibited in the highest degree. Whoever goes to any of them for an immoral purpose, goes to his mother, and is guilty of a hundred Brahmin-slaughters. Brahma-Vaivarta, Prakriti-Khaṇḍa 30.201–11; Sen, I, 171–72.

A person whose heart is set upon objects owned by others, particularly the wives of others . . . apprehends danger at every step. Brahma-Vaivarta, Kṛiṣṇa Janma-Khaṇḍa 35.87; Sen, II, 258.

O foremost of men! See those who ravished others' wives, killed by Yama's servants. Mārkaṇḍeya 14.77; Dutt, p. 71.

A man should not speak with another man's wife when forbidden to talk, nor should he commit adultery. Agni 227.40; Dutt, II, 815.

Incest likewise was forbidden.

One who commits incest with a daughter-in-law and a daughter is sent into *Mahājvāla* hell. Vishnu 2.6.12; Dutt, p. 131.

You have committed an incest on your daughter. Consequently, I forsake you, base and mean. And now go away on account of your doings. Matsya 1.48.53–56; A Taluqdar of Oudh (pseud.), I, 143.

Having visited an unmarried girl, a *Chaṇḍāla* woman, one's own daughter, and the wives of one's *Sapiṇḍa* relations, a man should commit suicide. Agni 173.50–54; Dutt, II, 665.

Ravishers of their mothers are born as eunuchs in every birth. They are never redeemed. Brahma-Vaivarta, Kṛiṣṇa Janma-Khaṇḍa 59.64–76; Sen, II, 334.

A daughter of Brahmā says to her father:

"A daughter has been classed among mothers, as stated in the Vedas. How is it that you, being the author of the Vedas, are about to ravish your daughter?" Brahma-Vaivarta, Kṛiṣṇa Khaṇḍa 35.47–56; Sen, II, 256.

There are passages in the Purāṇas that show consideration for a daughter.

The birth of a daughter is highly meritorious. Matsya 154.414–17; A Taluqdar of Oudh, (pseud.), II, 99.

My daughter is very dear to me; and I cannot make her feel hurt. Matsya 1.29.10; A Taluqdar of Oudh (pseud.), I, 89.

The king was more attached to his daughter than to his sons. Brahma-Vaivarta, Kṛiṣṇa-Janma Khaṇḍa 41.111–25; Sen, II, 285.

Certain requirements on the part of the daughter are demanded for the happiness of her parents.

No progeny can be born without a woman . . . In the Śāstras at many places, it has been said, that a girl is equal to ten sons. If she is not modest and good, she is the cause of pain to her people and is useless. The birth of such a girl who is a source of pain and disgrace to her parents is always repented and regretted. Matsya 2.154.156–164. A Taluqdar of Oudh (pseud.), II, 88–89.

There are many verses suggesting that a father should show great care in the selection of a bridegroom for his daughter.

One ought to marry one's daughter to a man who is well-qualified as regards his family, birth, age, beauty, good qualifications and wealth. Matsya 154.414–17; A Taluqdar of Oudh (pseud.), II, 99.

A father gives his daughter to a suitable bridegroom. Brahma-Vaivarta, Kṛiṣṇa Janma-Khaṇḍa 114.31–41; Sen, II, 507.

Anyone who gives his daughter to a man unqualified, old, ignorant, poor, foolish, deformed, wrathful, foul-mouthed, cripple, blind, deaf, dumb, paralysed, impotent, sinful, or recluse, is guilty of Brahmin-slaughter. Anyone who gives his daughter to a Vaiṣṇava well-talented, tranquil, learned and youthful, gets at once the benefits of ten grand horse-sacrifices. Brahma-Vaivarta, Prakriti-Khaṇḍa 16.81–97; Sen, I, 134.

The father is relieved from anxiety by making over his dear daughter to a suitable bridegroom. Brahma-Vaivarta, Gaṇeśa-Khaṇḍa 4.1–12; Sen, II, 6.

Expression is given of the affectionate regard of a lonely father for a daughter who has been married and has left her father's home.

Himāchala felt very lonely and dejected in the absence of Pārvatī, as often is the case with the father of the bride. Matsya 154.497; A Taluqdar of Oudh (pseud.), II, 103.

The selling of a daughter was forbidden.

Whoever sells his daughter in emergency or merely for the sake of filthy lucre, goes to the Hell . . . where he is bitten by crows and vultures. Brahma-Vaivarta, Prakriti-Khaṇḍa 16.98–99; Sen, I, 134.

Whoever sells his daughter for gain dwells in the pit of flesh, and eats it for as many years as there are hairs on the skin of the body of his daughter. Brahma-Vaivarta, Prakriti-Khaṇḍa 30.27–41; Sen, I, 166.

There is no salvation for the person who sells his sons or daughters. Agni 153.1–4; Dutt, I, 593.

A man loses his caste by . . . trading on the person of one's own daughter. Agni 168.28–38; Dutt, II, 644.

With regard to the liberty of a girl to choose her own husband the Brahma-Vaivarta Purāṇa says:

A girl should never of her own accord solicit a husband. Brahma-Vaivarta, Kṛiṣṇa Janma-Khaṇḍa 114.31–41; Sen, II, 507.

Yet other Purāṇas do allow a young woman to choose a husband.

A girl is at liberty to make her own choice, and to be united with a husband, in the absence of any such relation to give her away in marriage. Garuda 95; Dutt, p. 268.

A king should not punish a girl who chooses her own husband according to the rites of a Gāndhārva marriage. Agni 227.40–45; Dutt, II, 815.

A girl who desires to marry a high class man should be given to him in marriage; and after marriage if the girl be confined in the house, she would remain all right. Matsya 2.227.130; A Taluqdar of Oudh (pseud.), II, 246, 247.

Both the Garuda and the Mārkaṇḍeya Purāṇas say that a girl should be given only once in marriage:

A girl should be given only once in marriage and anyone carrying away a married girl should be dealt with as a common felon. Garuda 95; Dutt, p. 268.

Where a man, after having given his daughter to someone, gives her to a second person,—truly that man is thus divided into many portions, and swept along in a stream of burning corrosive. Mārkaṇḍeya 14.68; Pargiter, p. 81.

It is the father who gives his daughter in marriage; and after that she is to remain faithful to her husband.

A girl shall be clean in body and spirit, frugal in her expenses, and faithfully nurse the man she has been given to by her father in marriage. Agni 222.19–23; Dutt, II, 795.

Although the importance of marriage for daughters is greatly emphasized, nevertheless the Purāṇas contain evidence that not all daughters were married.

The king, hearing . . . that his daughter had no intention to marry . . . began to pass his time without giving away his daughter in marriage. Thus the daughter lived . . . protected by her father and mother. Devī Bhāgavata 5.17.27–31; Vijnanananda, p. 412.

Among the persons who ought to be invited to the feast of *Naimittika Śrāddha* (that is, for the deceased forefathers), a daughter's son was included.

It should be noted what class of people ought to be invited to the feast of Naimittika . . . especially a daughter's son. Matsya 1.16.5–13; A Taluqdar of Oudh (pseud.), I, 49.

A daughter's son had the power to save his grandfather through religious ministrations upon the latter's death.

That high-souled Yayāti in this way, through his magnanimous daughter's sons, was saved from fall; and after leaving the earth, that doer of great charitable deeds rose to Heaven, filling the earth with his renown. Matsya 1.42.28,29; A Taluqdar of Oudh (pseud.), I, 112.

The reward of performing the ceremony to the deceased forefathers, was that the man would obtain many daughters as well as sons and would become prosperous.

The performer of the ceremony [*Śrāddha*] becomes the father of many sons and daughters, thrives in trade and agriculture, and the tenantry prospers in his estate. Agni 163.28–39; Dutt, I, 628.

Despite these expressions of esteem for daughters, there are passages which show that daughters were not desired.

Absurd is the lasting good name of a house in which female children are born. Garuda 110; Dutt, p. 325.

A man is at liberty to marry a second wife . . . after eleven years of the marriage of a wife that has given birth to daughters only. Garuda 115; Dutt, pp. 351, 352.

It is to be noted that although an especially religious man prays for a beautiful wife and many sons and grandsons, yet in his prayer he expresses no desire for daughters or granddaughters.

May I be blessed with a beautiful wife and sons and grandsons in large numbers. Agni 209.55–63; Dutt, II, 746.

Not only the desire for sons but also the absolute necessity of having a son for the salvation of both a father and a mother is stated definitely.

Whoever is unmarried and void of sons . . . commits the . . . sin (Brahmin-slaughter). Brahma-Vaivarta, Prakriti-Khaṇḍa 30.160–71; Sen, I, 170.

There is no prospect in the after-birth of the sonless. Never, never will Heaven be his. Without son, there is none other who can be of help in the next world. Devī Bhāgavata 4.15–27; Vijnanananda, p. 9.

The sonless can never go to the Heavens; so he must get a son somehow or other. Devī Bhāgavata 2.6.36–48; Vijnanananda, p. 96.

The life of a woman who has no son, is useless. Brahma-Vaivarta, Gaṇeśa-Khaṇḍa 2.16–31; Sen, II, 4.

Asceticism and charity yield fruits which are reaped in the next world. But the birth of a good son, i.e., a son of noble blood, gives happiness in this world, as well as in the next. Brahma-Vaivarta, Gaṇeśa-Khaṇḍa 2.16–31; Sen, II, 4.

Śaturpā, the barren wife of Manu, lamented:

"Unless I get a son, I will take poison or enter into the flames." Brahma-Vaivarta, Gaṇeśa-Khaṇḍa 5.1–12; Sen, II, 8.

There is a very interesting tale concerning a certain king and his wife, who, failing to have a son, treated a daughter much as if she were a highly prized son.

With a desire to get a son; he [King Rabhya] made many presents. . . . When copious quantities of ghee were offered as oblations, there arose, from the fire, a girl beautiful in all respects. . . . The priest . . . presented her to the King, and said . . . "Take this girl, resembling a son, and be happy." . . . The King . . . went to his wife Rukmarekhā, and said . . . "Take this daughter." The Queen . . . felt the pleasures of having a son when she got in her arms that lotus-eyed beautiful daughter. The King next performed the natal and other ceremonies of the daughter, and did all other acts as if she had been a son to him. . . . That beautiful girl was nursed and cared after like a son. Devī Bhāgavata 6.21.32–53; Vijnanananda, pp. 558, 559.

A woman's joy in her husband and son is voiced in the following verse from the Brahma-Vaivarta Purāṇa:

"I am as much pleased as a woman who sees her husband after a long course of separation, or as a woman who sees her only son returning home after years." Brahma-Vaivarta, Gaṇeśa-Khaṇḍa 9.28–37; Sen, II, 22.

Much as a son is to be desired by a Hindu woman, nevertheless, her superior commitment is to her husband.

So there is none dearer than the husband to a woman. A son is dear to her, as he is the offspring of her husband. The husband is dearer to a woman than a hundred sons. Brahma-Vaivarta, Prakriti-Khaṇḍa 42.18–30; Sen, I, 203.

The Purāṇas teach, however, that a woman should recognize virtue as superior to a husband and sons.

A husband is, indeed, greater than the son. But virtue is greater than the husband. Brahma-Vaivarta, Gaṇeśa-Khaṇḍa 7.36–46; Sen, II, 14.

A reciprocal devotion to the mother is demanded of a worthy son.

A worthy son should not abandon his mother. Brahma-Vaivarta, Gaṇeśa-Khaṇḍa 16.20–32; Sen, II, 33.

Not only sons but also grandsons are included in the religious life span. It is to be noted also that the following passage continues the teaching found in the Laws of Manu (6.2–3; SBE, XXV, 198–99), namely, that the wife may accompany her husband when he resorts to the forest.

A house-holder having seen the birth of his grandson (a son's son) should resort to the forest. He may do that . . . either alone or in company of his wife. Agni 160.1–5; Dutt, I, 617.

The killing of a woman is forbidden.

A man loses his caste by killing . . . a woman. Agni 168.28–38; Dutt, II, 644.

The destroyer of a woman or that of a child is born as an earth-worm. Mārkaṇḍeya 15.18; Dutt, p. 73.

Under no circumstances is a woman to be killed. Matsya 1.47.106; A Taluqdar of Oudh (pseud.), I, 130.

Not only should women not be killed but also the Purāṇas say that they should be protected.

Women should always be protected with care; never to be killed. Devī Bhāgavata 7.25.57–77; Vijnanānanda, p. 679.

The ladies of the palace should be protected and served. Agni 224.33–42; Dutt, II, 803.

The king and the virtuous should protect the faithful wives; and they in their turn should help their husbands in matters of housekeeping. Agni 222.19–23; Dutt, II, 795.

A wise man preserves his youthful wife more carefully than his life. Brahma-Vaivarta, Kṛiṣṇa Janma-Khaṇḍa 114.64–71; Sen, II, 509.

The father of a woman shall protect her in her infancy; the husband, in her youth; and her son, in her old age; in absence whereof the duty of maintaining her shall devolve upon his friends and relations. Day and night, a woman shall not quit the side of her husband. Garuda 95; Dutt, p. 271.

The same teaching as that in the previous passage has already occurred in Manu (9.3; SBE, XXV, 328).

Along with remorse for the wrongs done in war to the many persons who are involved, King Yudhishṭira expressed concern for the tragic plight of women in war.

Not by any course of duties [*karma*] laid down for a house-holder [*gṛhastha*] shall I be able to expiate what sin has now accrued to me in respect of women whose relations were slain by me. Bhāgavata 1.8.51; Rau, I, 44.

In the Matsya Purāṇa it is gratifying to note that even enemy women are to be spared.

If thou art angry with male population hostile to thee, what is the fault of the women? Why art thou enraged with the women? . . . Hast thou not heard commonly said in the world that the women of the enemy should not be killed? Matsya 2.188.41–48; A Taluqdar of Oudh (pseud.), II, 180.

There are instances in the Purāṇas where women are bracketed with Śūdras.

A man having accidentally killed his chaste and innocent wife, should practise the penance similar to what has been prescribed for the murder of a Shūdra. Agni 173.13–18; Dutt, II, 660.

Even women and Śūdras are admitted to the privilege of practising the vow. Garuda 119; Dutt, p. 359.

The following words also occur.

Anyone who knows the rule of righteousness does not kill a dunce . . . or a woman. Bhāgavata 1.7.36; Rau, I, 35.

The murderer of a child, a woman, or an old or imbecile person, is chained down to the bottom of the hell, known as the Raurava. Agni 203.20–23; Dutt, II, 728.

There are verses in the Purāṇas which teach that in the higher stages of religious knowledge wives and all worldly attachments are only temporary and that they really contribute to the misery of mankind.

Non-attachment to one's sons, wives and domestic affairs . . . are but the components of right perception or knowledge. Agni 362.19–27; Dutt, II, 1336.

Wives, children, friends, and relations are but the passing shadows in the phantasmagoria of life. Garuda 115; Dutt, p. 348.

Wife, children, servants, houses, lands, riches, contribute much more to the misery than to the happiness of mankind. Vishṇu 6.5; Dutt, p. 444.

A high status for women was not encouraged by those authors of the Purāṇas who gave to the Hindu people a description such as the following concerning one of their most powerful gods:

She was horrified by the cruel Indra who also beat her and subjected her to great troubles, as one would do unto a helpless woman without a lord. Matsya 147.10–15; II, 55.

On the other hand, we must note in the Agni Purāṇa that though sometimes little value would seem to be placed upon woman yet the face of a woman is considered always pure.

The face of a horse or that of a goat is always pure; and likewise the faces of a woman, calf, bird, and a dog are always pure. Agni 155.1–10; Dutt, I, 599.

Also consideration is shown for the pregnant woman.

The seat, bed, marriage, wife, son, and alms-bowl of one's own are always holy. . . . A man should give way to a venerable person, a pregnant woman, or to a person carrying a heavy load, if come across on the road. Agni 154.13–31; Dutt, I, 596.

This Purāṇa also condemns the man who speaks disrespectfully of women.

A man loses his caste . . . by mixing with men who speak irreverentially of women. Agni 168.28–38; Dutt, II, 644.

Passages concerning widows are to be found in the Purāṇas.

The widow who practises self-control and austerities after the death of her husband, goes to heaven. A widow shall never feel any inclination to dwell in the house of a stranger, nor should she be querulous in her disposition. A widow as well as the wife of a man who is absent in a distant country, should never decorate their persons, and live in a temple and worship the gods for their husband's good. A wife in the latter case shall wear a few ornaments for the good of her husband. Agni 222.19–23; Dutt, II, 795–96.

A widow should not anoint her body with oil. She should not see her face in the looking-glass or behold the face of any other man. She should not witness an opera, dance, a grand festival or see the face of a dancer, a singer or a well-dressed man. She should always listen to pious narratives. Brahma-Vaivarta, Kṛiṣṇa Janma-Khaṇḍa 83.102–24; Sen, II, 407.

A Brahman is warned not to eat food offered by a childless widow:

A Brahman who . . . eats food offered by a childless widow commits Brahman-murder. Brahma-Vaivarta, Prakriti-Khaṇḍa 30.172–82; Sen, I, 170.

We have evidence that the advice of the sage Aurva prevented a pregnant woman from performing *Satī*.

When her aged husband died, she prepared herself to die with him, but by the sage Aurva who knew her to be pregnant, she was prevented (from the act). Bhāgavata 9.8.3; Rau, II, 134.

Yet on the other hand there is evidence that a woman performed *Satī* even when she was leaving a mere boy an orphan. The boy Paraśurāma says:

My mother died on the funeral pile of her husband. I am now an orphan. Brahma-Vaivarta, Gaṇeśa-Khaṇḍa 30.7–20; Sen, II, 57.

The Devī Bhāgavata declares:

Those who are born . . . of widows . . . are always to be avoided. Devī Bhāgavata 3.27.2–3; Vijnanananda, p. 230.

Widows are urged not to marry.

She who does not take a second husband after the demise of her first one, achieves fame in this life, and lives in the same region with the goddess Umā in the next. Garuda 95; Dutt, p. 269.

Men are warned not to marry widows:

Those who passed their days as the husbands of widows are reduced to those worms that are being eaten up by ants. Mārkaṇḍeya 14.83; Dutt, p. 71.

In the Bhāgavata Purāṇa we find a lengthy instance of *Satī*.

That great Queen Archis, his devoted wife . . . followed him to the forest, though very delicate and not fit to go into the forest. . . . On observing the body . . . of her own beloved Lord, completely destitute of life, consciousness, etc., the true wife wept over it but for a short time, and soon caused it to be placed on the funeral pile of fuel on the high edge of a hill. Having performed appropriate rites, she bathed in the waters of the river, and poured libations to her Lord of noble deeds, and then bowed to the gods in heaven witnessing from the sky, she thrice went round the pile, and contemplating her Lord's feet, threw herself into the fire. On seeing the chaste Archis follow Pṛthu, her Lord, . . . thousands of Goddesses with their consorts sang her praises. . . . They showered down flowers . . . and talked to one another in praise of her, while the celestial trumpets were blowing. The Goddesses said, "What a blessed wife is she, who with a full heart has followed the king of kings even as the goddess Lakshmī sought the Lord of sacrifices (Nārāyaṇa). This worthy lady certainly goes to higher regions by following her lord. See! Archis passes beyond us by virtue of her dutifulness." . . . He who with faith and attention reads this holy account to himself or to others or listens to it, would attain to the path of Pṛthu. Bhāgavata 4.23.19,21,22–23,24–26, 31; Rau, I, 142–43.

With regard to the subject of *Satī,* such scriptural support as Hinduism gave the rite is mainly in the Purāṇas. Edward Thompson says:

Suttee was for the aggrandizement of the husband, who took with him when he died the most valuable and personal of his possessions. . . . We may look on suttee as almost inevitable from the premise of Hindu sociology and religion, that the husband stands to the wife in place of the Deity. Suttee, this surviving root from the darkest ages of savagery, was bound to blossom and fruit terribly, for a host of subsidiary considerations fed it. Families boasted . . . of their suttees, and tried to surpass rival families. Jealousy made an old man unwilling that a young and lovely woman should survive him. . . . Sordid greed—desire to avoid sharing a dead man's possessions with his widow—was considered by Rāmmohan Roy one of the causes that led to the increase of suttee in Bengal over a century ago. Hindu writers commonly blame Mahommadan lawlessness; women were unsafe, and it was best to preserve their honour by burning them when their protectors died. . . . But the main source of encouragement lay deeper than greed, deeper than even glorification of man. Hindu theology, with its doctrine of retribution pedantic in its exactitude, proved the woman left a widow a sinner whose previous life had brought upon her in this one the heaviest of all punishment in the loss of her visible God. Widowhood, then, must in rigorous justice be an experience so desolate and crammed with misery that it was better to perish in the flames that consumed the husband's corpse. . . . The widow who mounted the pyre passed from the condition of a sinner to one of beatification; her dying curse or blessing had absolute power and unfettered course. After her death prayers were made to her manes, and those prayers were sure of fulfilment. Her dying redeemed her ancestors from hell; and she enjoyed everlasting communion with her lord. . . . Everything conspired to point the widow along one path—that which led to the red glow of the funeral pyre.[30]

The custom of *Satī* seems to receive sacred sanction in the Purāṇas.

The princess again followed him in death, and in agreement with sacred precepts once more mounted cheerfully his funeral pyre. Vishṇu 3.18; Dutt, p. 235.

Where is that intelligent lady, fit to be adorned, who wants to live even for a moment as a widow which makes her unadorned and look low in the eyes of the people? Matsya 2.210.21; A Taluqdar of Oudh (pseud.), II, 214.

As the body of her husband together with the hut is being consumed by the fires, the virtuous wife Gāndhārī standing outside, will enter into that fire to follow her Lord. Bhāgavata 1.13.57; Rau, I, 70.

[30] Thompson, *Suttee,* pp. 46–50.

It is stated that a woman will go to heaven if she burns on her husband's funeral pyre.

The widow who burns herself in the same funeral pyre with her husband also goes to heaven. Agni 222.19–23; Dutt, II, 796.

It is very remarkable that the poets allow a woman the power to save her husband, yea even a wicked husband.

If a woman enters into fire with her husband, she reclaims him, even if he be guilty of Brahmanicide, ingratitude, or of other vile iniquities. Garuda 52; Dutt, p. 142.

Today medical men and women in India continually have to combat many harmful features of the ancient Hindu system of medicine. A large part of the population still treat disease as produced by an asterism or some earthly omen. Certainly the study and practice of medicine should not be hampered by ignorant fanaticism. The Purāṇas contain medical advice which may be of value for the cure of children having certain ailments. It is lamentable, however, that there are not more words of advice on child care direct from Hindu mothers in this period of Hinduism. Their words on the topic of health might have been of great value. Just how valuable most of the priestly writers' words on child care were may be deduced from a few of the following examples:

A child is subject to be possessed by the monstress Kākolī on the fourth day of its birth. The disease is marked by such symptoms, as the jerking of limbs, loss of appetite, foaming at the mouth, and upturned position of the dilated pupils. The remedy consists in smearing the body of the child with an unguent, composed of the scrapings of ivory, the cast-off skin of a snake, and the urine of a horse. Agni 299.5–9; Dutt, II, 1106.

The virtue of a topaz consists in removing the sterility of a woman, and in crowning her with the glory of maternity. Garuda 74; Dutt, p. 203.

A paste of Śṛingī and Ativisha mixed with honey, or honey and pulverized Ativisha alone, should be applied on the tongue of a child suffering from cough, catarrh or from inflammatory fever incidental thereto. Agni 283.1–4; Dutt, II, 1038–39.

Kaśyapa . . . began to counsel his wife how a pregnant woman should live. . . . A pregnant woman should not often go and sit at the root of a tree, nor should she sit on a broom-stick or a pestle. She should not enter or plunge herself in deep waters, and should also avoid living in a solitary house, sitting upon an ant-hill, and also depression of mind. She should not write by her nails, charcoal or ashes, on the floor, and should avoid much sleeping and labour. She should also abstain from sitting in a place covered with coal, chaff and bones, as well as from quarreling and yawning. She should not keep her hair unkempt, nor her person unclean, nor should she sleep with her head towards the north. She should never doff her garments, and should not allow her mind to be afflicted or her feet to remain wet. She should avoid much laughing and the use of inauspicious words. She should serve her preceptor, do pious deeds, and bathe in lukewarm medicated water. She should take great care of herself in every way, should wear fine ornaments, worship Vāstu (household deity), keep herself pleased, and devotedly serve her husband. She should give alms to the poor, and worship Gaurī (the wife of Śiva) on the third day of a bright fortnight. A woman, and particularly one who is in the family way, if she follows such a course, begets amiable, valiant, and long-lived children; otherwise there is always a danger of miscarriage. Matsya 1.37–48; A Taluqdar of Oudh (pseud.), I, 24, 25.

A repetition of the Ṛikrunning as "Pramandina; etc.," ensures the safe delivery of a woman undergoing the travails of childbirth. Agni 259.27–32; Dutt, II, 946.

A woman suffering from incessant miscarriage . . . should bathe an image of god Vishṇu placed on a lotus-flower. A woman whose issues die in childhood, should perform the rite under the boughs of an Aśoka tree. Agni 265.1–4; Dutt, II, 980.

It is evident that much magic has been handed down in the Hindu scriptures; but often true nobility of character and profound thought are to be noted in the same document that contains magic.

The Purāṇas expound upon the signs of the Zodiac and other omens, which are supposed to affect the problems of women.

A married couple whose natal stars stand in the relation of Samasaptaka becomes fondly enamoured of each other. But a marriage can be safely contracted or celebrated where the Kṣetrapatis or the presiding planets at the nativity of both the bride and the bridegroom are friendly towards each other or stand in the relative positions of Dvidadasha and Tricone towards each other. The effect of such an union is prosperity in the married life, even if the stars be otherwise hostile. Marriage between a pair whose stars stand in the relation of Shaṭaka or Ashṭaka towards each other is always prohibited, like an inauspicious marriage celebrated at the setting of Venus or Jupiter, as the effect of such an union would be the death of both the bride and bridegroom. A marriage ceremony gone through when the sun is in the house (Kṣetra) of Jupiter or in the event of the latter being within the mansion of the former is attended by the widowhood of the bride. The celebration of a marriage ceremony should be postponed for three weeks or four months as the case might be in the event of any planet hastily leaving any particular sign of the Zodiac (Atichāra) or gradually receding from its position. A penance or marriage ceremony is strictly forbidden when Jupiter takes the above-said movements. Similarly a marriage ceremony should not be celebrated in the months of Pausha and Chaitra or on the days of the lunar month known as the Riktā (except such days being Saturdays) nor when the god Hari would be enjoying his yearly sleep, nor on Tuesdays and Sundays, nor on the night of the new moon. But the evening is always auspicious, as then no stars exert their baneful influence. Marriage ceremonies should be celebrated under the auspicious influence of the asterisms such as the Rohiṇī, the Uttarās, the Mūlā, the Hastā, the Revatī, and when the sun is in the zodiacal signs of Libra or the Gemini. Agni 121.1–8; Dutt, I, 482–84.

The number of letters composing the names of both the man and the wife should be multiplied with the number of their Mātras and divided by four. The quotient, if even, would indicate the birth of a male child, while an odd quotient obtained in the aforesaid way would indicate the birth of a female child. Any remainder being left in the latter case would predict the death of the wife before that of her husband, while the one remaining in the former instance would foretell the survival of the wife. Agni 141.3–5; Dutt, I, 553.

Obeisance to the goddess Vajraśṛiṅkhalā! . . . Drink the blood of my enemy out of the cup of a human skull. . . . Obstruct the eastern quarter of the sky, O thou goddess with bloodshot eyes, besmeared with ashes, clad in bloody clothes, and equipped with the bolt of thunder! . . . Keep in control the demon-world. . . . O thou goddess of mighty prowess . . . who art encircled by a wall of liquid thunder drippling down from thy dishevelled hairs . . . protect me from all malignant stars and planets! Protect me from (the influences of) all diseases; keep me secure from the infinite harms and evils that beset human life. Agni 141.9–20; Dutt, I, 555, 556.

A woman named after an asterism, a plant, or a stream . . . should be deemed as a curse. Agni 244.1–6; Dutt, II, 884.

A woman whose small toe does not touch the ground, should be shunned as death. Agni 244.1–6; Dutt, II, 884.

In certain places we find that a high ethical standard is taught for estimating women.

Beauty and good character become a cause of happiness; for that reason she who is without character, is to be forsaken. Mārkaṇḍeya 69.34; Dutt, p. 295.

A woman . . . fond of quarreling with her neighbors or relations, or excessively greedy, or foul-mouthed, should be deemed as a curse. Agni 244.1–6; Dutt, II, 884.

A woman conversing with a person at a forbidden place, and on a forbidden topic, should be liable to a fine of a hundred paṇas, while a man found guilty of such an offence, should be punished with a fine double in value of the latter. Agni 258.68–71; Dutt, II, 941.

An unchaste woman has no place beneath the face of the sun. Everyone is released from his sins after his sufferings. But an unchaste woman is never released, so long as the sun and the moon exist. . . . All the sins of the world dwell in an unchaste woman. There is no sin greater than she. Brahma-Vaivarta, Kṛiṣṇa Janma-Khaṇḍa 23.25–36; Sen, II, 201.

The life of an unchaste woman in India is quite useless. Brahma-Vaivarta, Kṛiṣṇa Janma-Khaṇḍa 23.37–49; Sen, II, 202.

An unchaste woman . . . is a blot on her family. Brahma-Vaivarta, Kṛiṣṇa Janma-Khaṇḍa 23.78–91; Sen, II, 203.

Warnings against the unchaste woman are numerous and explicit.

No wise man believes a vile woman. No one is her friend. Brahma-Vaivarta, Prakriti-Khaṇḍa 16.41–51; Sen, I, 132.

A man who eats food cooked by a prostitute . . . commits the sin of the murder of a Brahman. Brahma-Vaivarta, Brahma-Khaṇḍa 16.43–52; Sen, I, 53.

A man should not eat the boiled rice . . . prepared by a public woman, . . . a woman who lives with her paramour . . . a ballet dancer . . . a corrupt woman. Agni 168.1–12; Dutt, II, 641.

If such a person is again found talking to women, he should be fined a tola of gold or silver. But there is no serious crime in talking to actresses in private, or walking with them in private; for, it is their profession, and they should therefore be fined something for doing so, for they earn their livelihood by prostituting their bodies. Matsya 2.227.122–23; A Taluqdar of Oudh (pseud.), II, 246.

Only an unchaste woman troubleth her husband; a chaste woman doth not. Brahma-Vaivarta, Brahma-Khaṇḍa 6.36–46; Sen, I, 17.

An unchaste wife is troublesome to her husband like his enemy. A woman of sharp tongue and a woman of bad character are both unchaste. Brahma-Vaivarta, Gaṇeśa-Khaṇḍa 2.16–31; Sen, II, 4.

The wife who wantonly breaks faith with her lord, should be caused to be torn to pieces by dogs specially trained for the purpose. Agni 227.40–45; Dutt, II, 815.

A scolding wife, wild, querulous and argumentative is but the blight of life. A wife, attached to another and fond of staying in another man's house, and who is not ashamed of her own depravity, is but the curse of life. A wife who appreciates and honours the good qualities in her lord and lives in loving submission to his wishes, is satisfied with the little she gets, is alone entitled to be called a beloved. An unchaste wife, an insincere friend, an argumentative servant, and a residence in a snake-infested chamber, are but the preludes of death. Walk not in the paths of the wicked; but sit in the assembly of the pious and the godly. Garuda 108; Dutt, p. 317.

Nevertheless, a wife, even though she be of bad character, must not be left unsupported by her husband.

As the wife must be favourably disposed towards the husband if he be of bad character, similarly is the wife of bad character to be supported (by the husband). Mārkaṇḍeya 69.59; Dutt, p. 297.

A chaste wife is highly praised in the Purāṇas. Under no circumstances is she to be forsaken.

He who forsakes a chaste and undegraded wife in her youth, is sure to incarnate as a woman, and to suffer the pangs of widowhood in his six successive rebirths. Garuda 107; Dutt, p. 313.

The fire and the sun, though they are foremost of the effulgent, cannot even hold candle to a chaste woman in point of lustre. Brahma-Vaivarta, Gaṇeśa-Khaṇḍa 44.11–27; Sen, II, 89.

Polygamy appears in the Purāṇas.

Pāṇḍu had another wife named Mādrī. Vishṇu 4.14; Dutt, p. 291.

The sons of [a] Brāhmaṇa father should be entitled to four, three, two and a single share respectively, according to the castes of their respective mothers; or in other words, a son by a Brāhmaṇa mother would take four, a son by a Kshatriya mother would take three, a son by a Vaiśhya mother would take two, while a son by a Shūdra mother would take a single share only. Agni 256.11–12; Dutt, II, 922.

The elder co-wife shall be the companion of her lord, inasmuch as the younger one does not enjoy that privilege. Garuda 95; Dutt, p. 271.

Yayāti had two queens. Matsya 1.24.52; A Taluqdar of Oudh (pseud.), I, 78.

King Kaikaya had ten daughters, who all were married to Satrājita. Matsya 1.45.22–24; A Taluqdar of Oudh (pseud.), I, 121.

Pushkara said: "A Brahman may take four wives; a Kshatriya, three; a Vaiśhya, two; while a member of the Shūdra caste is not allowed to have more than a single wife." Agni 153.1–4; Dutt, I, 592.

Ajamīḍha had three wives. Matsya 1.49.41–44; A Taluqdar of Oudh (pseud.), I, 148.

The King had fifty queens, the best of women, most fortunate and possessing a never-fading youth. Brahma-Vaivarta, Kṛiṣṇa Janma-Khaṇḍa 41.111–25; Sen, II, 285.

Kṛiṣṇa had sixteen thousand queens. Agni 276.3–8; Dutt, II, 1013.

By the pleasure of the Lord Mahādeva all those girls were blessed to have Lord Kṛishṇa as their husband. Matsya 2.194.11–20; A Taluqdar of Oudh (pseud.), II, 194.

On the other hand, there is evidence that a wife was not always happy to have a co-wife.

It may be he has made some other beautiful woman as my co-wife. . . . She thought that having a co-wife would be more painful than her widowhood. Devī Bhāgavata 1.5.76–82; Vijnanananda, p. 17.

Despite the many verses which sanctioned polygamy, we find that polygamy is reported as a ground for losing caste.

A man loses caste by taking many wives. Agni 168.28–38; Dutt, II, 644.

In the Purāṇas, as also in previous sets of documents, female slaves are mentioned.

By dedicating female slaves, servants, ornaments, cows, land, horses and elephants to an idol, a man acquires wealth and fortune, and goes to heaven after death. Agni 211.63–72; Dutt, II, 758.

A man by forcibly visiting a female slave, should be liable to a fine of ten paṇas. Agni 258.72–73; Dutt, II, 941.

The precise prohibition against women's acquisition of knowledge of the sacred scriptures which was enjoined in Manu (9.18) is reiterated in the Matsya Purāṇa.

Women are by their very nature meek and weak. Women cannot study the Śāstras. Matsya 2.154.156–74; II, 88.

The women are not entitled to utter the Veda Mantras; and hence they are not invested with the holy threads. Agni 152.9–12; Dutt, I, 591.

The Bhāgavata Purāṇa speaks of "ignorant women and children" (1.19.29; Rau, I, 100). This Purāṇa states that women "are incapable of weighing evidence" (1.11.41; Chatterjee, p. 364). Yet the Garuda Purāṇa states that a woman baffles the best wisdom of the wise (Garuda 109; Dutt, p. 323).

Warnings against women's managerial ability are found in the Purāṇas.

Dwell not in a country where there is no law, or in which the central government is vested in a more than one responsive head, or which is governed by a woman, or an infant. Garuda 115; Dutt, p. 351.

The strength of a woman lies in her tears. Garuda 115; Dutt, p. 350.

The prohibition against knowledge for women seems to have been overcome in some instances. A very high estimate of a certain queen is recorded.

King Yuḍhishtira . . . gladly approved of the queen's words, which were sanctioned by righteousness and reason, and characterised by mercifulness, compassion, sincerity, justice and nobleness. Bhāgavata 1.7.49; Rau, I, 37.

We find also the instance of Saunatī, daughter of Devala and wife of Brahmadatta, who succeeded in overcoming the restriction against learning the Brahma lore.

She became learned in the Brahma lore. Matsya 1.20.26; A Taluqdar of Oudh (pseud.), I, 65.

For generations India has put handicaps in the way of woman's education; but this restriction has not been totally effective in stifling woman's intellectual training. Throughout the centuries a few women have fought for a chance to secure mental enlightenment. Today Indian women are forging ahead in an inspiring manner.

The actual birth of a child is declared to defile the people in the house.

People of all classes are defiled for a period when there is a childbirth in the house. Matsya 1.18.1–5; A Taluqdar of Oudh (pseud.), I, 60.

According to the Purāṇas women accompanied their husbands to the temples.

One who, in company of one's wife and sons, in a temple of Viṣṇu, hears about the sixteen kinds of ordinances, attains the realm of the Lord Viṣṇu, and remains there for one kalpa. Matsya 2.289.17; A Taluqdar of Oudh (pseud.), II, 368.

Kukudmin in the company of his wife went to hear the song of the great Brahman. Agni 273.13–16; Dutt, II, 1004.

Even as in the Vedic period, so also in the Puranic there is evidence that women appeared in public assemblages.

. . . in the noble assemblage which will be attended in that sacred city, in company of their beautiful ladies. Matsya 1.69.10–12; A Taluqdar of Oudh (pseud.), I, 205.

Women traveled and engaged in trade. However, they were not encouraged to travel abroad.

Freight and tolls should not be collected from women and wandering mendicants. Agni 223.23–29; Dutt, II, 799.

One who takes a girl away to a foreign land after marrying her in his own country is a thief and should be killed. Matsya 2.227.129; A Taluqdar of Oudh (pseud.), II, 246.

Miserliness is condemned for both men and women.

The man or woman who exercises miserliness goes to the lower regions. Matsya 1.62.34; A Taluqdar of Oudh (pseud.), I, 192.

The Purāṇas urge great care in the construction of a woman's home.

The doorway being blocked by a filthy drain or other impurities causes sterility to women. If there be any obstruction in the shape of pillar, it indicates difficulties to the wife. Matsya 2.225.10–14; A Taluqdar of Oudh (pseud.), II, 298.

Fireplaces built for cooking purposes on the east and west cause the death of the owner and widowhood to the womenfolk, and cause also many fears. Matsya 2.254.9–14; A Taluqdar of Oudh (pseud.), II, 295.

If Kautaki trees, milky trees, Aśana trees and the straight trees be planted in the house in the above mentioned directions respectively, then it means misery to the lady of the house and her children. Matsya 2.255. 20–24; A Taluqdar of Oudh (pseud.), II, 298.

The presence of goddesses in the home is besought.

Rest in peace in this house, O thou beautiful goddess who art the daughter of the god Prajāpati. . . . Rest in peace in this quadrangle. . . . O thou goddess of good fortune and gentle demeanours, stay in this house! O thou bedecked with garlands of celestial flowers, and who art worshipped by all and everywhere, increase my offspring and possessions. . . . May I live to witness the realization of my heartfelt desires! May population thrive, and elephants, horses and beasts in general increase in numbers! And may we have more and more wealth every day, by thy gracious blessings. Agni 247.1–23; Dutt, II, 891, 892.

Madhusūdana! as your household is never bereft of the goddess Lakshmī, similarly let not mine be devoid of my wife. Matsya 1.71.8; A Taluqdar of Oudh (pseud.), I, 214.

Detailed description of the Tripura fort is given in the Matsya Purāṇa.

The inner compartments for women resounded with the sounds of tinkling bells on their anklets; and these were more beautiful than the Heavens. In these compartments, there were many resting-places . . . tanks, banyan trees, . . . pools, lakes, gardens and forests. Matsya 2.130.21–26; A Taluqdar of Oudh (pseud.), II, 4.

On the other hand, reference is made to what appears to have been quite different arrangements for the housing of women.

Women confined in the houses like so many domesticated *Kokilas* [cuckoos] pent up in cages. Matsya 2.188; A Taluqdar of Oudh (pseud.), II, 180.

According to the Purāṇas the wife whom a Hindu husband considers ideal to have in his home is pictured in considerable detail.

She who speaks sweetly to her husband and is a clever manager of household affairs, is a true wife. She who is one in spirit with her lord, and devotes her whole self to his happiness, is a true wife.

He whose wife decorates her person with sandal paste, and perfumes her body after her daily ablution, talks little and agreeably, partakes small quantities of food, is ever fond of him, and is constantly engaged in doing acts of piety and virtue with a view to bring happiness and prosperity in the house, and is ever ready to yield to the procreative desires of her lord, is not a man, but the lord of heaven. Garuda 108; Dutt, p. 317.

Noteworthy is the statement of a modern educated Hindu, Narayanaswami Aiyar, concerning a husband's attitude with regard to the conducting of his household. "Each man thinks he is the master of his household. No! He is but the servant of the Lord who has placed him in charge of the household as His proxy. . . . Each one has to keep in mind . . . the lowest dust of the feet of the Lord in reigning over his family." [31]

In the Purāṇas the wives of Brahmans share in the honor and worship which the Brahmans constantly demand for themselves:

The wives of Brāhmaṇas should be worshipped and propitiated . . . whenever there would be anything amiss and regarding the increase of . . . childbirths. Agni 263.17–26; Dutt, II, 975.

Afterwards, the worshipper should bedeck the Brāhmaṇa along with his consort with fine clothes . . . and should look upon him as the moon in the company of Rohiṇī. Matsya 1.57.22,23; A Taluqdar of Oudh (pseud.), I, 175.

He [the worshipper] should bathe in the morning, and worship a married Brāhmaṇa couple. Agni 178.13–16; Dutt, II, 682.

[31] Aiyar, PLMS, p. 240.

Brāhmaṇas, with their wives should be adored by the devotee and by his consort. Matsya 1.62.32; A Taluqdar of Oudh (pseud.), I, 192.

The kingdom in which a forlorn Brāhmaṇa's wife weeps and suffers, is destroyed with all its subject people. Agni 222, 15–18; Dutt, II, 795.

There is no preceptor in the three worlds so great as he who gives us knowledge or he who initiates us in the mantras. Either of them is a lac of times greater than the father, and a hundred times greater than the mother. . . . It is mentioned in the Vedas that as the mother is greater than the father, so is the preceptor's wife a hundred times more adorable than the preceptor. The ravishment of the preceptor's wife is a hundred times more scandalous than the violation of one's mother. Brahma-Vaivarta, Brahma Khaṇḍa 10.44–55; Sen, I, 32.

The preceptor, as well as a Brahman husband and a wife, should be propitiated with presents of clothes, etc., whereby the penitent would enjoy all the comforts of this world, and attain salvation in the next. Agni 178.17–20; Dutt, II, 682.

Not only must seven Brahman wives be worshipped along with their husbands, but those Brahman wives are to perform the ceremony for a woman whose children have not survived and to offer prayer.

What should be done at the time of the ablution of a woman whose offspring do not survive?

The Lord said: "Seven Brāhmaṇa ladies, along with their husbands, should be worshipped with garlands, clothes, ornaments, etc., according to the means of the devotee. These women should have no bodily defects. Afterwards, the Brāhmaṇa women should perform the ablution ceremony of the woman whose children do not survive, and recite the following words:

"May this child be long-lived! May this progeny of this woman be long-lived!" Matsya 1.68.1–2,25–28; A Taluqdar of Oudh (pseud.), I, 201, 203.

Since Hindus cherish such reverence for Brahman priests and their wives, what an opportunity these Brahman members of Hindu society could exert if they were able to spread an enlightenment which would make for healthful and happy living!

Rigid caste distinctions forbade intermarriage with women of another caste.

If a low caste man wants to marry a high caste girl and does so, [he] would be punished with death. Similarly a high class woman marrying a low caste man should be punished with death. Matsya 2.227.131; A Taluqdar of Oudh (pseud.), II, 247.

A marriage should take place only between the members of the same class, the union of a person belonging to a higher class with one of the lower being always forbidden. Agni 150.14–18; Dutt, I, 587.

Sacrifices and religious ceremonies should not be performed by a husband in the company of a wife not belonging to the same caste as himself, a privilege which is reserved for his wives of the same caste. Agni 153.1–4; Dutt, I, 592.

The Purāṇas state rules regarding property settlement.

A woman, a servant, and a son—all these three have been said to be poor; for, the wealth acquired by them belongs to their master. Matsya 1.31; A Taluqdar of Oudh (pseud.), I, 94.

A woman is protected by her father in infancy, by her husband in youth, and by her son in old age. She has no separate and independent living. Garuda 115; Dutt, p. 351; see also Manu 9.3, SBE, XXV, 328.

A son begotten by a sonless man in another man's wife under a *Niyoga* (authority to beget offspring), should inherit the properties of both his natural father and the husband of his mother, as such a son can offer cakes of obsequies to both of them. A son begotten by a man in his own married and lawful wife, is known as an *Aurasa,* while a *Putrikā Suta* (a daughter's son who by agreement becomes a son of her father) should be deemed as ranking equally with a son of the former class. A son begotten in the wife of a man by one belonging to his own Gotra or by anybody else, is known as a *Kshetraja* son, while a son clandestinely begotten in the paternal house of a woman, is called a *Gūḍha-Utpanna* (born in secret). A son born in the womb of a maiden girl is called a *Kānīna,* and naturally belongs to the father of the girl (maternal grandfather). . . . A son born of a married woman by another, whether she had menstruated or not, is known as a *Paunarbhava*. . . . A child filiated by a person is called a *Kṛitrima* (artificial) son. A child voluntarily offering himself as a son to another, is called a *Dattātman*. . . . A son deserted by one and filiated by another, becomes an *Apaviddha* son to the latter. The sons enumerated above are all competent to offer cakes of obsequies and libations of water to their fathers, whether natural or adopted, and to inherit the properties respectively left by them.

The rule, laid down above, shall apply to sons born of mothers, belonging to the same castes as their husbands. A son begotten by a Shūdra out of lust in a female slave, should be entitled to a share in the property left by his deceased father. . . . The wife, daughters, parents, brothers, their sons, persons belonging to the same Gotra, Bandhus, disciples (in the case of a Brahmachārin), should be successively deemed as heirs to such a sonless man; and each of these succeeding relations should inherit his property in the absence of one immediately preceding him in the order of enumeration. This rule shall hold good in the case of the sonless of all castes. Agni 256.13–23; Dutt, II, 922, 923, 924.

A husband is not bound to repay or restore to his wife an estate or a property forming her *Strīdhana,* which he has appropriated in the time of famine, or sold for his medical treatment, or for the purposes of religious acts, or in the event of its being stolen by thieves. A husband marrying a second wife (*Adhivinnā*) in the life-time of the first, and without having assigned any separate property to her as her *Strīdhana,* should settle on her a *Strīdhana* equal in value to what had been settled on his first wife, or a half thereof in the event of the first wife having not been similarly provided for. Agni 256.30–36; Dutt, II, 925.

The six kinds of *Strīdhana* which form the separate property of a married woman, are the *Adhyagni* (gift made to a woman near the nuptial fire or at the time of marriage), the *Adhyāvāhanika* (gift made to a woman at the time of leaving her father's house for her husband's), gifts made by her husband or friends, gifts made by her father, gifts made by her mother and gifts made by her brother. Agni 209.22–27; Dutt, II, 742.

A gift made by a man to his own mother is a hundred times more meritorious than a gift made to an outsider, while the one made to one's father carries a thousand times more merit than the latter. Similarly a gift made by a man to his own daughter, brings him merit which lasts for the eternal time. Agni 209.28–36; Dutt, II, 743.

The king shall manage the properties of a widow who is the mother of a minor child or of those who have no legitimate guardians or relations of their own to protect them in their periods of widowhood. Properties settled on widows who had been faithful wives during the covertures of their marriage, and who are unable, out of ill health or incapacity, to manage their estates to their own benefit, shall also pass under the wardenship of the sovereign. And any attempt on the part of their relations to rob or to encroach upon a portion thereof, should be meted with the punishment like an act of theft. Agni 223.17–21; Dutt, II, 799.

The mothers (father's wives) not having received anything from their husband or father-in-law by way of their *Strīdhana,* should have a share in the division in the event of equal allotments having been made to each of the sons. Agni 256.1–10; Dutt, II, 921.

The property given to a man by his parents is his own, while his mother should be entitled to an equal share with the sons in the event of the partition having been made by his grandfather. The married brothers are bound to provide for the marriage-expenses of an unmarried daughter of their deceased father, and to give her a fourth part of a share. Agni 256.1–12; Dutt, II, 922.

The estates given a woman by her father, mother, husband or brother, as well as those presented to her near the nuptial fire, or those which fall under the denomination of *Adhibedanikas,* are the four classes of *Strīdhana* recognised by law. The Badhus of a woman dying without any issue, should inherit the estate presented to her by her friends and relations, as well as those which are known as the *Anvādheyaka.* The husbands of all castes, should inherit the *Strīdhana* left by their respective wives dying without any issue, while their daughters should be deemed as the legal heirs to such properties in the event of their having any female child; otherwise the property would revert to the father of the deceased. A man by taking back a property, or an estate, formally assigned and made over to his daughter, should be liable to punishment, whereas he is bound to defray the expenses incidental to her marriage and maintenance. Agni 256.30–36; Dutt, II, 925.

The Purāṇas expound upon the dangers of woman's love:

The three kinds of wine are called the *Gauḍī,* the *Paishṭī* and the *Madhvī,* the fourth sort of wine being the woman. It is the wine of woman's love that alone can intoxicate the three worlds. Wine, only when drunk, produces intoxication,—whereas a woman, simply being looked at, may madden the senses of a man, and enshroud his consciousness in the darkness of nescience. Hence a man should refrain from even beholding a woman, as she is wine to his eyes. Agni 353.9–15; Dutt, II, 1301.

There are many verses in the Purāṇas that show high respect for parents. Reciprocally, the love of mothers and fathers for their children is reported.

With their countenance beaming with affection, they brought presents, like children to their parents. Bhāgavata 1.11.4,5; Rau, I, 56.

By devotion to the mother one gets happiness in this world; by devotion to father, in *Madhyaloka* (the mid-region) . . . and by devotion to *Guru,* the preceptor, in *Brahmaloka.* Matsya 2.210.11; A Taluqdar of Oudh (pseud.), II, 213.

O father! a mother does never become hostile towards the sons, even when they become so. Mārkaṇḍeya 106.25; Dutt, p. 413.

A father and a mother well-guard their sons. Matsya 2.220.44; A Taluqdar of Oudh (pseud.), II, 234.

The mother is the emblem of the earth, and the greatest of all benefactors, male or female. There is no friend or relation greater than the mother. Brahma-Vaivarta, Kṛiṣṇa Janma-Khaṇḍa 72.105–15; Sen, II, 372.

You are kind, as mothers are towards their children. Devī Bhāgavata 7.28.4–45; Vijnanananda, p. 689.

How can a mother curse her sons, when they grow disobedient! Mārkaṇḍeya 106.32; Dutt, p. 414.

The mother is naturally merciful to her child. Devī Bhāgavata 11.18.41–59; Vijnanananda, p. 1112.

Fallen *Gurus* are not to be abandoned. And mother should not be forsaken, even if she does a great vicious crime; for, she is superior to all on account of her bearing the son in her womb and nourishing him. Matsya 2.227.148; A Taluqdar of Oudh (pseud.), II, 248.

The worship of female ancestors is to be included in religious ceremonies.

Then the oblations of water should be cast for the propitiation of the souls of one's father, grandfather and the great grandfather, together with those of his mother, grandmother and the great grandmother. Agni 115.10; Dutt, I, 451.

Sixteen kinds of women are to be regarded as mothers.

She who suckles the child, she who wields the child in her womb and gives him food, the wife of the preceptor, the wife of the tutelary deity, the father's wife, the daughter, the brother's daughter, the sister, the daughter-in-law, the mother-in-law, the paternal grandmother, the maternal grandmother, the brother's wife, the mother's sister, the father's sister, the maternal uncle's wife. These . . . are the daughters of

Brahmā, vested with Divine attributes. They are accomplished in every matter and adored in the three worlds. They are not ordinary beings. Brahma-Vaivarta, Gaṇeśa-Khaṇḍa 15.34–44; Sen, II, 32–33.

There are many laws in the Purāṇas regarding marriage-regulations:

A man should not marry a woman belonging to his own Gotra, or to a family acknowledging the spiritual leadership of the same *Ṛishi* as his own. Marriage with a woman is not forbidden where the bridegroom is not related to her within seven degrees in the father's line or five degrees on the side of her mother.

The Brāhma form of marriage is characterised by the giving away of the bride to a man of good and noble parentage and possessed of excellent virtues, and who has been specially invited and requested by her father for that purpose. This sort of marriage should be regarded as the best form of uniting a man and a woman in holy wedlock, as it is supposed to carry the bride's forefathers to heaven. In the *Ārsha* . . . form of marriage, the bride is given away with the presents of a couple of bullocks to the bridegroom; while in the virtue-giving *Prājāpatya* form, the bridegroom, or his relatives on his behalf ask for the hands of the bride. In the *Āsura* form of marriage which is always commendable, the bride is sold for value, while the *Gāndhārva* form is characterised by the union of a man and a woman out of mutual love. Marriage by forcibly carrying away a woman in battle is called the *Rākshasa,* while a marriage by practising fraud on the woman while asleep or otherwise insensible is known as the *Paiśāca.*

On the day of the marriage ceremony an image of Śacī should be made of clay brought from the potter's house, which should be worshipped on the banks of a tank on the same day. A bride should be taken to the house of the bridegroom amidst peals of music and shouts of general joy. A marriage should not be celebrated when the god Keshava would be enjoying his yearly sleep, nor in the months of *Pausha* and *Chaitra,* nor on Tuesdays and lunar days marked by the conditions known as the *Vistis.* Likewise the settings of Venus and the Jupiter and the eclipse of the moon, asterisms in conjunction with the sun, the Saturn, and the Mars, and the astral condition known as the *Vyatipāta* are inauspicious for the celebration of a marriage ceremony. Agni 153.12–16; Dutt, I, 593, 594.

An unmarried girl belongs to the clanship of the same *Ṛishi* as her father, while a married woman goes off by the Gotra of her husband. A woman, if unmarried, should offer libations of water to the souls of her departed forefathers, while a married woman should propitiate the souls of her departed manes, both on her father's and husband's sides, with libations of water. Agni 158.17–26; Dutt, I, 608.

He must marry a maiden who is a third of his age, one who has not too much hair, but is not without any, one who is not very black nor yellow complexioned, and who is not from birth a cripple or deformed. He must not marry a girl who is vicious or unhealthy, born of a low family, or suffering from any disease; one who may have been badly trained, one who talks improperly, . . . one who has a beard and has got a masculine appearance; one who speaks thick or thin, or croaks like a craven, who has got eyes without eye lashes, or [in]sufficiently covered with them; one who has got legs covered with hairs, thick ankles; one who has dimples in her cheeks when laughing. The learned should not marry a girl who has got a tender countenance, who has got white nails, and who has got red eyes. The wise and prudent should not marry one whose hands and legs are heavy, who is a dwarf, or who is very tall, or one whose eyebrows meet, or whose teeth are far apart and resemble tusks. O king, a householder should marry a girl who is at least five degrees distant in descent from his mother and seven degrees from his father. Vishṇu 3.10; Dutt, pp. 197, 198.

Some consideration is given in the Purāṇas to prohibiting a man from marrying under false pretenses.

The man who would negotiate the marriage of a bridegroom, knowingly screening his faults and defects from the guardians of the bride, should be punished with a fine of two hundred paṇas, no matter whether such a marriage has been formally celebrated or not. The man who would give in marriage to a man, a girl who has been previously united with another in lawful wedlock, should be liable to a fine of twelve hundred and fifty paṇas. Agni 227.1–17; Dutt, II, 812.

The man who hiding his faults marries a girl is considered not to have married at all and should pay 200 paṇas to the king. Matsya 2.227.14–22; A Taluqdar of Oudh (pseud.), II, 240.

Marriage difficulties could be discussed at a king's court.

A king's court shall entertain suits in which the legality of a marriage or the fulfilment of any condition appertaining thereto, is contested, or sought to be enforced either by the husband or the wife; and such a suit shall be denominated as a marriage-suit. Agni 253.13–30; Dutt, II, 905.

Conditions are specified under which a man may remarry.

A man is at liberty to marry a second wife in the event of his first having had no issue after eight years of wedlock; after nine years of that one whose children die in their infancy . . . and instantly when the first is foul-mouthed and tries to give him a bit of her mind. Garuda 115; Dutt, pp. 351, 352.

Despite the provision whereby a husband could remarry under certain circumstances, nevertheless not every husband did remarry after having found that his first wife was childless.

There he married a noble lady, named Chaitrā. He did not marry any other lady, in spite of his not getting any children from his wife Chaitrā. Matsya 1.44.31; A Taluqdar of Oudh (pseud.), I, 117.

Conditions were specified under which a wife could and could not be discarded.

A husband is at liberty summarily to discard a wife addicted to the habit of drinking wine, or afflicted with an incurable disease, or found to be inimically disposed towards him. O ye holy sages! a wife blest with the gift of sweetness of speech, tender, and graced with all those peculiar and excellent virtues which are found only in women, should be maintained and provided for at all hazards. The threefold benediction of God reigns in the household where the husband and the wife live in perfect harmony; and paradise is the house which harbours such a true, loving and virtuous pair under its roof. . . . Whoever discards a good and chaste wife, shall give her a third portion of her ornaments before formally effecting a separation. Garuda 95; Dutt, pp. 269, 270.

Conditions or circumstances under which a woman is permitted to marry again are enumerated.

. . . (1) the moral degradation of her husband, (2) his death, (3) renunciation by him of all worldly pursuits, his resorting to a monastery, (4) and his impotency. The widow of a man can marry the brother of her husband if living and willing to take her as his wife, while in the alternative she may marry whomsoever she pleases. The asterisms under whose benign influence a marriage ceremony should be celebrated and gone through, are the three *Pūrvas,* the asterisms presided over by the gods of fire and wind and the *Rohiṇī*. Agni 153.5–7; Dutt, I, 593.

Men are urged to marry. A mother says to her son:

"O son! Why hast thou foregone the pleasure of blessed matrimony? And why dost thou roam about cheerless and disconsolate without being bound in holy wedlock with an eligible bride?" Garuda 88; Dutt, p. 244.

A man who is not married cannot perform sacrificial duties.

The wifeless man, O King, is not entitled to perform his sacrificial duties, be he a Brāhmaṇa, Kshatriya, or Vaiśhya. Mārkaṇḍeya 71.11; Dutt, p. 302.

It is equally incumbent upon a husband and upon a wife not to forsake each other.

In forsaking thy wife, thou hast not done a graceful act; for, even as wives cannot desert their husbands, so too men cannot forsake their wives. Mārkaṇḍeya 71.11; Dutt, p. 302.

Very important is it for a man to have a wife.

Without wife a man cannot adore the gods, the ancestral manes, the servant and the guests. In the absence of a wife, or when united with a bad wife, the wealth even when acquired by men and brought to their house, is spent away. It is directly seen that men cannot accomplish their desired objects without wives. The husband and wife, when they jointly carry on pious observances, attain to threefold virtues. As a man satisfies his ancestral manes with offspring, the guests with food, and the immortals with adoration, so with all these should he protect his chaste wife. Mārkaṇḍeya 21. 74–77; Dutt, p. 103.

The wife is the most powerful incentive of men to the observance of the law and the attainment of merit. Especially is the law forsaken on her being forsaken. Mārkaṇḍeya 71.9; Dutt, p. 302.

A lovely wife becomes a cause of happiness. Mārkaṇḍeya 69.33; Dutt, p. 294.

The various advantages for a woman of securing a good husband are enumerated.

The women who get good husbands give peace and comfort to both their paternal and maternal families; and their lives become crowned with success. It is difficult for a woman to get a good husband. Without virtue, even a tolerable husband is not obtained; because, the natural course of women is to enjoy the company of their husbands for all their lives. The husband of a woman in spite of his being poor, unfortunate, illiterate and void of all fortune, is like a God to her. Without any effort, *dharma,* unlimited pleasures, and wealth to maintain one's life, are all found in husbands. Matsya 1.154.156–74; A Taluqdar of Oudh (pseud.), I, 89.

The woman who is blessed with her husband, sons and wealth . . . is completely fortunate; and the one bereft of them is extremely unfortunate. Matsya 1.154.156–74; A Taluqdar of Oudh (pseud.), I, 89.

A husband helps a woman to attain to "wished-for regions."

A woman has not separate sacrifices, *Śrāddhas* or fasts. By serving their husbands they attain to wished-for regions. Mārkaṇḍeya 16.61; Dutt, p. 82.

A husband is highly desirable for a woman.

O chaste and noble lady! As the husband is the most excellent course for woman, you should always set your heart upon serving your husband. Mārkaṇḍeya 16.62; Dutt, p. 82.

I know full well that there is no better refuge to women than their husbands. Devotion to them leads to benefit both in this world and in the next. Mārkaṇḍeya 16.66; Dutt, p. 82.

The husband being pleased with her, a woman becomes glorious both in this world and in the region of the dead, and attains to felicity. The husband is like a deity to woman. Mārkaṇḍeya 16.67; Dutt, p. 82.

The husband is the wife's friend. Devī Bhāgavata 9.45.1–63; Vijnanananda, p. 980.

The husband . . . supports his wife. He preserves her. He bestows the desired things to her. He increases her happiness. Devī Bhāgavata 9.45. 1–63; Vijnanananda, p. 980.

The husband . . . always nourishes his wife, and keeps her in comfort and happiness. Devī Bhāgavata 9.45.1–63; Vijnanananda, p. 668.

The husband is the friend of his wife, her refuge, her god and spiritual guide. Brahma-Vaivarta, Kṛiṣṇa Janma-Khaṇḍa 57.1–14; Sen, II, 329.

Women's safeguards of happiness are their husbands. Therefore women, who are helpless creatures, ought always to serve their husbands. Devī Bhāgavata 9.45.1–63; Vijnanananda, p. 980.

There is no friend in the world so dear to a woman as her husband. The gods or even the religious preceptor are not so dear to her as her husband. Even virtue is not greater, nor is wealth more precious to her, than her husband. In fact, the husband is unsurpassed. Brahma-Vaivarta, Kṛiṣṇa Janma-Khaṇḍa 17.87–96; Sen, II, 169–70.

To a woman, her husband constitutes her god. The husband is as pure as the gods, and represents all virtue. Brahma-Vaivarta, Kṛiṣṇa Janma-Khaṇḍa 57.15–25; Sen, II, 329.

Husband was her God. Bhāgavata 1.7.47; Chatterjee, p. 248.

Sāvitrī said: "To women, husband is their god; husband is their great refuge. Husband is their all in all. Therefore a virtuous woman should follow her lord. Father, brother and sons are the givers of limited things; but the husband is the giver of things unlimited. Who is there who does not adore her lord? It is proper of me to go to the place where my husband is taken, or where he goes himself. I ought to follow him by all my power. Deva! when I shall not be able to follow my lord in your custody, I shall give up my life." Matsya 2.210.17–20; A Taluqdar of Oudh (pseud.), p. 214.

A woman has only to honor her husband in act, thought and speech to reach the same region to which he is elevated; and she thus accomplishes her object without any great exertion. Vishṇu 6.2; Dutt, p. 433.

O Nārada! the woman who is devoted to her husband, God and preceptor, and observes this ordinance, and eats at night only on Sundays, undoubtedly reaches the solar region. Matsya 1.97.19; A Taluqdar of Oudh (pseud.), p. 265.

A woman should not be disobedient to her husband. Complete devotion is demanded from her.

The woman who is disobedient to her husband on account of being proud of her brothers, etc., should be driven out of the house by the king. Matsya 2.227.132; A Taluqdar of Oudh (pseud.), II, 247.

A woman who frowns at her husband, or abuses him, goes to the hell of meteors or torches, and dwells there for as many years as the hairs on the body of her husband. Brahma-Vaivarta, Prakriti-Khaṇḍa, 31.10–21; Sen, I, 173.

A wicked woman who does not know the merits of her husband, adopts the evil path. Ablution in all holy waters, initiation in all ceremonies, circumambulation round the world, asceticism, vows and gifts of all kinds, fasts, worship of the preceptor or the gods, and other difficult rites are not equal in point of merit to a sixteenth part of the devotion of a woman to her husband. Brahma-Vaivarta, Prakriti-Khaṇḍa 42.18–30; Sen, I, 203.

The sacred and imperative duty of a wife is to carry out the commands of her husband, and to live in perfect obedience to his wishes. Garuda 95; Dutt, p. 270.

By being whole-mindedly intent upon serving her husband, a woman reaps the religious merit earned by a man by worshipping deities, his ancestral manes and guests, and by the performance of pious rites. Mārkaṇḍeya 16.63; Dutt, p. 82.

Whether her husband is (outcaste) or not, wealthy or not, is a matter she entirely ignores. She is constantly engaged in his service. Brahma-Vaivarta, Brahma-Khaṇḍa 6.36–46; Sen, I, 17.

A woman of noble rank, be her husband ugly, fallen, ignorant, poor or diseased, regards him like Viṣṇu. Brahma-Vaivarta, Gaṇeśa-Khaṇḍa 44. 11–27; Sen, II, 89.

A chaste woman ever ministers to her husband like his mother. Brahma-Vaivarta, Gaṇeśa-Khaṇḍa 2.16–31; Sen, II, 4.

The devotion of a woman to her husband was carried to extremes.

The sight and touch of a chaste woman who always eats the refuse of the food of her husband, and drinks water with which his feet are washed, are desired always by the gods. Brahma-Vaivarta, Kṛiṣṇa Janma-Khaṇḍa 57.15–25; Sen, II, 329.

It is stated that mutual love does not always exist between husbands and wives.

Mutual love between the husband and the wife is rare in the three worlds. Brahma-Vaivarta, Kṛiṣṇa Janma-Khaṇḍa 126.48–58; Sen, II, 544.

It is only rarely . . . when a couple is fondly attached to each other that the wife is true at heart. Garuda 114; Dutt, p. 340.

Nevertheless a faithful husband and a faithful wife are unhappy in each other's absence.

A clever woman is consumed by the fire of mental agony caused by the separation from her husband. . . . Without her husband, a chaste woman is not inclined to eat or drink. Brahma-Vaivarta, Kṛiṣṇa Janma-Khaṇḍa 17.87–96; Sen, II, 169.

The wife of an absentee husband shall renounce all frolics, and forego the pleasures of mixing in society, or of sight-seeing and merry-making. She shall not smile, nor attend to her daily toilette; nor shall she stay in another's house till the return of her lord. Garuda 95; Dutt, p. 270.

As thou never leavest the side of thy goddess Lakshmī, O Lord, may I never feel the pangs of separation from my wife. Agni 177.3–7; Dutt, II, 677.

The characteristics which a woman desires in a husband are enumerated.

A woman wants to secure the society of a youthful, humorous, calm, affectionate, handsome, talented, wealthy and clean person as her lover or husband.

A woman never desires the society of an ill-natured, diseased, ungenerous and indiscreet gallant. Brahma-Vaivarta, Gaṇeśa-Khaṇḍa 20. 35–40,41–50; Sen, II, 40.

A man desires the following type of bride:

A woman who loves her husband with her whole soul, and the hue of whose cheeks resembles that of the Madhuka flower, and whose arched eye-brows do not meet each other over the roof of the nose, should be considered as a desirable bride, though possessed of other objectionable features. Agni 244.1–6; Dutt, II, 884.

The death of a wife is among the causes of unhappiness.

The death of one's own dear wife, humiliation at the hands of one's own relations, a debt unpaid and undischarged, a service of the low and the vulgar, and desertion by friends in one's evil days, are the five things which, though not fire in themselves, consume one's vitals. The thoughts of a starving family, a scolding wife . . . are like sword blades to the heart. Garuda 115; Dutt, pp. 347, 348.

The ideal Hindu wife is pictured in glowing terms.

A wife who is not proud of her charms, is a true wife. Garuda 115; Dutt, p. 351.

A loving sweet-speaking wife . . . dispels misery in the world. Garuda 115; Dutt, p. 348.

She was faithful to her husband, kind, sincere, pure and gifted with every female accomplishment, humility and discretion. Vishṇu 3.18; Dutt, p. 232.

The wife whose heart leaps up at sight of her husband, and who casts down her eyes when looked at by him, or casts her coy and timid glances aside at the time of seeing her husband's face, but still cannot take her eyes away from it, and freely gives out all her little stores of secrets,—the wife who is yielding both in body and mind to the wishes of her husband, and nestles herself around her husband's neck on his first return to home, and over-powers him with long and loving kisses, speaks nothing but truth when asked about anything, and feels a happy thrill running through her body at a simple touch of her husband's hand which ultimately resolves itself into little dew-drops of love-perspiration, dresses herself in neat but not costly costumes, shows signs of superb satisfaction on receipts of small presents, deems it a boon for her name to be uttered by her husband, places on her bosom anything sent by him simply for the fact of its having been hallowed with his touch, sleeps after finding him reposing in sweet sleep, and wakes before his waking, and rouses him up in sleep, if necessary, by gently pressing his thighs, should be deemed as a loving wife. Agni 224.3–18; Dutt, II, 801–2.

CHAPTER VI: THE MAHĀBHĀRATA

THE GREAT Epic of the Mahābhārata depicts the social life of India with special emphasis on the Kshatriyas. A. A. Macdonell tells us that

The epic kernel of the Mahābhārata, or the "Great Battle of the descendants of Bharata," consisting of about 20,000 çlokas, describes the eighteen days' fight between Duryodhana, leader of the Kurus, and Yudhishṭhira, chief of the Pāṇḍus, who were cousins, both descended from King Bharata, son of Śakuntalā. Within this narrative-frame has come to be included a vast number of old legends about gods, kings, and sages; accounts of cosmogony and theogony; disquisitions on philosophy, law, religion and the duties of the military caste. These lengthy and heterogeneous interpolations render it very difficult to follow the thread of the narrative. Entire works are sometimes inserted to illustrate a particular statement. Thus, while the two armies are drawn up prepared for battle, a whole philosophical poem, in eighteen cantos, the Bhagavadgītā, is recited to the hero Arjuna, who hesitates to advance and fight against his kin. Hence the Mahābhārata claims to be not only a heroic poem (*kāvya*), but a compendium, teaching in accordance with the Veda the fourfold end of human existence (spiritual merit, wealth, pleasure, and salvation), a *smṛiti* or work of sacred tradition, which expounds the whole duty of man, and is intended for the religious instruction of all Hindus." [1]

In another work, the same eminent professor calls the Mahābhārata "a moral encyclopaedia in Indian literature." [2]

The Kshatriyas fought not only the battles against invaders of the land but likewise often the priests for their right to think and to criticize. The Brahmans' attempt to deny the right of thought to Kshatriya women also was not always successful. In this heroic age the poets of the Mahābhārata portray, on the whole, womanhood which was noble, intelligent, and active. In this document we

[1] Macdonell, HSL, pp. 283–84.

[2] Macdonell, *India's Past,* p. 88.

glimpse women in the home, at court, on the battlefield, and in intellectual and spiritual capacities. Although in some of the earlier Hindu documents women are sometimes pictured as helpless females, in the Mahābhārata we find many accomplished women. Not only are they beautiful in appearance, but they possess real tact and graciousness of character. We find heroines suggested as examples for womanhood. We note that the Brahmans had not stamped out all spontaneous, tender relationship between husbands and wives. There are examples of mutual trust in one another and of sadness resulting from the separation of husband and wife.

High praise for the devoted wife is found in the Mahābhārata, even as in the Laws of Manu and the Purāṇas.

> She is the true wife who is a good house-wife. She is a true wife whose heart is devoted to her husband. She is a true wife who is faithful to her husband.
>
> A man's half is his wife. The wife is her husband's best of friends. . . . The wife is the source of salvation.
>
> Those who have wives can perform religious acts. Those that have wives lead domestic lives. Those that have wives can be happy; and those that have wives can achieve good fortune.
>
> The sweet-speeched wives are their husband's friends on the occasion of joy; they are as fathers on occasions of religious acts; they are as mothers in the hours of illness and woe.
>
> Even in the deep forest, the wife is the refreshment and solace of her roaming husband. He who has a wife, is trusted by all. The wife, therefore, is man's great means of salvation. Ādi Parva 1.74.39–43; Dutt, I, 109.
>
> My wife is dearer to me than life itself. Vana Parva 3.52.44; Dutt, III, 79.
>
> To be ever engaged in serving her husband is a higher duty to a woman than sacrifices, asceticism, vows and various charities. Ādi Parva 1.160. 24; Dutt, I, 226.
>
> . . . my beloved wife. Vana Parva 3.192.31; Dutt, III, 287.
>
> This is our beloved wife, dearer even than life. Like a mother she is to be cherished; and like an elder sister she is to be respected. Virāṭa Parva 4.3.13; Dutt, IV, 3.

. . . a dear wife. Śalya Parva 9.17.54; Dutt, IX, 33.

No man, even in anger, should ever do anything that is disagreeable to his wife; for, happiness, joy, virtue and everything depend on the wife. Ādi Parva 1.74.50; Dutt, I, 108.

Aṅgirasa's wife possessed good behaviour, beauty and accomplishments. Vana Parva 3.224.1; Dutt, III, 332.

The friend of an exile is his companion; that of a householder, is his wife. Vana Parva 3.312.64; Dutt, III, 447.

In all descriptions of misery there is no medicine similar to a wife; this is the opinion of all the physicians. Vana Parva 3.61.29; Dutt, III, 89.

To a man aggrieved there is no friend equal to a wife that serves as a remedy. Vana Parva 3.61.30; Dutt, III, 89.

You are much respected and beloved by your husband. Udyoga Parva 5.90.92; Dutt, V, 133.

What could be greater evil than (to witness) the death of sons and wives! Vana Parva 3.193.19; Dutt, III, 290.

Causing quarrels between husband and wife ought to be avoided, as well as the sinful ways of life. Udyoga Parva 5.35.43; Dutt, V, 51.

A husband is a woman's refuge. Under smoother circumstances and in a difficult situation a father is the refuge. Udyoga Parva 5.176.8; Dutt, V, 241.

Devoted to her lord, that highly blessed lady always practised high vows. Practising the severest penances, she was always truthful in her speech. . . . She came by spiritual knowledge and power . . . the highly intelligent Kuru dame. Strī Parva 11.16.2–4; Dutt, XI, 16.

Subservience of the wife to the husband is recorded in numerous passages. Her complete devotion is demanded.

Wives are always at the command and disposal of their husbands. Sabhā Parva 2.67.46; Dutt, II, 88.

It behooves the lady, treated fairly or unfairly, not to be angry with her husband. Vana Parva 3.70.12; Dutt, III, 105.

I never bathe or eat or sleep till he, that is my husband, has bathed, or eaten, or slept. Vana Parva 3.232.24; Dutt, III, 345.

Avoiding all excitement and carelessness in the presence of men, conceal your mind by observing silence. You should not stay, or talk, long even with your sons. . . . Therefore worship your husband, adorning yourself with costly garments and ornaments, and besmearing yourself with unguents and perfumes. Vana Parva 3.233.10,12; Dutt, III, 347.

The best ornament of a woman who is without the ornaments, is her husband. Destitute of such an ornament (as the husband), she does not shine, although she is beautiful. Vana Parva 3.68.19; Dutt, III, 102.

Men learned in the Vedas have declared that whether the act be sinful or sinless, it is the duty of the wife to do what her husband commands. Ādi Parva 1.22.27; Dutt, I, 174.

The woman who being commanded by her husband to raise offspring, will refuse to do it, will commit sin. Ādi Parva 1.122.19; Dutt, I, 174.

It is the highest and eternal duty of women,—namely, to sacrifice their lives, and to seek the good of their husbands. Ādi Parva 1.160.4; Dutt, I, 226.

We note that Queen Gāndhārī (Ādi Parva 1.110.13–15; Dutt, I, 160), who shared in the affairs of state, bandaged her eyes that she might not have any joy which was denied her blind husband. Such a denial, to be sure, may seem fanatical and foolish today. The modern woman probably would handle the situation by making her eyes serve for her husband that he might enjoy a richer life. However, the old Indian story shows the wife's rare understanding and deep sympathy for her husband.

In the Mahābhārata, as well as in the Purāṇas, eight types of marriage are described. In the first four the father gives his daughter to a husband. These are called the Brahmanic forms. The fifth kind is purchase, or demon-marriage; the sixth form, *Gāndhārva,* or love-marriage; the seventh, capture-marriage; the eighth, marriage by stealing. Among the savage tribes of the world the carrying-off of a married woman often has been considered heroic; but not so according to the Mahābhārata. Meyer points out that "the Brahmanic form, the warrior form, and the *Gāndhārva* form are lawful: either separately or mingled they are to be followed." [3] Meyer also states that "the mutual contract concluded with holy

[3] Meyer, SLAI, I, 57.

words by the wife and the husband is declared to be weightier than that concluded by kinsfolk." [4]

Bhīṣma said:

"The wise have said that after inviting an accomplished man, a maiden may be bestowed on him decked with ornaments and accompanied with valuable presents as much as lie in the power of the bestower to give.

"Others may bestow their daughters by accepting a couple of kine. Some again may bestow their daughters by taking a fixed sum, and some again take away maidens by force.

"Some marry with the consent of the maidens; some, by dragging them into consent; and some by obtaining their parents' consent. Some again obtain wives as presents.

"The learned men praise the eighth form of marriage. But the *Svayaṃvara* is highly spoken of by the kings. But the sages have said that the wife taken by force amidst an assemblage of kings after defeating them is to be highly prized. Therefore, O kings, I carry away these maidens by force." Ādi Parva 1.102.8–12; Dutt, I, 150.

The Brahmans may choose their wives from the three upper castes, the warriors from two, but the Vaiśya shall choose only from his own caste. If a Brahman begets offspring with a Śūdra wife, he must observe penance. That injunction in the Mahābhārata differs from the Law Book of Manu, for in 3.13 ff. it is held that "for this crime there is no atonement." [5] In the Mahābhārata the children of wives from different castes "are on an equality with one another (all take the father's caste)." [6] This is not so in the Agni Purāṇa.

A child born of parents belonging to different castes would get the caste of its mother. Agni 150.11; Dutt, I, 587.

The *Gāndhārva,* or marriage by the mutual vows of the betrothed without witnesses, is illustrated in the Mahābhārata by the story of Śakuntalā. After plighting her troth to the King Dushyanta, the latter promises his wife Śakuntalā everything; but leaving her, he forgets his promise to send for her. Years afterward Śakuntalā goes to her husband's palace and, presenting their son to him, is distracted by misery when the King fails to remember that

[4] *Ibid.,* p. 59. [5] *Ibid.,* p. 57. [6] *Ibid.*

he has promised that the son of their marriage shall be heir to the throne. His wife finally reminds him that the gods have known what he has done, and will judge him. The poet who gave this story to the Hindus excuses the King's initial failure to recognize Śakuntalā and their son under the pretext that the word of the mother would not have been sufficient to have convinced the people that this was his son. This incident shows how easily such marriages without witnesses could be disavowed.

Along with the explicit injunctions found in the Laws of Manu whereby the selection of a husband was imposed upon the father of the young woman, we find prevalent in Hinduism the question of *Svayaṃvara,* or self-choice. This free choice of a suitor seems to have been practiced chiefly, if not exclusively, among royal maidens of the Kshatriya caste. On this question of *Svayaṃvara,* Hopkins believes that this knightly form in the Epic is not a survival from primitive times, but a later growth. As regards this, Meyer believes Hopkins is right.[7] The *Svayaṃvara* is pictured in such a story as that of Kuntī (Ādi Parva 1.112.1–13; Dutt, I, 162), who hangs a garland around Pāṇḍu. The story of Draupadī in the Mahābhārata pictures the securing of a husband by means of a contest of skill in weapons (Ādi Parva 1.187–94; Dutt, I, 257–67). We note such passages as the following:

> Choose whom you like for your husband. I will (afterward) on (due) deliberation give you away (to him). . . .
>
> That father who does not give away his daughter in marriage, is blamed. Vana Parva 3.292.33,35; Dutt, III, 419.

> The *Svayaṃvara* of the daughter of the illustrious Devaka took place. Droṇa Parva 7.144.9; Dutt, VII, 239.

> All the Kshatriyas, celebrated in the world, O amiable sister, have come for your hand. O blessed girl, these powerful men will (try to) shoot the mark. Among these (heroes) you shall choose as your husband him who will (be able to) shoot the mark. Ādi Parva 1.188.24; Dutt, I, 258.

> She was desirous of choosing her own husband. Udyoga Parva 5.177.15; Dutt, V, 242.

---

[7] *Ibid.,* p. 78; see also *Journal of the American Oriental Society,* XIII, 168, 169, 357, 360.

A maiden named Keshinī, of peerless beauty, O king, with the desire of a good husband, resolved to choose one in a *Svayaṃvara*. Udyoga Parva 5.35.6; Dutt, V, 49, 50.

In the account of the maiden Damayantī (Vana Parva 3.57.22–32; Dutt, II, 85) she showed intelligence in recognizing her lover, Nala. Because of her beauty the gods themselves desired Damayantī and disguised themselves as her suitors. When they were lined in a row, however, Damayantī discovered that one lotus in the hand of a suitor was drooped slightly. She knew that this was a human hand, and thus placed her garland on her true lover.

The later devotion of Damayantī to her lover also is recorded in one of the most heroic stories in the Mahābhārata. After several years of happy wedded life Nala became possessed by the demon Kālī (Vana Parva 3.59–76; Dutt, III, 86–115). The fond husband took to gambling and lost all his possessions. He even abandoned Damayantī. There are pathetic accounts of his grief at leaving her asleep in the forest. Damayantī was terror-stricken when she awakened and found herself alone. She roamed the forest in search of her husband and called to him:

Hero, valiant, knowing duty,
  To honour faithful, lord of earth,
If thou art within this forest,
  Then show thee in thy proper form.
Shall I hear the voice of Nala,
  Sweet as the draught of *Amṛita,*
With its deep and gentle accent,
  Like rumble of the thunder-cloud,
Saying "Daughter of Vidarbha!"
  To me with dear and blessed sound,
Rich, like Vedas, murmured flowing,
  At once destroying all my grief? [8]

As time passed on, Nala failed to appear and Damayantī became wasted in form. The princess is described as follows:

Like the young moon's slender crescent,
  Obscured by black clouds in the sky;

[8] Macdonell, HSL, p. 297.

Like the lotus-flower uprooted,
All parched and withered by the sun;
Like the pallid night, when Rāhu
Has swallowed up the darkened moon.[9]

Having been transformed into a dwarf, Nala finally became the charioteer of the king of Oudh, who was seeking for Damayantī's hand. The princess declared she would accept the king only on condition that he was able to drive five hundred miles in a single day. Nala helped the king to do this and was rewarded with the secret of skill in playing dice. Damayantī recognized Nala. The latter played again at dice, and this time won back his kingdom. Nala was reunited with Damayantī; and years of happiness followed.

In this Hindu epic we also find another noteworthy instance of a maiden's *Svayaṃvara* in the story of Sāvitrī (Vana Parva 3.292–98; Dutt, III, 418–30). This daughter of Aśvapati, king of Madra, chose Satyavān as her husband. "She too, having got a husband after her own heart, rejoiced exceedingly" (Vana Parva 3.294.17; Dutt, III, 421). He was the son of a blind and exiled king. Sāvitrī made this choice despite the fact that the sage Nārada had warned her that the prince could live only one year. Her husband took her to the forest home of his father. For a year they were happy; but as the fatal day of her husband's death drew near, her anxiety grew great. One day, while going to cut wood, Satyavān became exhausted. His soul was taken by Yama; but Sāvitrī followed the god. Yama at first granted some of her wishes, but not the life of her husband. Sāvitrī, however, was so persistent that at last Yama granted life to Satyavān, and the loving couple lived happily once again.

As in the Laws of Manu, so in the Mahābhārata, elder brothers and sisters must marry before the younger ones. To do otherwise causes loss of caste; and penances for this sin must be performed (12.165.68–69). In Mahābhārata (12.35.27) we find that if the elder brother is killed or has become ascetic, the younger brother may wed.

[9] *Ibid.*, p. 298.

Evidence of the happy life of a certain young girl is recorded.

That youth (Kacha) daily gratified Devayānī who was also in her youth with singing, dancing, and playing on various kinds of instruments.

He gratified . . . Devayānī . . . with the presentation of flowers and fruits, and serving her as an obedient servant. Ādi Parva 1.76.24,25; Dutt, I, 114.

Daughters are praised in the Mahābhārata.

He had three daughters of great religious merit. Vana Parva 3.218.4; Dutt, III, 326.

The daughter of Kuntibhoja, Pṛithā, had large eyes. She was endued with beauty and every accomplishment. She was of rigid vows, devoted to virtue; and she possessed every good quality. Ādi Parva 1.112.1; Dutt, I, 162.

Some men think that father's affection for his son is greater; others (think that father's affection) for his daughter (is greater); but mine is equal. Ādi Parva 1.159.37; Dutt, I, 225.

Man desires son, daughter and wife for himself. Ādi Parva 1.160.3; Dutt, I, 226.

The son is even as one's own self, and the daughter is like unto the son. Anuśāsana Parva 13.45.11; Roy, X, 24.

Not only daughters but also daughters-in-law are equally praised.

There is no difference between a daughter and a daughter-in-law, as that between one's own self and a son. Virāṭa Parva 4.72.6; Dutt, IV, 79.

In the Mahābhārata we have a beautiful picture in which a father allows his little daughter to listen to words of wisdom expounded by a wise Brahman.

My father formerly kept a learned Brāhmaṇa with him. I sat on the lap of my father. That learned Brāhmaṇa used to recite unto me these truths, sweetly consoling me therewith. Vana Parva 3.32.59,61; Roy, II, 73, 74.

However, there is another account in which a daughter is commissioned by her father to wait upon a Brahman.

"O highly wise one, I have a renowned daughter, Pṛithā by name. That damsel is endowed with good manners, is observant of vows, chaste and self-controlled.

"She, without despising you, will wait on you and minister to your comforts. And you also will be pleased with her (graceful) manners."

Saying this, and duly worshipping that Brāhmaṇa, he (the king) went to his daughter Pṛithā, endued with large eyes, and said to her thus:—

"This highly fortunate Brāhmaṇa, O child, wishes to dwell in my house. . . .

"O child, you will minister to this Brāhmaṇa with great skill. And you will act in such a way as not to belie my words.

"What this highly-energetic, reverend and ascetic twice-born one devoted to the study of the Vedas, asks for, will be given him without any pride.

"A Brāhmaṇa represents the highest energy and the highest devotion; and it is in virtue of the devoutness of the Brāmaṇas that the sun shines in the heavens. . . .

"O child, now this highly fortunate one is entrusted to your care. You should be particularly careful in ministering to him." Vana Parva 3.302.10–13, 14–16,18; Dutt, III, 434.

As regards the inheritance of a deceased father, a daughter shall be treated equally as well as a son.

The son is even as one's own self, and the daughter is like the son. How therefore, can another take the riches when one lives in his own self in the form of his daughter? Anuśāsana Parva 13.45.11; Dutt, XIII, 113.

The similarity of this provision that both son and daughter shall share equally in a father's estate, may be noted in Manu (9.130). The property given by her father to a Brahmanic wife is to be inherited by her daughter if the wife has no son.

Whatever riches the *Brāhmaṇī* wife may acquire by gift from her father, should be taken by her daughter, for the daughter is like the son. Anuśāsana Parva 13.47.25; Dutt, XIII, 116.

Despite these expressions of praise for daughters, we find evidence that a male child was considered more desirable than a female child.

Draupadī gave birth to a daughter also, named Śikhaṇḍinī, and she was transformed into a male child.

She was thus transformed into a male child by a Yaksha, named Sthūṇa, who did it from the desire of doing her good. Ādi Parva 1.63.124–25; Dutt, I, 88.

Let mine be a son, and not a daughter. Udyoga Parva 5.190.4; Dutt, V, 258.

Greater than the desire for a male offspring, however, was the desire of acquiring truth.

Truth is more meritorious than the birth of one hundred sons. Ādi Parva 1.74.101–4; Dutt, I, 110.

On the whole, the predominant view concerning a marriageable maiden in the Epic period probably was that she should be chaste, that she should show implicit obedience toward her parents, and that she should depend upon them for the selection of her husband. However, in India today there is a very noticeable new tendency for the young men and women to exercise their own preferences in selecting their partner for life.

In the Mahābhārata the maiden who "spoils her virginity" is to be punished.

The maiden who spoils her virginity incurs three-fourths of the sin of Brahmanicide, while the man who knows her incurs a sin equal to a fourth part of that of Brahmanicide. Śānti Parva 12.165.43; Dutt, III, 245.

With regard to marriage, there is, on the whole, in the Epic a high sense of morality. The ideal bridegroom shall be chaste and shall be led into wedlock through religious motives, not lust. Great anxiety on the part of the parents is expressed over finding a desirable bridegroom for their daughter. The father must give his daughter in marriage; for the Mahābhārata definitely states (13.24.9) that he who does not give his grown-up daughter to a worthy wooer is guilty of Brahman murder. Meyer reports that "a wife must in no wise be bought or sold"; [10] anyone doing so is greedy and evil-minded. However, history shows that such acts were not uncommon. In *Deutsche Rundschau,*[11] Sohm points out that among the Germanic forefathers the free gift of the bride was invalid and

[10] Meyer, SLAI, I, 62.

[11] 1878, p. 99.

that only the purchase-marriage was valid according to law.[12] Meyer reminds us that even in the law literature it comes out more or less incidentally in many places that marriage by purchase was general.[13] However, the upper classes seem to be ashamed of it. The Mahābhārata recommends that continuously from the wedding day the hearts of the bride and bridegroom shall be bound in tender mutual love.

The love life of man and woman is woven intimately with religious edicts into the sacred scriptures. In the Epic, as likewise in other Indian scriptures, there is much description concerning sexual relations of women and men. Meyer writes: "When women become ripe for love—this for the Indian is no romance, but a practical chapter in the physiology of sex." [14] It is praiseworthy that in the Epic there is no child-marriage in the "narrative parts." [15] The heroes and heroines of the Mahābhārata are adults.

In the prophetic parts of the Mahābhārata there are warnings of the dire effects of child-marriages.

> O King, no one died in early age, and none took to wife before attaining to age. Ādi Parva 1.64.17; Dutt, I, 88.

The Mahābhārata predicts that in the *Kālī Yuga* there will be fearful deterioration.

> Unholy both in thought and deed, men take pleasure in envy and malice. The earth becomes full of sin and immorality.
>
> Girls of seven and eight years of age, give birth to children, and boys of ten or twelve years beget offspring. Vana Parva 3.188.51.60; Dutt, III, 276.

> Girls of five and six will give birth to children; and boys of seven or eight years of age will be fathers. Vana Parva 3.190.49; Dutt, III, 283.

The public woman appears in the Mahābhārata. However, the continence of man is praised. India often has been called a land of contrasts. The public woman passes through the pages of Hindu sacred scriptures—praised with song in one breath, but condemned in another. In the Mahābhārata adultery is explicitly condemned.

[12] Meyer, SLAI, I, 101.
[13] *Ibid.,* p. 100.
[14] *Ibid.,* I, 215.
[15] *Ibid.,* p. 217.

As you have sinfully ravished a girl who has no husband, all the women of your families will become unchaste. Karna Parva 8.45.12; Dutt, VIII, 90.

Yet we find the following words concerning the god Indra:

Ahalyā, the wife of a *Ṛishi,* herself of good reputation, was ravished by Indra while her husband was alive. Udyoga Parva 5.12.6; Dutt, V, 15.

Even when forsaken by their husbands, chaste women are commanded not to be angry.

Although fallen into great calamity, the chaste women guard themselves by their own efforts, and thus undoubtedly obtain heaven.

Again, chaste women, even if they be forsaken by their husbands, do never become angry; rather they hold their lives shielded by virtuous behaviour.

She should not be angry, forsaken as she was by a person, who himself was foolish, overtaken by distress, and also destitute of all happiness. Vana Parva 3.70.8–10; Dutt, III, 105.

The husband even may kill the adulterer. A part of the fivefold *dharma* (13.141.26) is refraining from adultery. Meyer points out that "naturally in the Epic . . . the ascetic shines in the most glorious of haloes; and great is the worth and the might of his utter renunciation of sex." [16] Meyer, however, shows that the Epic emphasizes that "even the strictest penitents are not proof against woman." [17] The Mahābhārata states:

By forsaking an unchaste wife one does not incur sin. By such treatment the woman herself may be purified while the husband may avoid sin. Śānti Parva 12.35.30; Dutt, XII, 48.

According to the Mahābhārata (12.35.25–26) a wedded wife must not be abducted; penance must be made for such an offense. This, as we know, is contrary to the estimation of such an act in several other cultures. Among the Germanic forefathers, Meyer points out, such an act "was looked on as a glorious deed." [18] Among pre-Islamic Arabs, American Indians, and in the knightly age of Europe it was considered praiseworthy.

The unfortunate status of female servants is reported.

[16] *Ibid.,* p. 258. [17] *Ibid.,* p. 260. [18] *Ibid.,* p. 77.

There is a class of persons called Sairindhris, who enter the service of others. Other females, however, (that are respectable) do not do so. Virāṭa Parva 4.3.17; Roy, III, 5.

Again and again in the Epic the conquest of the senses is stressed as the highest end. Lustful looking upon women is vigorously condemned, as well as unlawful sexual union.

Those men of foolish understanding who cast wicked eyes upon the married wives of other men, become cursed with congenital blindness on account of that sinfulness of theirs.

Those men who, moved by desire in their hearts, cast their eyes on naked women, those men of wicked acts take birth in this world to pass their whole lives in one continuous disease.

Those men of foolish and wicked acts who indulge in sexual union with women of castes different from their own,—those men of little wisdom, —have to take birth in their next lives as persons shorn of virility. Anuśāsana Parva 13.145.50–52; Dutt, XIII, 300–301.

The Epic warns that a man should not embrace any woman other than his own wife (12.193.11; 13.107.50; 13.144.10–11,13).

Polygamy is a feature of society clearly acceptable in Epic India.

Polygamy is no fault with men. Women only commit sin by taking more than one husband. Ashwamedha Parva 14.80.14; Dutt, XIV, 94.

He had two wives, proud of their beauty and of their youth. Vana Parva 3.106.9; Dutt, III, 163.

To marry more than one wife is not sin among men. It is very sinful for a woman to take a second husband after the first. Ādi Parva 1.160.36; Dutt, I, 227.

It is ordained that a husband can have many wives; but we have never heard that a wife can have many husbands. Ādi Parva 1.197.27; Dutt, I, 268.

He repaired to the forest with his wives, saying, "Whatever of paddy, wheat, gold, animals and women there are on the face of the earth are not sufficient for even one single man.

"Knowing such to be the fact, one should betake to contentment." Thus having renounced all his desires, and cultivating contentment, the Lord Yayāti retired into the woods. Droṇa Parva 7.63.8–10; Dutt, VII, 94.

That one (King Śaśabindu) of illustrious soul has a hundred thousand wives; and each of these wives was blessed with a thousand sons. Droṇa Parva 7.65.2; Dutt, VII, 95.

With him were four thousand women all wedded to him. Vana Parva 3.122.6; Dutt, III, 183.

He enjoyed for a long time the sweet company of his two wives. Ādi Parva 1.75.47; Dutt, I, 113.

Bharata begot on his three wives nine sons. But none of them was like his father; and Bharata was not satisfied with any of them.

Thereupon their mothers, becoming angry, killed them all. Ādi Parva 1.94.20,21; Dutt, I, 136.

The enmity and sorrow that so often afflict polygamous wives is reported (1.124; 5.35.31,32).

. . . the grief of one who . . . is a co-wife. Sabhā Parva 2.68.81; Dutt, II, 92.

The wife is exhorted to remain faithful to one husband.

Dīrghatamas said:

"From this day I make this rule among men, that every woman shall stick to one husband only all through her life." Ādi Parva 1.104.31; Dutt, I, 154.

All venerable persons are to be respected, as also the women who are devoted to one husband. Vana Parva 3.204,5; Dutt, III, 307.

As all too frequently throughout the world's literature, the view of woman as a chattel appears in the Mahābhārata. Slave girls are mentioned frequently (4.34.5; 8.38.5,7; 5.86.8; 2.51.8,9; 14.85. 18; 2.35.53; 12.29.65; 15.14.4; 39.19; 17.1.14; 18.6.12–13; 12. 29.133; 3.185.34). A woman slave can be won by a game of dice.

When you have been won (by us) at dice and made our slave, you are to live amongst our serving women as you best can. Sabhā Parva 2.67.33; Dutt, II, 88.

Meyer points out that in the Mahābhārata slave girls "are the natural gift for Brahmans." [19] Woman is often considered as property.

A wife's duties in the care of the household are described at some

[19] *Ibid.*, II, 509.

length in the Mahābhārata (12.228.60; 13.11.10–13). In the Epic a daughter-in-law must fear the father-in-law and dignity must be observed between them (5.37.5).

O gentle ladies, is your treatment towards your fathers-in-law gentle and considerate? Udyoga Parva 5.30.35; Dutt, V, 38.

The daughter-in-law said:—

"You are the senior of my senior, since you are the deity of my deity. You are, indeed, the god of my god." Ashwamedha Parva 14.90.76; Dutt, XIV, 109.

The daughter-in-law must not give orders in the presence of her mother-in-law or her father-in-law (12.228.76). Meyer points out that there are some very beautiful relations "between the parents-in-law and the daughter-in-law. Especially with her husband's mother the younger woman has affectionate, and even intimate, relations. The Epic poetry often touches on this subject; and there is never heard one note of that song of the mother-in-law that we know so well." [20]

In certain passages the Mahābhārata indicates that the position of the widow was not a happy one. After the death of her husband, Satyavān, Sāvitrī said:

"I am as good as dead without my husband." Vana Parva 3.296.52; Dutt, III, 426.

The miserable life of a widow is depicted in the following passage:

Women serve no purpose when their husband is dead. She who lives without her husband, lives a miserable life. . . .

Death is preferable to one who has lost her husband. . . .

She who lives even for a moment after being separated from her husband,—that sinful woman, lives in great misery and in hell. Ādi Parva 1.121.20,21,27; Dutt, I, 172, 173.

Yet there are other verses which indicate that sometimes widows were protected.

He [the King] maintained widows, orphans, the maimed and the poor. Ādi Parva 1.49.11; Dutt, I, 69.

---

[20] *Ibid.*, II, 404.

That son who does not maintain his mother in her widowhood, meets with disgrace. Vana Parva 3.292.35; Dutt, III, 419.

The custom of widow immolation, which was not present in Vedic times, is noted in the Mahābhārata. There is an instance of four wives all of whom committed *Satī*.

Devakī, Bhadrā, Rohiṇī and Madirā threw themselves on the bodies of their lord.

The four wives of that heroic son of Śūra ascended the funeral pyre and were consumed with the body of their husband. All of them attained to those happy regions which were his.

The son of Pāṇḍu burnt the body of his uncle together with those four wives. Mausala Parva 16.7.18,24–25; Dutt, XVI, 8.

After the death of Pāṇḍu, children having survived, two of his wives, Kuntī and Mādrī, debate as to which one should practice *Satī*.

"Therefore, my body shall be burned with that of the king. O revered sister, do not refuse me your permission to what is agreeable to me." . . .

Having said this, the daughter of the king of Madra, the lawfully wedded wife of that best of men, Pāṇḍu, ascended the funeral pyre of her lord. Ādi Parva 1.125.31,33; Dutt, I, 179.

Edward Thompson is of the opinion that the few instances of *Satī* in the Mahābhārata are "later interpolations." [21] Meyer states that

Widow burning is really foreign to the Epic; the cases which do happen to be found are rare exceptions, and undoubtedly belong, at least in far the greatest part, to later revisions. . . . In isolated cases, . . . such a death by self-sacrifice of the woman undoubtedly happened from early times in Aryan India . . . and the Kshattriyas in particular, the fore-fathers of the Rājputs, who are endowed with the strongest feeling for private property in regard to their wives, may have known it. . . . The widows of Droṇa, Drupada, and the still so young Abhimanyu, go on quietly living, (11.25.19,20,23), to say nothing of others.[22]

With regard to inheritance by the widow the Mahābhārata says:

The highest sum that the husband should give the wife is three thousand coins. This wealth that the husband gives to the wife, the latter may spend or dispose of as she likes.

---

[21] Thompson, *Suttee,* p. 19.

[22] Meyer, SLAI, II, 412, 413, 414.

Upon the death of the childless husband, the wife shall enjoy all his riches. Anuśāsana Parva 13.47.23,24; Dutt, XIII, 116.

Meyer states that "the woman is often found inheriting her husband's property in spite of many opposed views." [23]

In the Mahābhārata a widow of the upper classes must not make a new marriage. In the higher castes, at least in the noble and the Brahmanic castes, this custom was prescribed by the higher rule of conduct at the time the Epic was built up. Also, it still reflects here and there other and probably older conditions, when in these circles, or at least among the Kshatriyas, another marriage of the widow or of an outcast woman was the custom. Thus it was apparently a matter of course for Damayantī to take another husband when Nala had disappeared (3.70 f.).

Another important and complicated problem of the status of woman at this period in the sacred scriptures of Hinduism is polyandry. Meyer maintains that in the Epic "only one or two cases of it are found; and these are exclusively cases of a community of wives among brothers." [24] However, the five famous brothers, heroes of the Mahābhārata, have one wife in common, named Draupadī. Nevertheless, if we trace the origin of these five brothers, we plainly see that they are "unauthorized stranger intruders of a later date." [25] Thus Meyer believes that the Pāṇḍavas were of non-Aryan stock; and in an article in *Wiener Zeitschrift für die Kunde des Morgenlandes,* Winternitz also leans toward this view, as he calls the Pāṇḍavas a "non-Aryan mountain tribe." [26] As proof of polyandric marriage [27] Winternitz points out Mahābhārata (1.191) and Arjuna's speech in which Arjuna holds it quite wrong even to think of making Draupadī the wife of himself alone. Meyer is of the opinion that "polyandry is utterly repugnant to Indian feelings." [28] And furthermore, like legendary traditions of polyandric marriages in other countries, there is evidence in the Epic of earlier or still existing conditions of hetaerism; but he believes that "such mythical tales of earlier times often seem . . . to be altogether too bold to be used as wholly credible grounds of proof." [29] Meyer

[23] *Ibid.,* p. 406. [24] *Ibid.,* I, 108. [25] *Ibid.*
[26] *Ibid.,* p. 109. [27] *Ibid.,* p. 107.
[28] *Ibid.,* p. 108. [29] *Ibid.,* p. 115.

admits that there is "left always a certain doubt" about this question.[30] Yet he points out that Draupadī's marriage was reluctantly made. He believes that from the passages brought forward by Winternitz and others, polyandry in India really cannot be deduced.[31]

In the Epics, as well as in the other scriptures of Hinduism, there are many beautiful pictures showing children's tender regard for their parents. The mother becomes the important center of the family life. Indeed in the Mahābhārata the mother is the foremost of all superiors.

O foremost of all men learned in the precepts of virtue, it is said that obedience to superiors is a cardinal virtue. Of all superiors the mother is the foremost. Ādi Parva 1.198.16; Dutt, I, 269.

Many scholars feel that women held a more important position in Epic days than in later times. The Mahābhārata several times exhorts children to be respectful and obedient to mother as well as to father.

The son who obeys the commands of his father and mother, who is humble and a well-wisher of his parents, and who loves them, is the best of sons. Ādi Parva 1.85.25; Dutt, I, 127.

Rāma tried to serve his old parents. Vana Parva 3.213.13; Dutt, III, 322.

Return soon to the side of your parents, and be . . . diligent in honouring your father and mother; for, I do not know, if there is any virtue higher than this. Vana Parva 3.214.13; Dutt, III, 323.

O Karṇa, never do such acts as will lead to the injury of your own self, your friends, your sons, your wives, your mother, and your father. Vana Parva 3.300.1; Dutt, III, 432.

You are worthy of my worship as my mother. Protect me as your son. Vana Parva 3.46.47; Dutt, III, 71.

Listen therefore to the advice of your father and of your mother. Udyoga Parva 5.138.25; Dutt, V, 191.

A mother's affection toward her children is emphasized.

Women give birth to their children with great pain to themselves; and

---

[30] *Ibid.*

[31] *Ibid.*, p. 109.

. . . they bring them up with great affection. Vana Parva 3.204.12; Dutt, III, 307.

And furthermore, a woman feels affection not only for her son but also for her son-in-law.

Every woman feels a very great affection for her son-in-law. Ādi Parva 1.116.11; Dutt, I, 166.

The function of the mother in the propagation of the species is recognized.

Some consider the mother to be superior; and some again consider the father as such. The mother, however, performs the most difficult thing; for, she propagates the species. Vana Parva 3.204.17; Dutt, III, 307.

However, it is stated:

The mother is but a sheath of flesh (within which the son dwells). The son, sprung from the father, is the father himself. Ādi Parva 1.74.109; Dutt, I, 110.

Even the wise and holy *ṛishis* admitted that women are necessary.

Even *Ṛishis* cannot create men without women. Ādi Parva 1.74.51; Dutt, I, 108.

The Mahābhārata reëmphasizes the dependence of women, which is to be found from the Brāhmaṇas onward.

The slave, the son, and the wife,—(these three) are always dependent. They can have no wealth; for, whatever they possess belongs to their master. Sabhā Parva 2.71.2; Dutt, II, 94.

Women are never independent. Ādi Parva 1.174.22; Dutt, I, 242.

Also women are warned not to be curious.

Curiosity is the worst thing in a chaste woman. Udyoga Parva 5.39.80; Dutt, V, 64.

On the other hand woman's intelligence seems to be valued.

O highly-intelligent lady! Vana Parva 3.29.1; Dutt, III, 41.

In this world the nature of women is very subtle. Vana Parva 3.71.6; Dutt, III, 106.

. . . hearing this her speech, pregnant with sense, and consisting of weighty letters and words. Udyoga Parva 5.136.12; Dutt, V, 188.

Great sorrow is expressed by a wife because of separation from her husband:

Thus bewailing, the consort of that high-souled monarch began to search her dear lord in that forest, infested with wild beasts. Vana Parva 3.63.18; Dutt, III, 91.

What is the use of my life, separated as I have been, from that foremost of men? How shall I live today, afflicted with sorrow for my husband. Vana Parva 3.64.90; Dutt, III, 95.

A husband is presented as being a necessity for a woman.

A woman without a husband will always be liable to be sinful. Ādi Parva 1.104.32; Dutt, I, 154.

In the Epic there is an instance of the violent treatment of a woman.

While she was piteously praying . . . he dragged her forcibly by her black hair. Sabhā Parva 2.67.32; Dutt, II, 88.

When the Kshatriya caste was almost exterminated, it was the women who saved that caste from extinction.

When the earth was thus in olden time made Kshatriya-less by that great *Ṛishi,* the Kshatriya women raised children by the Brāhmaṇas, learned in the Vedas.

They went to the Brāhmaṇas not lustfully, but from virtuous motives. It is said in the Vedas that the son so raised belongs to him that had married the mother.

Thus it was that the Kshatriya race was again brought into existence all over the world. Ādi Parva 1.104.5–7; Dutt, I, 153.

Warning is given against marriage between persons whose ages differ greatly:

A husband of sixty years can never be agreeable to a young wife. Sabhā Parva 2.64.14; Dutt, II, 83.

The Mahābhārata pictures scenes of bloody battle where women come in for a full share in the horrors of war.

. . . that field of battle, terrible to look at . . . and it resounded with the cries of elephants and horses and men and women. Strī Parva 11.16.4,7; Dutt, XI, 16.

The Kuru ladies were plunged into indescribable distress. . . . The cries of those grief-stricken ladies . . . seeing the dead bodies . . . they are running here and there in a body towards their sons and brothers and sires and husbands. Strī Parva 11.16.15–19; Dutt, XI, 16,17.

Those Kuru ladies . . . bewildered with sorrow, are running here and there. . . . Some amongst them, heavily sighing and repeatedly bewailing, are stupefied by grief, and are giving up their lives. Many of them, seeing the bodies (of their sons, husbands, or sires) are weeping and lamenting. Others are striking their heads with their own soft hands. Strī Parva 11.16.44–48; Dutt, XI, 18.

I heard the piteous cries of my mother and other women of the Vrigu race as they were being massacred by the Kshatriyas. Ādi Parva 1.182.5; Dutt, I, 252.

. . . the ravisher of soldiers' wives. Virāṭa Parva 4.25.3; Dutt, IV, 32.

Women are included in the booty of war.

O repressors of foes in battle, upon you I shall confer women adorned with ornaments, plentiful riches and other things that you may like. Virāṭa Parva 4.34.5; Dutt, IV, 41.

In the Mahābhārata woman is shown as a peacemaker pleading for mercy on enemies.

She forbade her brave son of steady heart from fighting any longer. Ashwamedha Parva 14.84.20; Dutt, XIV, 99.

In a story in the Ashwamedha Parva we find Queen Dusshala urging Arjuna to be merciful:

You should show mercy to this child, forgetting the Kuru prince (Duryodhana) and the wicked Jayadratha. . . .

Taking him [the child] with me, O King, I have come to you desirous of the safety of all the warriors! Do you listen to these words of mine.

This child of that wicked enemy of yours has now come to you, O mighty-armed hero. You should, therefore, show mercy to this infant. . . .

Be pleased with the child whose friends and kinsmen have all been killed and who himself knows nothing of what has taken place. Do not yield to anger.

Forgetting his [the child's] disreputable and cruel grandfather, who offended against you so highly, it is but fit that you should extend your grace towards this child. Ashwamedha Parva 14.78.35,37–38,40,41; Dutt, XIV, 91.

Meyer maintains that "the woman of the warrior nobility stands proud, strong and honoured wherever Brahman hands and later influences have not smirched her." [32] However, it is also stressed again and again in the Mahābhārata that the man's duty is to shelter the woman (4.21.40–43; 14.90.45 ff.; 5.39.83; 5.38.10,11). Not only do we find beautiful, mild, tender, and long-suffering women pictured in the Mahābhārata but there are also women of energy, strong will, and daring pride. The Mahābhārata quite clearly shows that Kshatriya women were not veiled. In the Epic women may have an important share in the events of their time. Queen Gāndhārī appears in the Council Chamber. Sanjaya says to King Dhṛitarāṣṭra:

"I shall not tell you anything in secret, for then, ill feeling against me may enter within you, O king. Have our sire of great vows, and Queen Gāndhārī brought here.

"They will be able to remove any ill-feeling . . . (you may harbour against me), acquainted as they are with virtue and skilled as they are in foresight. In their presence shall I tell you everything. . . ."

Gāndhārī and Vyāsa were brought there by him, who was then spoken to. They quickly entered the Council Chamber. Udyoga Parva 5.67.6,7,8; Dutt, V, 105.

In a passage in the Mahābhārata we note that where there are no male heirs, maidens shall be made rulers.

Install on their thrones the daughters of those that have no sons. Śānti Parva 12.33.45; Dutt, XII, 47.

It is reported that women go hunting and cattle branding with the men (3.239 ff.; 12.126.9; 1.114.9–11). Women take part in picnics and festivals.

In the Mahābhārata it is stated that woman is the light of the house.

Worthy of worship, highly blessed, virtuous, forming the light of their homes—such are the wives, who are the visible embodiments of house-

---

[32] *Ibid.*, II, 439.

hold felicity. It is therefore, that they should be specially protected. Udyoga Parva 5.38.11; Dutt, V, 59.

However, the texts also say that woman is untrue, unreliable, dangerous, of a bad magical nature, weak, and the root of all evil. Let us look at a few samples of such condemning verses:

Women generally speak falsehood. Ādi Parva 1.74.72; Dutt, I, 109.

Where a woman, or where a child, or where a wicked man is the guide, there . . . persons (who make themselves guides) are as helpless as a stone in a river, which sinks. Udyoga Parva 5.38.43; Dutt, V, 60.

Milk is possible in cows, devotion is possible in the Brāhmaṇas; unsteadiness is possible among women. Udyoga Parva 5.36.57; Dutt, V, 55.

Women, kings, serpents, one's own lord, enemies, enjoyments,— . . . for what wise man is it proper to put any reliance on these? Udyoga Parva 5.37.57; Dutt, V, 58.

A woman, a cunning and deceitful person, one that is lazy, one that is fierce, one that is wrathful, one that is vain of his own power, a thief, one that is ungrateful should never be trusted; nor should an atheist. Udyoga Parva 5.39.74,75; Dutt, V, 64.

Men should never trust women, even if they be wedded wives. Ādi Parva 1.235.31; Dutt, I, 315.

All men, attached to children, wives, kinsmen and relatives, sink in the miry sea of sorrow, like wild elephants, when shorn of strength, sinking in a miry slough. Śānti Parva 12.174.27; Dutt, XII, 261.

The permission which was granted to man in Manu (8.112) to speak falsehood to women at the time of marriage and on certain other occasions was carried over into the Mahābhārata.

There is not sin, if falsehood is spoken to women, in marriages, or to save kine, or the Brāhmaṇas. Droṇa Parva 7.191.49; Dutt, VII, 340.

Despite passages condemning women, we find lines showing respect:

Those who are harsh towards the Brāhmaṇas, women, blood relations, and cows fall . . . like ripe fruits from their stalks. Udyoga Parva 5.36.60; Dutt, V, 55.

They who do not . . . cherish their kinsmen, guests, friends, sons, wives, and servants, for such negligence are consumed with sin. Vana Parva 3.2.56,57; Dutt, III, 5.

A woman cannot offend. Virāṭa Parva 4.24.10; Dutt, IV, 31.

O blameless lady. Vana Parva 3.31.25; Dutt, III, 45.

There is a passage which says that woman is unreliable in confidential matters.

In matters of secrecy, a woman, a fool, a boy, a covetous man, a mean-minded person, and he in whom signs of insanity are marked must not be consulted. Vana Parva 3.150.44; Dutt, III, 220.

However, on the whole women in the Mahābhārata are active and influential.

Modesty is one of the virtues appropriate to a Hindu woman (5.90.87). Other desirable traits for the ideal Hindu woman are stated. The goddess of prosperity, Śrī, declares that she is to be found in beautiful and admirable women:

I live in those women who are given to truth and sincerity and who adore the gods. I do not live with those women who do not look after household furniture and provisions . . . and who always utter words against the wishes of their husbands.

I always avoid those women who are fond of the houses of other people and who have no modesty. On the other hand, I live with those women who are devoted to their husbands. . . .

I always live with those women who are truthful . . . who are handsome and lovely in appearance, who are blessed and who are gifted with all accomplishments. I always avoid such women who are sinful and . . . impure . . . who have no patience or fortitude, and who are fond of dispute and quarreling; who are indolent and sleepy and always inclined to lie down. Anuśāsana Parva 13.11.11,12,13,14; Dutt, XIII, 21.

The admirable Sāvitrī is described as follows:

By her ministrations, good qualities, affections, self-control, and good services to all, she pleased everyone.

She delighted her mother-in-law by administering to her physical comforts, and (covering her with) all sorts of robes. And she pleased her father-in-law by worshipping him as a god, and by controlling her words.

Similarly, by agreeable words, by skilfulness, by sweet disposition, and by ministering to him in private she delighted her husband. Vana Parva 3.294.19–21; Dutt, III, 421.

Proper treatment of women in the home is indispensable to prosperity and happiness. This tendency reaffirms almost verbatim that which is in Manu (3.56–60).

> Women should always be adored and treated with love. There where women are treated with honour, the very gods are said to be propitiated.
>
> There where women are not adored, all acts become fruitless. If the women of a family, on account of the treatment they receive, indulge in grief and tears, that family soon becomes extinct.
>
> Women are deities of prosperity. The person that desires affluence and prosperity should honour them. By cherishing women one cherishes the goddess of prosperity herself, and by afflicting her, one is said to pain the goddess of prosperity. Anuśāsana Parva 13.46.5,6,15; Dutt, XIII, 114, 115.

In the Mahābhārata women of the higher castes receive the most privileges. In a polygamous household the wife who is of the Brahman caste is considered the most honorable and head wife. Meyer points out that

> The bathing and adorning of the husband, the tooth-cleaning, and the anointing, the sacrifices to gods and forbears, and all else that is done in the house on works of holy law,—all this, no other may ever care for, so long as she is there. . . . Food and drink, wreath, clothing, and ornaments must be handed to the husband by the Brahman woman, for, she is the most important.[33]

The Brahman is supposed to wed a woman only of the three higher castes. If he weds a Śūdra woman, he must perform penances. The son of a Brahmanic woman gets a larger inheritance than those of lower-caste wives.

The same self-seeking, dominating character of some Brahmans which is found in other Hindu scriptures continues in the Epics. Priestly pride often asserts itself unrelentlessly; and sometimes this is done at the expense of women. In general the Brahman does not hesitate to set up a superior position for himself. Special privileges are accorded Brahmans. We must remember, however, that the

[33] *Ibid.,* I, 66.

Mahābhārata frequently stresses that there are some things permitted to gods and holy men which are not allowed to ordinary persons. Meyer points out that

> The priestly caste in Old India was not so very distinguished for its chaste living. . . . In the Epic, however, what is told of them does not give a particularly unfavorable picture of their sexual morality. That they anyhow preached a loftier sexual ethic is . . . shown by numerous passages in the Epic.[34]

The Brahman, of course, must not be angered or spoken of scornfully. The humblest services must be rendered him by women as well as by men. Meyer points out that the Brahman dwells upon the word "give." [35] Yet the very dwelling upon this word actually may have helped morality. After all, it was the Brahmans who urged the giving away of the bride without a purchase-price. Meyer states that

> In Brahmanic literature there often can be found a higher view of woman; and the not seldom lofty moral doctrine which in Brahmanic circles along with all kinds of irritating trash was partly built up in independence, partly, however, taken over from outside, in very many aspects was to woman's advantage also.[36]

Therefore not all Brahman priests can be condemned. Likewise, we must not be over-critical with regard to the Brahman's life of begging. The Mahābhārata points out that the taking of gifts by Brahmans is good; "the taker wins the same merit as the giver" [37] (13.121.14). Thus the Mahābhārata suggests that the giver should consider it an opportunity to win spiritual favor through his act. Meyer declares that "it is the strivings of this very priestly caste that India has to thank, in spite of much that is so unpleasing, for an infinity of good and lovely things in the domain not only of the intellectual but also of the ethical." [38]

In the Mahābhārata is the highest praise for women and at the same time the bitterest denunciation. Despite prohibitions which the priests attempted to enforce upon the women of the Epic, on the whole these women stand out significantly. They are resolute

[34] *Ibid.*, I, 248.
[35] *Ibid.*, p. 67.
[36] *Ibid.*, II, 440.
[37] *Ibid.*, I, 14.
[38] *Ibid.*, I, 68.

and spiritual. They are not isolated, but are in close contact with the events of their time. They are capable and serviceable members of society. As a matter of fact the Epic seems to have produced far more outstanding portraits of women than of men. Meyer is of the opinion that

The Epic gives us glimpses enough to show us that in those times the woman held in general a more important position than she did later. . . . Or perhaps rather: that in the world of the Mahābhārata, which at least grew up out of an original Kshattriya poetry, the woman was in far higher esteem than she was when controlled by more priestly notions and conditions.[39]

As in every previous set of the sacred scriptures of Hinduism, so also in the Mahābhārata there is to be found a considerable emphasis on the feminine aspect of divinity.

. . . Aditi, the mother of the gods. Śalya Parva 9.45.17; Dutt, IX, 86.

Those destroyers of foes . . . those illustrious mothers . . . the mobile and immobile universe is permeated by those Auspicious Ones. Śalya Parva 9.46.1,2; Dutt, IX, 89.

The images of gods and goddesses sometimes smile, sometimes tremble. Bhīṣma Parva 6.2.26; Dutt, VI, 3.

O goddess worshipped of all! . . . O giver of victory! O Umā! I bow to you. You are the Vedas . . . You are the highest virtue. Bhīṣma Parva 6.23.6,9,10; Dutt, VI, 29.

O great goddess, with my inner soul purified, I adore you. Through your grace, let victory always attend me in the field of battle. . . .

You are consciousness. You are sleep. You are illusion. You are modesty. You are beauty. You are twilights. You are the day. You are Sāvitrī. You are the mother.

You are contentment. You are growth. You are light. You support the sun and the moon. You make them shine. You are the prosperity of those that are prosperous. Bhīṣma Parva 6.23.13,15,16; Dutt, VI, 29, 30.

He mentally hymned the divine Durgā, the goddess of the three worlds. Virātā Parva 4.6.1; Dutt, IV, 7.

O great goddess! The persons who remember you in the crossing of

[39] *Ibid.*, p. 208.

waters and in the forest and wilderness are never afflicted with calamity.

You are fame and prosperity. You are fortitude and success. You are modesty and knowledge. You are offspring and intellect. You are evening and night. You are light and sleep. You are lunar beam and beauty; and you are forgiveness and mercy.

When worshipped, you remove men's fetters, ignorance, loss of sons, loss of wealth and disease, death and dread. Virāṭa Parva 4.6.22–24; Dutt, IV, 8.

Goddesses were of very great significance to the Hindus of the Mahābhārata. It is interesting to note that after the tragic depression into which some Brahman priests attempted to thrust India's women, the Epic literature again and again considers goddesses and women holy. For generations these very stories of illustrious women and poetic goddesses have helped to stir Hindu women with hope and faith.

CHAPTER VII: THE BHAGAVAD GĪTĀ

AMONG the sacred scriptures of Hinduism the Bhagavad Gītā has probably been most highly esteemed, not only by Hindus but also by people of other faiths. Certainly world literature would be the poorer without it. Also, without it the concept of religion in Hinduism would suffer; for in the Bhagavad Gītā is found a new formulation of religion in terms of devotion. There was reached the revelation of God through human personality. Thus the emphasis on the Hindu religion came to be a personal devotion to a personal deity—in contrast with the Nature-Worship of the four early Vedas, the worship of deities through sacrifice, as in the Brāhmaṇas, and the speculations on an impersonal *Brahma-Ātman,* as in the Upanishads.

Woman receives little attention in this highly revered document; yet perhaps this is quite natural, inasmuch as the setting of the Gītā is a battle scene. However, in the Gītā the deity Kṛishṇa offers an assured salvation to women, as well as to the two lower castes, Vaiśyas and Śūdras.

Even those who are born of the womb of sin—women, Vaiśyas, and Śūdras too—if they resort to me, go on the highest way. Bhagavad Gītā 9.32; Hill, p. 188; [1] compare Dutt, 6.33.32; VI, 45.

Although in this passage women are classed along with Śūdras, it is very important to note that there is another opinion offered by an intelligent contemporary Hindu that "women are not on a level with the Shūdras, for, from the womb of a Shūdra there cannot be born a Brāhmaṇa or a Kshatriya or a Vaiśhya." [2]

The Bhagavad Gītā preaches against lawlessness—the corruption of women being one of the serious instances and causes of social confusion.

[1] Hill, tr., *The Bhagavadgītā.*

[2] Sastri, *The Vedic Law of Marriage,* p. 28.

When lawlessness prevails, O Kṛiṣṇa, the women of the family become corrupt; when women are corrupted, there appears caste-confusion. 1.41; Hill, p. 108.

The following verse suggests a certain depreciatory attitude toward woman and the home:

Unattachment, independence of child, wife, home, and the like . . . these are declared to be knowledge. 13.8–11; Hill, p. 224.

The deity Kṛishṇa identifies himself with motherhood and, too, with ethical virtues which are especially exemplified by women, as well as with other aspects of life.

The Blessed Lord said: . . .

"I am the father of this universe, the mother, the creator, the grandsire." 9.17; Hill, p. 185.

"All-seizing Death am I, and the Source of things to be; of female powers, Fame, Fortune, and Speech, Memory, Intelligence, Steadfastness, Long Suffering," 10.34; Hill, p. 199.

CHAPTER VIII: THE RĀMĀYAṆA

INDIA has been called "the natural birthplace of poetry and song." [1] Just as the Mahābhārata has been termed "the *Odyssey* of the Hindus," so the other Epic of ancient India, the Rāmāyaṇa of Vālmīki, has been characterized as "the *Iliad* of the East." In comparing it with the Mahābhārata, Monier-Williams points out that the purity of the text of the Rāmāyaṇa "has been exposed to risks, which the longer Epic has escaped. Its story was more popular and attractive. It was shorter, and far less burdened with digressions; it had more unity of plot; its language was simpler and presented fewer difficulties. As a result of these circumstances it was more easily committed to memory. Hence it happened that, even after the final settlement of its text, it became orally current over a great part of India." [2] The Rāmāyaṇa is one of the most effective of all Hindu sacred writings. It makes the following claim for itself:

> Whoe'er this noble poem reads
> That tells the tale of Rāma's deeds,
> Good as the Scriptures, he shall be
> From every sin and blemish free.
> Whoever reads the saving strain,
> With all his kin the heavens shall gain.
> Brahmans who read shall gather hence
> The highest praise for eloquence.
> The warrior, o'er the land shall reign.
> The merchant, luck in trade obtain;
> And Śūdras listening ne'er shall fail
> To reap advantage from the tale.
>
> Bāla Kāṇḍa 1.1; Griffith.[3]

---

[1] Reed, *Hindu Literature; or, The Ancient Books of India,* p. 153.
[2] Monier Monier-Williams, *Indian Wisdom,* p. 336.
[3] Griffith, tr., *The Rāmāyan of Vālmīki,* p. 6.

The Rāmāyaṇa enjoins the lifelong inseparability of wives and husbands.

According to the Vedas and various other sacred texts, wives are inseparately blended with their husbands. Kiṣhkindhyā Kāṇḍa 4.24; Dutt, II, 759.[4]

There is nothing more cruel for women than the forsaking of their husbands. Ayodhyā Kāṇḍa 2.24; Dutt, I, 261.

A woman without her husband cannot live. Ayodhyā Kāṇḍa 2.29; Dutt, I, 274.

In the Laws of Manu and in the Mahābhārata it is taught that a wife should reverence her husband as if he were a veritable deity. This teaching is reaffirmed in the Rāmāyaṇa.

Verily, unto women cognizant of virtue, a husband, whether he has any merits or not, is a very deity. Ayodhyā Kāṇḍa 2.62; Dutt, I, 363.

A husband is a deity unto the wife. Ayodhyā Kāṇḍa 2.39; Dutt, I, 303.

They that love their husbands, whether living in the city or the forest, whether well or ill disposed towards them, attain great state. Wicked, or libidinous, or indigent, a husband is a supreme deity unto a wife of noble character. Than the husband a greater friend find I none, O Sītā, who is worthy of being served both in this world and the next, and who is like imperishable asceticism. But bad women, whose hearts hunger after carnality, and who lord over their husbands, do not get acquainted with the virtues and demerits (of their husbands); and range at their will. Surely women of this sort who are given to doing evil acts, reap infamy, and fall off from righteousness. But worthy women like thee, furnished with excellences, see a superior and better world, and range the celestial regions, like pious people. Therefore, following this one, and adopting the course of chaste women, do thou prove the associate in virtue of thy husband. And then shalt thou attain both fame and religious merit. Ayodhyā Kāṇḍa 2.117; Dutt, I, 498.

The Rāmāyaṇa teaches that a wife is incomparably the best gift that a man can have.

The wise say that there is no other gift better than that of a wife in this world. Kiṣhkindhyā Kāṇḍa 4.24; Dutt, II, 759.

---

[4] Unless otherwise stated, the quotations used are from Dutt, *A Prose English Translation of the Rāmāyaṇa.*

The dependence of a woman upon her husband, son, and relatives is continued from the antecedent Laws of Manu.

One of the refuges of a woman is her husband. A second is her son, and a third is her relatives; and a fourth she has none. Ayodhyā Kāṇḍa 2.61; Dutt, I, 362.

A wife's service to her husband is enjoined as the best method of attaining unto Heaven.

The woman, who serves not her husband, being engaged in excellent religious rites and fasts, shall fare wretchedly in the life to come. And a woman gets at the excellent abode of the celestials by serving her husband. Ayodhyā Kāṇḍa 2.24; Dutt, I, 262.

The social pressure for the urgency of marriage is so great that elder brothers should marry before the younger brothers.

Those . . . who . . . marry before their elder brothers are married, do . . . go to hell. Kiṣhkindhyā Kāṇḍa 4.17; Dutt, II, 739.

Adultery is condemned in the Rāmāyaṇa.

Those who kill their friends and elope with their preceptor's wives, do always visit the land of the vicious. Kiṣhkindhyā Kāṇḍa 4.17; Dutt, II, 739.

Even that important Vedic deity Indra suffered punishment for the violation of Ahalyā, the wife of the *ṛishi* Gautama.

Brahma then told Indra that his defeat was due to the curse uttered against him by Gautama for his violation of Gautama's wife, Ahalyā. Uttara Kāṇḍa 7.9; Sen, III, 488.

The slaying of a woman is condemned.

The sin . . . reaped by slaying . . . a woman, a boy, or an old man. Ayodhyā Kāṇḍa 2.75; Dutt, I, 401.

In 2.67 virgins are mentioned as beautifully attired and enjoying their play in gardens.

Virgins decked in gold . . . repair to gardens for purposes of sport. Ayodhyā Kāṇḍa 2.67; Dutt, II, 379.

In the Rāmāyaṇa a mother is to be honored as much as is a father.

A mother should be as much regarded (by a son) as a father is. Ayodhyā Kāṇḍa 2.101; Dutt, I, 460.

. . . dear as a father or a mother. Ayodhyā Kāṇḍa 2.118; Dutt, I, 498.

Here, as in the Mahābhārata, young women are pictured as waiting-maids:

Mithilā's lord gave many hundred thousands of kine . . . as well as an hundred damsels adorned, endowed with elegance, to form goodly waiting-maids. Bāla Kāṇḍa 1.74; Dutt, I, 168.

Incest is forbidden.

Śāstras sanction the destruction of one who under the influence of passion ravishes his own daughter, sister and younger brother's wife. Kiṣhkindhyā Kāṇḍa 4.18; Dutt, II, 742.

In the Rāmāyaṇa (3.13) woman is called unstable and restless.

This hath been the nature of the fair sex from the commencement of creation, that they gladden him that is well off, and forsake a person in adversity.

And women imitate the instability of lightning, the sharpness of weapons, and the celerity of the eagle [*garuda*] and the wind. Araṇya Kāṇḍa 3.13; Dutt, II, 535.

The main theme of the Rāmāyaṇa is the story of Sītā, who has come to be the ideal woman for the followers of the Hindu religion. This Epic begins with a description of Ayodhyā, the city ruled by the mighty King Daśaratha. He has three wives, Kauśalyā, Kaikeyī, and Sumitrā. Their respective sons are Rāma, Bharata, and Lakshmaṇa. Sītā, the daughter of King Janaka, ruler of Videha, is the wife of Rāma. We read of their happy marriage in verses such as the following:

The wise Rāma, in the company of Sītā, with his heart dedicated unto her, passed many a season in delight. And Rāma's beloved Sītā, as having been bestowed upon him by his sire, by her loveliness, and her perfections as much as by her loveliness, went on enhancing his joy. And her lord came to exercise a double influence on her heart. And by her own heart, the daughter of Janaka, Mithilā's lord, resembling a goddess in grace, and like unto Śrī (goddess of wealth) herself in loveliness, completely read his inmost sentiment. . . . The excellent princess looked graceful, even like the lord Vishṇu, the chief of celestials on being joined with Śrī. Bāla Kāṇḍa 1.77; Dutt, I, 176.

As King Daśaratha feels old age creeping upon him, he decides to make his favorite son, Rāma, the heir apparent.

Born of my eldest wife, worthy of myself, thou crowned with the best qualities, thou art worthy son, O Rāma, dear unto me. Ayodhyā Kāṇḍa 1.3; Dutt, I, 189.

This decision is received gladly by all the King's subjects with the exception of one of his wives, Kaikeyī, who wishes her son, Bharata, to become the ruler. Kaikeyī is so unhappy that she goes to the "anger-chamber."

What sensible woman can rejoice in the advancement of a co-wife's son! Ayodhyā Kāṇḍa 2.8; Dutt, II, 210.

A wicked adviser, Mantharā, reminds Kaikeyī that she always has been the favorite wife of her husband. Thereupon, Kaikeyī becomes increasingly angry because her son is not to be the King's heir.

Having fully ascertained her course, that weak one, being angry, lay down upon the floor, knitting her eyebrows. The ground was strewn with garlands and excellent ornaments which Kaikeyī had cast away; and they adorned the earth, as the stars adorn the welkin. Clad in a soiled garment, binding fast her braid, she lay down in the anger-chamber. Ayodhyā Kāṇḍa 2.10; Dutt, II, 209.

The aged King Daśaratha is unhappy when he learns of Kaikeyī's determination to stay in the anger-chamber. Kaikeyī demands a promise, namely, that her son Bharata shall be the king's successor and that Rāma, the son of the co-wife, shall be banished for fourteen years. Daśaratha begs Kaikeyī not to demand this promise, but Kaikeyī insists. The following day, instead of proceeding to the consecration of Rāma, the king announces Rāma's fate. As a dutiful son, Rāma calmly accepts his enforced exile.

Realizing that because of the banishment of Rāma she will become a sonless wife, Rāma's mother is filled with grief.

A sonless woman has only one cause of mental affliction. Her only sorrow is "I have no child and nothing else, my son. I have not experienced in my life that blessing and pleasure which women generally feel when their husbands are devoted to them. I have sustained my life so long, O Rāma, only with the hope that I shall have a son. Myself, being the eldest of all the queens, I shall have to hear unpleasant and heart-rending words from the co-wives who are all younger than I. There can be no greater misery for women than this my boundless grief and lamentations. Thou being present, they have reduced me to this miserable plight, I do not know what else they will do, thou being away. There is death certain for me. O my darling! Being disregarded by my husband, I have been greatly insulted. I am equal to the maid-servants of Kaikeyī, or even inferior to them. Those who serve me or are obedient unto me, shall not even speak with me when they will see the son of Kaikeyī (installed). She is always of fretful temper. How shall I, reduced to misery (on account of thy exile) eye the face of Kaikeyī, uttering harsh words?" Ayodhyā Kāṇḍa 2.20; Dutt, II, 247.

There is to be no questioning of the king's orders.

Husband is the deity and master of the wife as long as she lives. So the monarch, being the lord, can deal with thee and me in any way he likes. Ayodhyā Kāṇḍa 2.24; Dutt, II, 262.

Kauśalyā must continue to serve her husband.

Even those who do not worship and bow unto the celestials, should serve their husbands, being intent upon their welfare. Such is the virtue that should be always pursued by women according to the Vedas and Smṛitis. Ayodhyā Kāṇḍa 2.24; Dutt, II, 262.

Rāma consoles his mother with the following words:

"Engaged in discipline and fasting, and devoted to the services of thy husband, thou shalt attain thy best desire on my return, if this foremost of pious men lives then." Ayodhyā Kāṇḍa 2.24; Dutt, II, 262.

Lakshmaṇa, the king's son by another wife, Sumitrā, decides to accompany his brother Rāma. Sītā likewise is determined to share the exile of her husband.

"O dear husband! Father, mother, son, brother, daughter-in-law,—all of them, abide by the consequences of their own actions. It is the wife alone, that shares the fate of her husband. Neither father, mother, son, friends, nor her own self is the stay of a woman in this or in after life; it is the husband alone that is her only support. If thou dost repair today unto the forest impregnable, I shall go before thee, treading upon the thorns and prickly grass. Confident, do thou take me with thee. There exists no sin in me that could justify forsaking. Under all circumstance unto a woman the shade of her husband's feet is preferable to the tops of a palace. . . . I have been taught by my father and mother to follow my husband in all conditions of life; and I shall carry out now what I have been taught. I shall not abide by any other counsel. I shall wend my way unto the forest impassable, devoid of men, inhabited by tigers and other voracious animals. Happily shall I live there, as if in my paternal house, giving no thought upon the prosperity of the three worlds, thinking only of the services that are to be rendered unto my husband. I shall sport with thee, O great hero, in that forest impregnated with the fragrance of flowers, tending thee constantly, having my senses subdued, and being engaged in austere performances. O great hero! Capable art thou to maintain many thousand others in the forest; what of me? Surely I shall go today to the forest with thee; there is no doubt about it; and thou shalt not be able to dissuade me from so doing. Undoubtedly I shall always live upon roots and fruits. Living with thee always, I shall not bring about thy affliction. Always I shall precede thee when walking, and shall take my repast after thou hast taken it. Willing am I to view mountains, rivulets, lakes and ponds. Being fearless in thy company, O my intelligent husband and great hero, I shall behold on all sides ponds filled with wild geese and ducks, and beautified with a collection of full-blown lotuses, and shall bathe there every day, pursuing the same vow with thee. And greatly gratified, I shall amuse there with thee, in this manner, even for hundred or thousand years. . . . I shall go there in that dense forest, full of deer, monkeys and elephants, and live there as if under my paternal roof, cleaving unto thy feet, and abiding in thy pleasure. Do thou accept my entreaty whose heart is entirely thine, knows none else, and is ever attached unto thee, and who am resolved to die, if forsaken by thee." Ayodhyā Kāṇḍa 2.27; Dutt, II, 270–71.

"The *vinā* [lute] without strings does not sound; and the car without wheels does not move. So, although having an hundred sons, a woman without her husband cannot attain happiness." Ayodhyā Kāṇḍa 2.39; Dutt, II, 303.

"I know that a woman's spiritual guide is her husband. Even if a husband should be poor and of a disreputable character, he should be ungrudgingly obeyed by the like of me." Ayodhyā Kāṇḍa 2.118; Dutt, II, 498.

"The asceticism of a woman is ministering unto her husband. . . . Women of this sort, firm in their husbands, are highly respected in the celestial regions by virtue of their pious acts." Ayodhyā Kāṇḍa 2.118; Dutt, II, 499.

The narrative points out that Sītā gains her desire not to be separated from her husband.

Sītā, attaining her desire, follows her husband like a shadow. Attached to virtue, she does not forsake him, even as the sun forsakes not Mount Meru. Ayodhyā Kāṇḍa 2.40; Dutt, II, 306.

As Rohiṇī, the favorite wife of the moon, followeth the moon, Rāma's beloved spouse,—like unto an embodiment of Divine power—dear (unto Rāma) as life itself, and engaged in acts of good, . . . and the best of wives, followed Rāma. Bāla Kāṇḍa 1.1; Dutt, I, 3.

The aged King Daśaratha is left distressed, after having complied with the unreasonable wishes of his jealous wife Kaikeyī. He refuses to see her and spends the remainder of his life with his bereaved wife Kauśalyā, mother of Rāma. Another co-wife, Sumitrā, comforts Kauśalyā with the assurance:

"O blameless one! O auspicious lady! You will again see your son, like unto the new risen moon, paying homage unto your feet with his head. Ayodhyā Kāṇḍa 2.44; Dutt, II, 315.

Finally, grieving for his son Rāma, King Daśaratha dies.

Meanwhile, Kaikeyī's son, Bharata, has not lived with his mother, but with his maternal grandparents. When summoned to succeed Daśaratha, he refuses and at once sets out for the forest of Daṇḍaka to search for Rāma, Sītā, and his brother Lakshmaṇa. Upon finding Rāma, Bharata begs him to return to Ayodhyā and become king. Rāma insists upon faithfully fulfilling the term of his exile and refuses to return. He takes off his gold-embroidered shoes and presents them to his brother, Bharata, signifying that he gives his inheritance to him. Bharata is forced to return alone; but he places the golden shoes of his brother Rāma upon the throne and keeps the royal umbrella over them. Only in their presence does he hold conferences and mete out justice.

Sītā is described in the forest of Daṇḍaka.

She is evidently eager (for rest). Of tender years, and unknown to hardship, she hath come to the forest rife with troubles, being urged by the love she bears unto her lord. Araṇya Kāṇḍa 3.13; Dutt, III, 535.

Meanwhile Rāma has decided to rid the forest of all the wicked giants who have terrorized the religious hermits living there. He succeeds in slaying thousands of demons. In so doing, however, he enrages their leader, Rāvaṇa. This demon changes one of his subjects into a golden deer. Upon seeing this unusual animal, Sītā asks Rāma and Lakshmaṇa to capture it. While they are in pursuit, Rāvaṇa disguises himself as an ascetic and forcefully carries Sītā away.

"By force I will carry off his wife Sītā, resembling the daughter of a celestial." Araṇya Kāṇḍa 3.36; Dutt, III, 589.

And the wicked (Rāvaṇa) with a shaking frame carried away the daughter of the king extremely distressed, speaking piteously, uttering lamentations, and putting forth endeavours (to free herself). Araṇya Kāṇḍa 3.53; Dutt, III, 633.

When Rāma returns and learns of Sītā's loss, he is grief stricken.

He holds his wife dearer than his life, and is ever attached unto her. Araṇya Kāṇḍa 3.37; Dutt, III, 592.

"Without Sītā I shall not breathe. . . . Without thee [Sītā] I shall renounce my life." Araṇya Kāṇḍa 3.61; Dutt, III, 651, 652.

"Without her even the heaven itself appears to me as desolate." Araṇya Kāṇḍa 3.62; Dutt, III, 654.

"My heart is sinking, not beholding her fine spotless countenance, having eyes resembling lotuses and smelling sweet. When shall I hear again, O Lakshmaṇa, the sweet, incomparable and auspicious accents of Vaidehī, intervened by smiles, and couched in an elegant and easy style!" Kishkindhyā Kāṇḍa 4.1; Dutt, IV, 696.

As time goes on, the sad plight of Sītā is described by Hanumat, the lord of the monkeys. She is forlorn and assailed by the demonic Rākshasa, yet is immovably faithful to her husband Rāma.

Thereupon he beheld there (Sītā) wearing a soiled cloth, poorly, greatly reduced by fast, sighing again and again, and encircled by a band of Rākshasas. She was (however) spotless like unto the rays of the moon on the first lunar day. And her graceful beauty could with great difficulty be perceived, like unto the flame of fire enveloped with smoke. And wearing a shattered and soiled yellow cloth, and divested of all ornaments, she appeared like a lotus-stalk without lotuses. Oppressed, racked with grief, weakened, and chaste as she was, she appeared like Rohiṇī possessed by Ketu [the dragon]. She was greatly reduced by fast, stricken with grief and anxious thoughts, disturbed with sorrow, and was poorly; and her eyes were always full of tears. Separated from her kith and kin and not beholding Rāma and Lakshmaṇa, but the Rākshasas, she appeared like a hind surrounded by dogs. Her braid of long hair resembling a black serpent falling on her back, it appeared as if the earth was filled with dark-blue forests on the disappearance of the rains. She was worthy of happiness only, and never knew of misery; and therefore she was (now) greatly oppressed with sorrow. Sundara Kāṇḍa 5.15; Dutt, V, 937–38.

Sītā says to Hanumat:

"I hope . . . that my husband shall soon regain me; for, pure is my soul, and he is gifted with many accomplishments." Sundara Kāṇḍa 5.37; Dutt, V, 997.

Hanumat reports:

"Sītā hath been keeping the life of a highly chaste damsel." Sundara Kāṇḍa 5.59; Dutt, V, 1075.

"These Rākshasas, and these trees enveloped with fruits and flowers—forsooth she doth not behold, but is engaged with all her heart in meditation, only touching Rāma. Husband enhanceth the beauty of a female more than the dress; (and therefore Sītā), beautiful as she is, doth not appear graceful in her husband's absence." Araṇya Kāṇḍa 3.16; Dutt, III, 942.

Sītā says to Rāvaṇa:

Hearing those words of that terrible Rākshasa,—Sītā, stricken with grief and of feeble voice, slowly replied. Racked with grief, engaged in asceticism and weeping, Sītā began to tremble. And that excellent damsel devoted unto her husband began to think of him. . . . That one of beautiful smile, said, "Do thou take back thy mind from me and place it in thy own wives. Like unto a sinner unworthy of praying for final emancipation, it doth not behoove thee to expect to come by me. Devoted unto one husband, I shall never perpetuate such an iniquitous act. I am born in a high [family], and have been married in a pious family." Having accosted Rāvaṇa thus, the well-known Vaidehī, turning her back, again spake unto him saying,—"I should not live with thee, since I am another's wife and chaste." Sundara Kāṇḍa 5.21; Dutt, V, 953.

"What shall I do without my lord of comely presence? Debarred from my husband's presence, stricken with grief, and not beholding Rāma, having dark-blue eyes, I shall soon meet with death." Sundara Kāṇḍa 5.26; Dutt, V, 967.

Many beautiful appellations are given to Sītā. She is called, "O stainless one" (5.56, Dutt, II, 1056); "O gentle damsel" (5.56, Dutt, II, 1057); "O exceedingly fair one" (5.56, Dutt, II, 1057); "O noble lady" (5.56, Dutt, II, 1057); "Exalted lady" (5.58, Dutt, II, 1064); "Worshipful dame" (5.34, Dutt, II, 986); "Illustrious wife of Rāma" (5.58, Dutt, II, 1068).

Hanumat assures Sītā of the unceasing devotion of her husband Rāma.

His heart is so much attached unto thee, that he does not drive away even flies, insects and snakes from his body. Rāma is always engaged in meditations, overwhelmed with grief; and he has no other thought but seeing thee. Rāma hath no sleep; and even when asleep that best of men awakes exclaiming in sweet accents, "O Sītā!" He always welcomes thee, sighing and saying, "O my dear love!", whenever he beholds any fruit, flower or any object liked by the ladies. O worshipful dame, he is always lamenting, exclaiming, "O Sītā!" And that high-souled son of the king, to regain thee, hath resorted to ascetic observances. Sundara Kāṇḍa 5.36; Dutt, II, 995–96.

While Rāma is burning the body of the vulture, Jaṭāyu, who had tried to save Sītā from Rāvaṇa's attack, he hears a voice from the pyre, which tells him how he may kill his enemies and regain his wife.

The devoted Sītā is described by Hanumat.

She was encircled by Rākshasas, worn out with grief and anxiety, and was like unto the rays of the moon shorn of their brilliance. And Vaidehī, having a beautiful waist, and devoted unto her husband, did not care for Rāvaṇa, proud of his prowess; and she was accordingly confined by him. And that graceful daughter of the king of Videha was, by all means, devoted unto her lord; and had all her thoughts centered in him, like unto

Paulomī [wife of Indra, the lord of the celestials]. . . . And I saw her in that garden, wearing a single piece of cloth, soiled with dirt, surrounded by the Rākshasas, and remonstrated with now and then by those ugly demons. . . . Engaged in thoughts touching her lord, she was lying on the earth, shorn of all grace,—like unto a lotus on the appearance of winter. She had not the least attachment for Rāvaṇa, and was resolved upon putting an end to her existence. Sundara Kāṇḍa 5.59; Dutt, II, 1076.

Vaidehī . . . [is] devoted unto her lord. Sundara Kāṇḍa 5.59; Dutt, II, 1076.

She (Sītā) is engaged only in thoughts touching thee (Rāma). Sundara Kāṇḍa 5.65; Dutt, II, 1090.

Sītā hath been keeping the life of a highly chaste damsel. Sundara Kāṇḍa 5.59; Dutt, II, 1075.

Thus I was accosted by Sītā, reduced to a skeleton, observing pious observances. Sundara Kāṇḍa 5.65; Dutt, II, 1091.

A group of monkeys then come to the rescue and build a miraculous bridge for Rāma. He leads his army across it to the abode of Rāvaṇa and slays his enemy. Sītā hears of her husband's victory.

The wise monkey Hanumat reports to Rāma.

Sītā, possessed by grief, and having eyes full of tears, expressed her desire to see thee. And I was told by her, confident of her previous trust, with profuse tears in her eyes, "I wish to see my husband." Yuddha Kāṇḍa 6.116; Dutt, VI, 1503.

Then to Bībhishaṇa, the messenger of the Rākshasas, Rāma tells of his desire to see his wife, Sītā.

Thereupon, sighing hard, and casting his looks upon the ground, he spoke . . . "Do thou speedily bring Sītā, the daughter of the king of Mithilā, bathed, sprinkled with celestial paste, and adorned with celestial ornaments." Yuddha Kāṇḍa 6.116; Dutt, VI, 1503.

Hanumat goes on Rāma's errand, and Sītā expresses a desire to see her husband without delay.

And beholding . . . Sītā . . . Bībhishaṇa . . . said, "O Vaidehī, may good betide thee! Sprinkled with celestial paste, and adorned with celestial ornaments, do thou ascend this car. Thy husband wisheth to see thee." Being thus addressed, Vaidehī replied unto Bībhishaṇa, "Without bathing even, I wish to see my husband." Hearing those words, Bībhishaṇa replied:—"It behoveth thee to do what thy lord Rāma hath said." Whereto the chaste Maithilī, regarding her husband as God, and filled with devotion unto her husband, replied, "So be it." Yuddha Kāṇḍa 6.116; Dutt, VI, 1503–4.

The Rāmāyaṇa then gives us the following picture of the husband and wife.

Rāma addressed the highly intelligent Bībhishaṇa . . . "Therefore, leaving behind the palanquin, let her come here on foot." . . . Being thus addressed by Rāma, Bībhishaṇa, being sorry, humbly brought Sītā near him. . . . As if hiding herself in her own person in shame, Maithilī, following Bībhishaṇa, approached her husband. And she, having a gentle countenance and always regarding her husband as her god, fixed her looks upon her lord's face out of surprise, joy and love. And beholding the gentle countenance of her dearest lord resembling the full moon, she removed her mental distress. Thereupon she appeared (beautiful), having the countenance of the clear moon. Yuddha Kāṇḍa 6.116; Dutt, VI, 1505.

At this point Rāma publicly announces his suspicion of Sītā's character.

Beholding Maithilī standing humbly by him, Rāma began to give vent to his pent-up feelings—"O gentle one! Destroying all the enemies in the arena of battle, I have subdued thy enemy—I have done all that can be accomplished by manliness!" . . . Hearing those words of Rāma, Sītā began to look wistfully like a hind, with eyes full of tears. And beholding his beloved spouse near him, and afraid of popular ignominy, his heart was broken into two. Thereupon he spoke unto the exquisitely beautiful Sītā . . . "I (always) anxious to have honour, have removed my insult,—as is the duty of man. May good betide thee!—Do thou know that all my labour in the battle-field, backed by the prowess of my friends, is for thee. To uphold the dignity of my well-known family, to remove the ignominy consequent upon thy being stolen away, as well as to wipe off my own insult, I have encompassed this. I have suspected thy character; thou (therefore) standing before me, art distressing me like unto a lamp before one who is subject to an eye-disease. . . . Do thou therefore proceed, O daughter of King Janaka, wherever thou likest to one of these ten quarters. I permit thee, O gentle one. I have nothing to do with thee. What powerful man, born in a high family, takes back his wife, considering her as friend out of lust, who hath lived long in another's house? Thou wert taken by Rāvaṇa on his lap, beheld by him with sinful eyes, how can I, taking thee back, bring disgrace upon my great family? The object with which I have gained thee back, hath been accomplished. I have got no attachment for thee—do thou go wherever thou wishest, O gentle one. I speak these [words] unto thee, impelled by my sense of duty. . . ." Thereupon hearing those unpleasant words from her beloved (husband) Sītā, always sensitive and who had never heard such unpleasant words, trembling like a creeper torn by the trunk of an elephant, began to weep, shedding tears profusely. Yuddha Kāṇḍa 6.117; Dutt, VI, 1506, 1507.

Being thus addressed by Rāma's harsh words, Sītā was greatly pained. And hearing those words of her lord . . . before the great assembly, Sītā was greatly humiliated with shame. . . . The daughter of King Janaka began to shed tears. Thereupon, wiping the tears off her countenance, she . . . addressed her husband. "Why dost thou, O hero, like a common man addressing an ordinary woman, make me hear these harsh and unbecoming words? O thou of long arms, I am not what thou hast taken me to be. Do thou believe me. I do swear by my own character. Seeing the ordinary women, thou art distrusting the whole sex. Do thou renounce this suspicion, since thou hast tried me. O Lord, though my person was touched by another, it was not in my power; nor was it a wilful act (of mine). Accident is to blame in this. My heart is under my control; and that is in thee. What could I do of my body which was subject to another and of which I was not the mistress! O thou the conferrer of honour! Our affection towards one another was increased by our living continually for a long time. Even then if thou hast not been able to understand me, I am ruined forever. . . . Thou dost not sufficiently honour my character, O thou conversant with characters. Thou art not sufficiently considering all my devotion and good conduct unto thee." Saying thus with accents choked with tears, and weeping, Sītā spoke unto Lakshmaṇa . . . "Make a funeral pyre for me. That is the only remedy for this disaster. Being thus branded with an unfounded stigma, I do not like to keep my life. To adopt the proper course for me who has been renounced before the assembly by my disaffected husband, I shall enter this [pyre]." Yuddha Kāṇḍa 6.118; Dutt, VI, 1508, 1509.

Lakshmaṇa, the slayer of enemies, being possessed by anger, looked towards Rāma. And understanding Rāma's intention by gestures and at his command, the powerful Lakshmaṇa prepared a funeral pyre. None dared there request; speak with, or even look at Rāma. . . . Thereupon circumambulating Rāma, standing with his head down, Sītā approached the burning fire. And bowing unto the celestials and Brāhmaṇas, Sītā, with folded hands, spoke before the fire:—"As my heart hath never gone away from Rāma, may thou protect me, O fire, the witness of the people. As Rāma considereth me vile, who have got a pure character, may fire, the witness of the people, protect me on all sides." Saying this, and going round the fire, Sītā, with undaunted heart, entered the flaming fire. The great assembly there, young and old, overwhelmed with grief, saw Sītā enter the flaming fire. . . . All the females began to weep. Yuddha Kāṇḍa 6.118; Dutt, VI, 1509, 1510.

Hearing the lamentations . . . the virtuous-souled Rāma, with a poor heart, and having his eyes full of tears, engaged in meditation for some time. Yuddha Kāṇḍa 6.119; Dutt, VI, 1510.

Thereupon the Deity of Fire, the witness of the people, spoke unto Rāma, saying—"O Rāma, here is thy Sītā. No sin hath visited her. Neither by word, mind, understanding, nor eyes . . . hath she deviated from thee. . . . She was in the solitary forest separated from thee, poorly, and having no control over herself; and hence she was carried away by the Rākshasa Rāvaṇa. Although shut up in the inner apartment, well-protected and guarded by the dreadful she-demons, she had always her mind in thee. . . . Although tempted in many a way and remonstrated with, she did not think of that Rākshasa in her inner mind. Her heart is pure; and she is not spoiled with sin. Do thou therefore take back Sītā." . . . Therefore hearing those words, the virtuous-souled Rāma, the foremost of the skilled in speech, with his eyes agitated with delight, meditated for sometime. Being thus addressed, the highly effulgent and intelligent Rāma, of unmitigated prowess—the foremost of the pious, spoke unto that best of celestials, saying—"Beautiful (Sītā) lived in the inner apartment of Rāvaṇa for a long time; so she needs this purification in the presence of all people. If I would take the daughter of Janaka without purifying her, people would say that Rāma, the son of King Daśaratha, is lustful and ignorant of the morality of the people. I know it full well that Sītā, the daughter of King Janaka, hath her mind devoted unto me, and hath not given it to anyone (else). As the ocean cannot go beyond its banks, so Rāvaṇa could not approach her, having expansive eyes, protected by virtue of her own chastity. The vicious-souled one could not, even by his mind, get Sītā, who was beyond his reach like unto the burning flame of fire. Her mind could not have been moved, although she lived in the inner apartment of Rāvaṇa. She belongs to none else. Sītā is mine, as the rays belong to the sun. The daughter of Janaka hath been purified before the three worlds. So I am incapable of renouncing her, as a self-controlled person cannot forsake his (own) reputation. It behoveth me to carry out the well-meaning words of you all, who have spoken out of affection." Saying this . . . the powerful Rāma . . . regaining his spouse, attained to happiness. Yuddha Kāṇḍa 6.120; Dutt, VI, 1513, 1514.

Though he was deceased, yet the voice of the aged King Daśaratha is heard.

The king spoke unto his daughter-in-law, who was standing before him with folded hands, saying, "It doth not behoove thee, O Sītā, to be enraged (with Rāma) for renouncing thee and for purifying thee . . . This was done by him ever wishing thy welfare. O daughter, to establish the purity of thy character, what thou hast done, is hard to perform. What thou hast done, shall glorify all other females. Though there is no necessity for giving thee any instruction as regards thy duty towards thy husband, still I should say that he is thy great god." Yuddha Kāṇḍa 6.121; Dutt, VI, 1517.

Thus again is reaffirmed the deep-seated Hindu conception that her husband is a woman's greatest deity.

In estimating the value for womanhood of this Epic poem, there is divergence of opinion. The unsupported suspicions concerning the character of womanhood which were expressed by the revered Rāma have not helped forward the ethical progress of womanhood in India. Let us examine the opinion of a writer on Indian life, Mrs. Sarangadhar Das. She points out that King Daśaratha's polygamous weakness was the original external cause of all the suffering endured in the Rāmāyaṇa. His plurality of wives brought about untold intrigue and jealousy leading to deep unhappiness among the women of the zenana. Whatever may have been the mores of the time, certainly today Rāma can hardly be considered chivalrous in having humiliated Sītā publicly. With regard to this matter Mrs. Das states:

They say that it was his duty, as a just and blameless king, to re-establish before his people beyond cavil or possible breath of slander the purity of their queen. But we may read into the incidents another meaning. This over-emphasis on the physical aspect of womanhood, this lack of confidence which is its natural result, attributed even to the noblest of Hindu kings, explains to some degree why it was possible for laws such as Manu's in time to gain complete ascendancy.[5]

On the other hand, Professor Macdonell has pointed out that "No product of Sanskrit literature has enjoyed a greater popularity in India down to the present day than the Rāmāyaṇa." [6] Another learned Professor, Moritz Winternitz, has even maintained that "scarcely any other poem in the entire literature of the world has influenced the thought and poetry of the nation for centuries." [7] Not only occidentals but orientals themselves have given this same high estimate of the powerful influence of the ideals expressed in the Rāmāyaṇa. In the Introduction to his translation of the poem, Manmatha Nath Dutt says:

The influence exercised by the Rāmāyaṇa upon the Hindus, reaching down to the lowest strata of society, is . . . immense. Truly of the Rāmāyaṇa it can be said in Baconian language, that it has come home to the business and bosoms of all men. . . . The Rāmāyaṇa has become a household word in Hindu society; and expressions embodying the memories of incidents celebrated in the epic, pass current amongst all ranks of the people, being mouthed alike by high and low, by prince and peasant, by the aristocracy and the nobility of the land, by merchants and mechanics, by cultivators ploughing the field, and by shepherds keeping the flock, by princesses and high-born dames in towering edifices, and by the women of the peasantry plying their daily tasks, by religionists and politicians, and men of letters,—in short by the community universally [pp. iii–iv].

With regard to the heroine of the Rāmāyaṇa, the same translator says:

Sītā steps forth—a divinity clad in flesh. Sītā would follow the fortunes of her lord. She considers it as the height of undutifulness to remain behind, continuing to enjoy the pleasures of the palace, while her beloved Rāma is leading a life of toil and privations in the remote woods. The daughter as well as the daughter-in-law of kings, brought up in the lap of luxury and amidst the soft ministrations of those pleasures that per-

[5] Das, PSIW, p. 49.
[6] Macdonell, HSL, p. 317.
[7] Winternitz, *A History of Indian Literature,* I, 476.

tain to a royal household, Sītā, the idol of every man's love and regards, boldly and with alacrity faces all the toils and terrors of a forest-life, in preference to remaining in Daśaratha's residence bereft of the company of her sweet lord [p. ii]. . . . Sītā, the best and fairest of her sex, the embodiment of all loveliness and grace physical and mental, she who rose from the sacrificial fire of inspiration—a goddess in all her manifold perfections and unsurpassed excellences, whose name carries in the very mention a world of pathos [p. iii].

Dutt adds that

Sītā has become the grand exemplar to Hindu women as the embodiment of purity, chastity, and wifely fidelity. She has furnished Hindu ladies with the highest and noblest conception of their duties in their various and manifold relations in life. Her empire is both wide and deep over the hearts of her sex, performing for their eternal behoof spiritual service of incalculable worth [p. iv].

CHAPTER IX: CONCLUSIONS

THE SACRED scriptures of Hinduism, as presented in the foregoing chapters in large measure by quoted passages, contain much material concerning woman. They show her from infancy onward —her varied relationships to mother, father, sisters, and brothers, to husband and husband's family, to her children, to her home, and to the community in which she lives, as widow, as slave, as teacher of men, as wielder of power. Some persons have highly estimated the value of the pictures of womanhood set forth in the sacred scriptures of Hinduism. For example Meyer asserts that as a loving wife and tender mother woman has nowhere else found greater and more heartfelt appreciation than in Old Indian literature. He feels that "from the world of the Old Indian books there is wafted to us a deeply ethical spirit, one might even say a wholesomeness, which has a very pleasing effect." [1]

However, many portions of the Hindu sacred scriptures have not contributed to the fullest measure of freedom for service among Hindu women, but often have caused real degradation. We have pointed out that at times the Hindu woman has been denied freedom of thought because of some of the limitations which are unquestionably present in certain passages. She has been fed ancient superstition and cruel fear in many instances. Sometimes direct relations with the Supreme Godhead have been denied to her. According to certain of the sacred scriptures which have been adduced, her husband, however evil he might be, nevertheless is to be revered as her god. Desire for sons in order to continue the religious observances of ancestors has been responsible again and again for child-marriages. Such unions often have caused tragic mortality among young girls. The religious belief that it is neces-

[1] Meyer, SLAI, I, 5.

sary to bear a legitimate son at the earliest possible moment often has caused the setting aside of a barren woman or the mother of girls only. R. W. Frazer says that "for all orthodox Hindus, marriage is a sacred union, and no woman can be divorced," but "she may be turned out of caste, and thus lose all social status." [2] Jealousy, intrigue, and deep sorrow often have resulted from bringing an additional wife into the home. A. R. Caton states that in modern India "polygamy is seldom practised, except because a first wife has not become the mother of a son or of sons." [3] One of the causes of female infanticide undoubtedly has been the fact that so often daughters have been considered of little value.

Today Hindu women are sometimes participants in offering girl children to temples, as they feel that this is repayment to a god for the bestowing of children. If the children manage to live to womanhood, they become temple dancers and singers. One of the social wrongs which is often pointed out by students of India's problems is that of the Devadasis (servants of the gods). Here we see clearly the influence of so-called "religious" thought on the status of women. Sir James Frazer suggests that, while still children, these women are dedicated to temples, "formally married, sometimes to the idol, sometimes to a sword, before they enter on their duties." [4] The report of the 40th Indian National Social Conference of 1927 shows that these dedicated women "supplement the meagre allowances which they get from temple service by performance on social occasions." [5] Such women can never be widowed, because they really have not been married. Amy Wilson-Carmichael declares, "Hence the auspiciousness of their presence at betrothals, marriages, feasts of all sorts." [6] *The Indian Social Reformer* points out that although the women apparently profess to be engaged in singing, dancing, and service in the temples or in private families, their duties involve a life of prostitution.[7] All this is done in the name of religion. Modern Hindu reformers are recognizing the evils of this practice and are making efforts to abolish it.

[2] Frazer, ITPP, p. 272.
[3] Caton, KP, p. 91.
[4] Frazer, *The Golden Bough,* I, 61.
[5] Caton, KP, p. 177.
[6] Wilson-Carmichael, *Things As They Are,* p. 189.
[7] February 8, 1930, p. 380. See also articles by Dr. Muthulakshmi Reddi and Dr. Jerbanoo Mistri in Caton, KP, pp. 177–98.

The religious teaching (Manu 4.212; 5.62) that childbirth is a process ceremonially unclean, has been one factor in bringing about conditions that have caused high mortality at that critical juncture. Hindu sacred scriptures also have tended to keep men and women from eating together. The social gathering of the entire family at meal times, with its beneficial exchange of ideas and its happy companionship, often has been denied Hindus. As we have seen from evidence cited (2.145), the Laws of Manu declared that a mother should be reverenced a thousand times more than the father. But in 5.139; 11.153; 11.224 woman is mentioned along with the Śūdras, the lowest of the caste groups. The prohibition against the remarriage of widows by Manu (9.64–65) has been one factor in helping to bring about the pathetic condition of many Hindu widows. Even today their desolation is often pitiable, especially that of the child widows. Orthodoxy has been responsible in many cases for denying education to girls. Sacred scriptures have been used by many a Hindu husband as sanction to repudiate his wife unjustly. Manu (8.299) permits a husband to strike his wife with a rope. Just as these sacred scriptures have been responsible for much misery suffered by Hindu women in centuries past, so they exert a tremendous influence today. In these writings are instances of stupid blundering and incorrect reasoning resulting in false deductions. In these teachings we find not only ignorance and fear but also jealousy and hate.

It would be unfair and untrue, however, to stop at that point in our evaluation. With regard to womanhood it is equally apparent, as we have evidenced abundantly, that in the sacred scriptures of Hinduism are many elements of strength. We have noted praise and admiration for the feminine. In these sacred scriptures are many instances of companionship and love between the sexes, and there is emphasis upon the sanctity of the family. Although some verses show laxity of moral values, yet in others is expressed the need of sexual purity. Certainly in the scriptures we find a deep reverence for the mother. In the early Vedas woman, for the most part, was unfettered, and she was allowed the privilege of giving religious instruction to her children. Apparently monogamy was practiced generally, and in many cases a girl was allowed the choice of a husband. Widows could remarry. Wife-burning is not found in the Vedas. There we find a wholesomeness and a sense of the worth of human life—of women as well as of men. Again and again the Hindu scriptures repeat that women are to be honored. Religious deeds are said to be useless if women are not honored and cherished. A close scrutiny of the sacred scriptures of Hinduism brings to attention the fact that in the very scriptures which at times stimulate hatred, urge war, foster superstition, and bring about arrogance, yet also are to be found words of wisdom which encourage humility, unselfishness, self-examination and self-control, patience and steadfastness, fearlessness and courage, purity, simplicity, thought and meditation, thankfulness, sincerity and earnestness, truth and truthfulness, temperance, happiness, joy, and righteousness.[8] Certainly, whatever in the Hindu sacred scriptures supports the ideal of equal comradeship and mutual benefits for men and women is worthy to be carried on in the nation's culture.

In considering the social condition of women at the present time in India naturally we must take into account many factors beside sacred scriptures. There is the tremendous size of the country; India totals 1,808,679 square miles,[9] and is often termed a "subcontinent." It is composed of various races and as many as 225 languages.[10] The climate of India ranges from the equatorial zone in the South to temperate zones and even to eternal snow in the Himalayas. Survivals of many prehistoric customs are recorded in the Hindu sacred scriptures. As Hinduism has grown up in a region of diverse peoples, it has absorbed characteristics from these widely varied tribes. In an article in *The American Journal of Theology* (XX, No. 1, Jan., 1916) Professor R. E. Hume states that

> The Indo-Aryans whose own objects of worship had been the superior nature-deities like the heaven, the sun, the moon, wind, rain, fire, dawn, etc., became one of many instances in the history of international intercourse where a people which had first conquered in a contest of military strength have later succumbed to the force of the ideas, the ideals, the practices of the vanquished.[11]

---

[8] See Hume, *Treasure-House of the Living Religions, passim.*

[9] India, *Census of India, 1931,* I (Part 1), 1.

[10] *Ibid.*, p. 350.

[11] Hume, article, "Hinduism and War," p. 35.

No one can begin to understand the status of Indian women today without noting the wonderful work accomplished by the All-Indian Women's Conference. Indeed K. M. Panikkar, the Foreign Minister of the State of Patiala and author of many books on India, wrote in the year 1938, "The re-examination of the principles of social life by Hindu women is . . . one of the most important features of Indian life today." [12] The women's movement in India is occupying itself with education, health measures, rural and industrial welfare schemes, problems of early marriage, purdah, the position of widows, women's franchise rights, and the representation of women in governing bodies. There are many educational centers in India today that are infusing a new spirit among women. Some of the most outstanding are those in Western India, the Indian Women's University at Poona, the Seva Sadan, which is active in both Bombay and Poona, Dr. D. K. Karve's Widows' Home in Poona, Pandita Ramabai Widows' Home in a village outside Poona, Parsi High Schools, and the Vanita Vishrams at Bombay, Ahmadabad, and elsewhere. In Madras are the Women's Christian College, St. Christopher's Training College, and the Queen Mary Government College. In Bengal at Calcutta we find the Bethune College, the Diocesan and the Loreto Missionary Colleges, and the Brahmo-Balika Shikshalaya. There are also the Widows' Home for Training Teachers and the School for Women's Industries. In the Punjab are the Lady MacLagan School, the Victoria School, the Queen Mary College, the Lahore College for Women, the Kinnaird College, and the Sikh Kanya Maha Vidyalaya at Ferozepore and Jullundur. In the United Provinces in Lucknow are the Isabella Thoburn College and School and the Martiniere School.

The outstanding women's organizations in India are in keeping with what Farquhar, as far back as 1912, pointed out as the rejuvenation of India. In this awakening there has been

> . . . a new attitude to women, fresh humanitarian feeling, and a consciousness that the new India . . . cannot be brought in without many reforms. . . . Hindus frequently declare that Hinduism, largely as a result of many decades of devastation and chaos, had fallen very low

[12] Panikkar, *Hinduism and the Modern World*, p. 77.

indeed by the opening of the nineteenth century. . . . Scholarship was seriously contracted; spirituality remained only in the great places of the land; a coarse ritualism was supreme in all the . . . centres of population; and the more repulsive features of the religion, such as gross idolatry, immorality, infanticide, *satī,* hook-swinging, and other tortures, were very much in evidence.[13]

A part of this awakening has been brought about by Western influence. However, one of the healthiest hopes for the spiritual life of present-day Hindus must be the reforms which are being effected within Hinduism itself. Already this internal development has produced the Social Reform Movement. Also it should be noted that "a vast Hindu literature has kept falling from the Indian press in all the chief cities during the last thirty years, editions of the sacred books, above all, of the Gītā, commentaries and translations both in English and the vernaculars."[14] As a result of turning to the actual documents for deeper study, there will probably be far fewer defenders of the entire ancient ritual of Hinduism. As Professor H. L. Friess and Professor H. W. Schneider point out,

The Hinduism which has been revived under the stimulus of Hindu nationalism is not the old Hinduism, but a modernized religion which has incorporated much of Western Science and morality, much of Christianity and much of "Young India." In this sense, Hinduism is today exhibiting some of its most ancient characteristics, its flexibility, its catholicity and its hold on the minds and habits of the people.[15]

When more intensive examination of the actual Hindu documents becomes widespread, the harmfulness of some pronouncements against womanhood surely will be exposed.

Undiscerning orthodoxy in Hinduism is therefore becoming less powerful. Still these sacred scriptures must be scrutinized more rationally than has yet been done before definite and lasting social reforms can affect the Hindu woman. No doubt the world might have been a better and happier dwelling place—not only for women but for men as well—had some parts of these so-called sacred scriptures never been written or, at least, not been considered "sacred." A positive reconstruction of the social status of women

[13] Farquhar, PH, p. 152. [14] *Ibid.,* p. 160.
[15] Friess and Schneider, RVC, p. 119.

might well have been made long ago. But the writings are inescapable facts; Hindus and world scholarship have inherited them. As the gifted Indian author Romesh Dutt says with regard to the Epics,

> Mothers in India know no better theme for imparting wisdom and instruction to their daughters, and elderly men know no richer storehouse for narrating tales to children, than these stories preserved in the Epics. . . . They have been the cherished heritage of the Hindus for three thousand years; they are to the present day interwoven with the thoughts and beliefs and moral ideas of a nation.[16]

Although the sacred scriptures of Hinduism contain some contradictions, yet world literature certainly would be the poorer without the poetry and the social and religious teachings contained in them. Edwin Arnold, the famous English author, said in speaking of the Bhagavad Gītā that "English literature would certainly be incomplete without possessing in popular form a poetical and philosophical work so dear to India." [17] From reading these scriptures countless Hindus throughout generations have been inspired to deeds of love, to a sense of the chastening power of grief, and to helpful lessons of morality. The very document which in certain passages has caused injury, in other instances has offered help to hearts that have nearly reached the breaking point.

These scriptures should be evaluated in the light which one civilization can appropriate from another. The early Vedas and the subsequent sacred literature of India must be considered in any comparative study of world religions. These scriptures can provide an enlightening glimpse of past days in the Middle East world. Also they may help in criticism of many phases of present-day life. The wisdom of certain passages may prove a valuable guide for future generations. Readers of these scriptures should seek to understand the circumstances under which the writings came into being, should detect those passages which are actual outgrowths of primitive life, those which are the direct influence of various historical movements, those which are but the reflections of an individual author's likes and dislikes or his search for greed and power. In this dis-

[16] *The Rāmāyaṇa and the Mahābhārata,* p. 381.

[17] Arnold, tr., *The Song Celestial; or, Bhagavad-Gītā,* pp. 9–10.

criminating process there may be detected some absurd and irrational doctrines. Thus inhumanities may be disposed of, and futile pronouncements abandoned. These sacred scriptures did not drop all neatly bound from the pens of gods and goddesses. They are the works of men and women—for history is the record of human development.

Since these sacred scriptures were written, no doubt, much of value has been lost. It is equally true that much that is injurious has been preserved. To be sure, this may be true of all sacred writings. It is to be hoped, however, that in the future, no one will attempt to uphold any harmful doctrine merely by saying that such conditions exist in other lands and in other religions. They do exist; but such doctrines should be discarded, and the sooner, the better.

It seems as though the people of India should cultivate a deeper realization of historical development. Professor Herbert W. Schneider has said: "Ideas have a natural soil and a physical habitat. Therefore, to understand both the origin and the fruit of an idea, one must examine the teeming world by which it was generated and into which it falls." [18] In other words, as this author so well states: "A living idea is understood when seen in terms of its environment. It is true,—ideas are members of that eternal world of lifeless forms; but this is the world in which ideas are entombed and enshrined. The world in which they live is the physical world, in which alone life is possible." [19] It would be a step forward in enlightenment, if everyone could realize that all sacred scriptures have a historical setting and that they should be studied and evaluated accordingly. In so doing, we should train ourselves to neither praise fanatically nor condemn ruthlessly. Concerning every doctrine everyone should inquire diligently and repeatedly, "Is it worthy spiritually, or is it harmful superstition?" In the course of history the settings of religious doctrines often have been disregarded and the doctrines have been applied to newly developed situations, which in the light of reason have no similarity to the original conditions. Hindus, as well as all other peoples, in turning their attention to the past should use for practical living today only that which is

[18] H. W. Schneider, *The Puritan Mind,* N.Y., Holt, 1930, p. 6.
[19] *Ibid.,* p. 7.

helpful and which will contribute to the enrichment of the future. Farquhar has pointed out that belief in the sacredness of custom has helped to shield the abuses of family life and of caste distinctions in India. He says that

> When a custom is believed to have come down from early times, the obligation to observe it seems to the ordinary Hindu to be absolutely beyond dispute. To break away from it, in his eyes is tantamount to a revolt against society. Hence child-marriage, compulsory widowhood, widow-burning, widow-drudgery, female infanticide and the thousand inhuman cruelties of caste were in the past regarded as inviolably sacred.[20]

To counteract the emotionalism and the supernaturalism in the Hindu faith, there should be an emphasis upon reasonableness. The traditional should be viewed in the light of the rational. Some of the past teachings necessarily must be rejected; some should be combined in new designs. In attempting to read the past, we must not think the picture too simple. Rather, we moderns should realize the complexity of the past and the diversity of present-day life. It takes courage for the followers of any religion to detect and to point out hypocrisy and ulterior motives in the authors of their sacred books. Those who study the past should also guard against too much romanticism.

Indian women should continually and intensively investigate life today in its actual setting. An analysis of the past, then, can be helpful, if studied in connection with present and changing conditions. Religion's concern should be not merely with other-worldliness but also with the actual problems of this world. Some traditions in the Hindu sacred scriptures have been of distinct value in enriching Hindu culture; but their social influence ever must be watched and evaluated. In each generation the times bristle "with urgent issues. Men and women are compelled to face them and to decide."[21]

In the sacred scriptures of Hinduism, as we have evidenced by abundant illustrations, the goddesses of the Hindu pantheon are highly praised. This phase of Hindu worship is potent today. Dhan

[20] Farquhar, PH, pp. 192–93.

[21] H. W. Schneider, *Science and Social Progress,* Archives of Philosophy, No. 12, Columbia University, New Era Printing Co., Lancaster, Pa., 1920, p. vii.

Gopal Mukerji tells a story illustrative of this fact. He quotes a Mr. Eagles as saying,

Sarojini Naidu gave me an insight into Hindu womanhood which I cannot be grateful enough for. In the West, you know, we have no notion of the veneration and appreciation of womanhood that people possess in this country. As the poetess told me, the worship of women is everywhere. She took me to the temple of Durgā, the mother of the universe; to Lukhmī, the Goddess of Abundance; to the house of Sarasvatī, the Goddess of Poetry and Wisdom. . . . Why, the whole country speaks in symbols! [22]

From the vast storehouse of Hindu sacred literature, then, it would seem as though Hindu mothers should teach their children only those ideas that are ennobling and that will lead to a high ethic. Many are the heroic efforts which, in the past, outstanding Indian women have made to do away with superstitious beliefs and harmful practices. Gallant women of today who have an intimate appreciation of modern needs and problems are valiantly fighting injustice toward their sex by intelligent methods. Such injustice may be found in some of the legalistic portions of the sacred scriptures which we have considered. It is the aim of progressive Indian women, and also of many intelligent and humanitarian men, to remove such injustices. The proportion of educated Indian women is still small; but the headway they have been able to make in the last few years has been remarkable. Surely greater numbers of Hindu women soon will come to see that the discarding of outworn and harmful ideology in Hinduism need not cause the coming generation to be less spiritual, but rather will inculcate a deep religious spirit which will bring about a freer and stronger growing faith in the spiritual. Intelligence should increase rather than diminish true piety in their homes. Hindu women should not feel that in questioning certain pronouncements in their faith they are showing disrespect to their ancestors or a lack of reverence for the sacred writings of their religion. K. M. Panikkar has well pointed out that "in asking for the renovation of social energies, the Hindus do not deny their past or question the wisdom of their ancestors." [23]

Hinduism often has been termed a way of life rather than a

[22] Mukerji, *Visit India with Me*, pp. 63, 64. [23] Panikkar, HMW, p. 115.

creed. All over the world, religion is needed for the winning of freedom for womanhood; that is, the kind of religion which is based upon a living faith in the value of reason and love. This intelligence and this love are to be found in the best of the Hindu sacred scriptures, as well as in the best documents of all the world's living religions. Such intelligence and love are not to be found in any religious documents which happen to have acquired the apellation "sacred," if in reality they are altogether faulty. Certainly, religion, as well as education and patriotism, will play its part in the further development of cultures.

Hindu women, then, should realize that antiquity reveals both greatness and limitations and that the Hindu heritage shows a development much like that of other religions. For instance, the Israelites were among the cruel warriors of ancient peoples. Yet in the Hebrew religion we find expressions of love, mercy, and high social ethics. Christians have learned to disregard the cruelties of the Old Testament and to look to the helpful messages of the prophets. Likewise, Islam presents contrasts of love and hate. Indeed, there is much in the Hindu scriptures which is base and crude; yet these same scriptures offer a wealth of material which is highly ethical and spiritual. Certainly Indian women should condemn any parts of the early writings which are harmful to health and happiness, to service and progress. Before accepting a regulation they should ask if it is compatible with rational living. If they are to use their scriptures as a basis or even as a part of any code of helpful moral guidance, they need to build up a new synthesis consisting of only those parts of the writings which are worthy. If we would build a sound life, it is necessary for all of us to examine our thoughts and beliefs, for the ideas which human beings allow in their minds so powerfully affect their behavior. It would seem as though the time has come, not only in India but also in all the civilized countries of the world, to cease to allow harmful religious teachings to degrade women. In the last analysis such teachings certainly will be injurious to the whole population. It must be kept in mind that women comprise one-half the population of the world. Everyone should realize also that when religious laws are handed down from generation to generation merely because of tradition, sometimes they tend to become more rigid and to assume unhealthy connotations which were not intended by the original writers. Manners and customs which have been handed down indiscriminately should be studied seriously before being applied to modern life. A sacred scripture cannot be discarded or utterly denounced merely because of a few perversive statements. Its entire context must be viewed. The practical influence of sacred scriptures also must not be overestimated. It should be understood that a situation which is supposed to have been the result of a religious law, in reality may have been the result of various other causes, such as sociology, economics, or psychology.

Certain it is that women of every faith should have the privilege of reading their sacred scriptures. Restrictions against this privilege are out of date in this modern world. Women should read all the scriptures of their religion—not alone those passages referring to the feminine. Before attempting to evaluate any sacred scriptures we moderns also would do well to read not only the words of our own faith but also those of other religions. We need to study the origins of all our common problems. We should try to find out how other civilizations have coped with similar situations. We ought to cultivate a finer discrimination between worth and worthlessness, between truth and falsehood. This would be a most effective way to help bring about social progress throughout the entire world. This can be accomplished by an understanding of the proper use of mythology and tradition. Religion today should not be a combination of harmful taboos, groundless fears, superstitions, charms, and hideous ceremonies.

It is evident that some of the subjection which has been inflicted upon Indian women throughout the ages has been brought about by those Brahman *ṛishis* who were unscrupulous. Certainly some of these so-called religious leaders did not observe the principle of respect for others. They hardly could have wished to impose upon themselves some of the indignities which they have inflicted upon women. Dhan Gopal Mukerji has said:

> The founders of caste were very astute aristocrats, who did not believe in equality. . . . It is a curious fact that Brahmans have very rarely

attained God in our history. Always it has been the other classes who have attained Him. We Brahmans compose the sacred books, but most of the prophets and incarnations of God are from other classes. . . . The only way to abolish caste would be to renounce the desire even for the highest caste.[24]

The same acute critic of Hinduism said of a certain type of Brahman priest that although he seems "to be occupied with holy things, in reality he has no time for God. . . . Half of them never do anything but sit down to this routine." [25] It is also to be noted that in all his writings the Brahman Mukerji gave high praise to the truly holy teacher.

Despite many words of wisdom and high praise for women, certainly among the verses given in this volume there are to be found cases of extreme cruelty and insult. Too long in India, as well as in some literature of every country, woman often has been referred to as a sort of chattel. It would seem particularly shortsighted for religious leaders to uphold doctrines which encourage women to be helplessly dependent. Harmful prohibitions directed against woman will turn out to be evils against society at large. The world sadly needs manhood and womanhood which results from full development of personality. As Professor Daniel J. Fleming has said, very few people "have begun clearly to vision, not a man-made world or even a woman-made world—but a world made just human." [26] To overcome age-long superstition is a difficult task; but by refusing to be mentally, spiritually, and physically injured and prevented from full growth, the Hindu woman can offer a real contribution to womanhood everywhere in the world.

It will do women no good to harbor bitterness over the grave injustice which so often has been done them in every land. Throughout the ages there has been much suffering—not only among women but also among innocent children. It is remarkable how patiently many Indian women have suffered throughout the centuries, and they should be praised for their noble spirit and for their moral fiber. But mere praise hardly helps to cure the evils and to prevent further innocent beings from like misery. Constructive ideas for

[24] Mukerji, *Caste and Outcast*, p. 93.
[25] *Ibid.*, pp. 121, 122.
[26] Fleming, *Building with India*, p. 61.

the abolition of misery will accomplish more than patient acceptance of evil. Hindu women should realize that harmful conditions are not inevitable, but, indeed, can and must be changed. Often people have not discerned clearly that a nation rises just as high as do its women. Woman's cause is inexorably bound up with civilization as a whole. All the potentialities of noble womanhood should be utilized in the evolution of society.

This matter of religion is no longer purely individual; for the world has become a relatively small globe. Modern scholarship is penetrating to the innermost secret places. Religious documents must be studied carefully if they are to continue as living works. Science is emphasizing the fact that we share all advancements and all handicaps. The world is becoming internationally conscious, though this process may seem painfully slow and even dubious to many people. Women must stand for what is right—not only in their own culture but also for a universal right. The emancipation of women, then, is of international concern. To be sure, cultures differ, and for centuries they will continue to differ. It may be that the trend will be to foster certain differences in order to give to civilization a rich diversity. But there are certain universal qualities which surely will be recognized and fostered. Men and women will endeavor to rid the world of harmful superstitions which result in disease and misery and of doctrines which hinder wholesome spiritual development. The world must be protected against any so-called religious doctrine that tolerates ignorance and disease. Preventable illness in India yearly causes the deaths of millions of people. Naturally, religious pronouncements are not responsible for all this misery; however, it is a fact that narrow religious superstitions which have been perpetuated in written scriptures often actually have hindered the spread of scientific medical care. If epidemics are not checked in any one locality, inevitably they sap the vitality of others. More and more, modern science must protect against such conditions; religion must assist rather than hinder this work. Religious men and women should be scientific; and scientific men and women should be religious. Harmful doctrines must be exposed and condemned because of their evil effects. Mankind must learn not to perpetuate such writings as "sacred" scripture. There always will be room in the world for holy men and women whose aim in their religious writings and in their manner of living is to further helpful, worthy causes which will be of benefit to humanity at large. That which is truly spiritual should benefit the world, not menace it.

Indeed, the good and the bad are interwoven in the Hindu writings, as well as in the writings of other peoples. There are some Easterners who find the highest expression of God in Hinduism. There are Westerners who believe, as did H. D. Griswold, that

> "By divers portions and in divers manners" God spake to the Hebrews through their prophets, so He spake, though less clearly, to the Vedic Indians through their *Ṛiṣis* and *Munis,* giving to both peoples more or less clear intimations of His nature and will, and making the very light which they received, however broken and partial, prophetic of a perfect illumination yet to come.[27]

Even though some ancient *ṛishis* have handicapped the progress of Hindu women in many instances, yet the women of India today must remember that such mistakes are human. Women, too, sometimes may have caused others to suffer. Cruel mothers-in-law, taking sanction from Puranic doctrine, often have been guilty of upholding unfair religious superstitions in order that their own love of power, selfishness, and jealousy might be satisfied. Often women have been the bitterest opponents of reform and actually have encouraged the continuation of their own slavery and dependence. Women must be made aware of vital statistics, of scientific causes and effects. They must note the facts and allow these facts to reveal actual conditions. They should be aware, for instance, of such government statistics as the following of 1931, which stated:

> Permission for Hindu widows to remarry is a natural corollary of the abandonment of the practice of *satī;* but though *satī* has gone, the social ban on the remarriage of the widow remains; and in every thousand Hindu women there are still 169 widowed, twenty-two of whom are under 30 years of age and over a quarter of those under 20.[28]

[27] Griswold, RRV, pp. 371–72.

[28] India, *Census of India, 1931,* I, 234.

In 1925 there was a loss of 196,181 mothers [29] out of eight million cases of childbirth. In India millions of babies die in the first year of life. Indian women should be aware of the fact that in 1936 it was estimated that only one out of every one hundred girls received an elementary education and that only one out of every one thousand girls received a secondary education.[30] There are nine million more males than females in this land.[31] Indian women should be equipped to read statements such as the following, given in the report of the Indian Statutory Committee: "The gap is at its widest in the age-group 10–20, and may not be unconnected with social customs and practices such as purdah and early marriage and unskilled midwifery." [32] It is true that some mothers-in-law have been the first to heap bitter slander upon child widows, holding them accountable for the death of their son. They have believed widowhood to be the punishment brought about by a horrible crime committed by the female in her former existence upon earth. Under the cloak of religion they have stood by and watched helpless young girls driven to ruin. Many instances have been reported in which an old widow has been cruel to a young widow. Frequently women have not taken advantage of the opportunities for freedom which have been offered to them; many young wives wish to accept the aids of modern medical science, but the elder women often resist. Before condemning man for his subjection of woman, it should be remembered that the conservative nature of woman likewise may be somewhat responsible for her status. But to call woman conservative may be an error; by some people she is termed even more adventurous than man. However, the fact remains that many a home exists in India in which women refuse to throw off the shackles of ignorance and superstition, despite the wishes of the men in their own families that their wives, daughters, and mothers shall be emancipated. So this problem is twofold; any chains which man may have placed upon woman have proven in the end to be a sad bond for both. Hindu men have suffered, too; and if these chains are not broken, they always will suffer. The

[29] Caton, KP, p. 50. Report of the Age of Consent Committee, 1928–29, p. 163.
[30] All-India Women's Conference, *Report*, p. 27.
[31] Indian Statutory Commission, *Report*, 1930, I, 50. [32] *Ibid.*

degradation of womanhood inevitably brings about the degradation of manhood also; such bondage produces impoverishment in national life. The mistakes of both men and women can be rectified only through united effort and education for both.

Fortunately, in the great drama of life woman will surely play a vital part. It is not likely that increased freedom to give to humanity all the service of which woman is capable, will in any way lessen her forgiving kindness or her patience and affectionate solicitude for her family. She ever will be a conservator of the human race. She deserves to have an effective voice in the control of living. More and more the Indian woman will demand not to be left in an ignorance forced upon her by fanatical religious doctrine. Portions of scriptures which prescribe indignities to any living being no longer deserve the appellation "sacred"; they should be prevented from spreading further suffering. Only that literature which contributes to worthful living is truly spiritual and valuable to mankind.

The coming years must find the Hindu woman with an increased capacity for creative living. She has many precious gifts that surely will help to rectify all-too-prevalent distressing conditions. She will enrich the thought and contribute to the service of her country. To gain this position in society she should strive; and in her striving she may take courage from the fact that although there were many *ṛishis* who wrote harmful words against womanhood, there were many others who did not seem to intend the feminine to be an object of subjection and degradation. This is evidenced by the important position which has been assigned to the feminine in the Hindu pantheon, as well as in the actual sphere of women in human life. It is to be hoped that of the literature which is being increasingly produced in India, more and more will reveal the gentle, powerful, truly noble Indian woman rightfully by the side of man in high dignity and helping to establish a kindlier social order. Indeed, such a literature well might be considered "sacred."

BIBLIOGRAPHY

TRANSLATIONS OF SACRED SCRIPTURES OF HINDUISM

THE VEDAS

Rig-Veda

Grassmann, Hermann, Rig-Veda; übersetzt und mit kritischen und erläuternden Anmerkungen versehen. 2 vols. Leipzig, Brockhaus, 1876–77.

Griffith, R. T. H., The Hymns of the Rigveda. 2 vols. Benares, Lazarus, Vol. I, 1920; Vol. II, 1926.

Macdonell, A. A., A Vedic Reader for Students; containing thirty hymns of the Rigveda in the original Samhita and Pada texts, with transliteration, explanatory notes, introduction and vocabulary. Oxford, Clarendon Press, 1917.

——— Hymns from the Rigveda; selected and metrically translated. London, Oxford University Press, 1923. "The Heritage of India Series."

Müller, F. Max, Vedic Hymns, Part 1. Oxford, Clarendon Press, 1891. "Sacred Books of the East," Vol. XXXII.

Oldenberg, Hermann, Vedic Hymns, Part 2. Oxford, Clarendon Press, 1897. "Sacred Books of the East," Vol. XLVI.

Peterson, Peter, Hymns from the Ṛigveda; edited with Sāyaṇa's commentary, notes and a translation. Bombay, Government Central Press, 1888; 2d ed., 1897; 3d ed., revised and enlarged by S. R. Bhandarkar, 1905; 4th ed., furnished with additional references by A. B. Dhruva, 1917.

——— A Second Selection of Hymns from the Ṛigveda; edited with Sāyaṇa's commentary and notes. Bombay, Government Central Press, 1899; 2d ed., revised and enlarged by Robert Zimmerman, 1922.

Thomas, E. J., Vedic Hymns; translated from the Rigveda, with introduction and notes. London, Murray, 1923. "Wisdom of the East Series."

Wilson, H. H., Rig-Veda Sanhitā. 6 vols. London, Trübner, 1850–88.

Yajur-Veda

Griffith, R. T. H., The Texts of the White Yajurveda. Benares, Lazarus, 1899.

Keith, A. B., The Veda of the Black Yajus School, entitled Taittiriya Sanhita. Cambridge, Mass., Harvard University Press, 1914. "Harvard Oriental Series," Vols. XVIII–XIX.

Sāma-Veda

Griffith, R. T. H., The Hymns of the Sāmaveda. Benares, Lazarus, 1907.

Stevenson, John, Translation of the Sanhitā of the Sāma-Veda. London, Oriental Translation Fund of Great Britain and Ireland, 1842.

Atharva-Veda

Bloomfield, Maurice, [Selected] Hymns of the Atharva-veda. Oxford, Clarendon Press, 1897. "Sacred Books of the East," Vol. XLII.

Griffith, R. T. H., The Hymns of the Atharva-veda. 2 vols. Benares, Lazarus, 1916–17.

Whitney, W. D., and C. R. Lanman, Atharva-Veda Saṁhitā. 2 vols. Cambridge, Mass., Harvard University Press, 1905. "Harvard Oriental Series," Vols. VII–VIII.

BRĀHMAṆAS

Eggeling, Julius, The Śatapatha-brāhmaṇa. 5 vols. Oxford, Clarendon Press, 1882–1900. "Sacred Books of the East," Vols. XII, XXVI, XLI, XLIII, XLIV.

Haug, Martin, The Aitareya Brāhmaṇam of the Rigveda. 2 vols., Vol. I, Sanskrit Text; Vol. II, Translation with Notes. Bombay, Government Central Book Depot; London, Trübner, 1863.

——— Reprinted, Allahabad, Pāṇiṇi Office, 1922. "The Sacred Books of the Hindus."

Keith, A. B., Rigveda Brāhmaṇas, the Aitareya and Kaushītaki Brāhmaṇas of the Rigveda. Cambridge, Mass., Harvard University Press, 1920. "Harvard Oriental Series," Vol. XXV.

Oertel, Hans, "The Jaiminīya or Talavakāra, Upaniṣad Brāhmaṇa," *Journal of the American Oriental Society,* XVI (Part 1, 1894), 79–260.

ĀRAṆYAKAS

Eggeling, Julius, The Brihad-Āraṇyaka, constitutes 14.1–3 of The Śatapatha-brāhmaṇa, in "Sacred Books of the East." XLIV, 441–510.

Keith, A. B., The Aitareya Āraṇyaka of the Rigveda. Oxford, Clarendon Press, 1909.

——— Sānkhayana, or Kauṣītaki, Āraṇyaka of the Rigveda. London, The Royal Asiatic Society, 1908. "Oriental Translation Fund, New Series," Vol. XVIII.

Müller, F. Max, "The Aitareya-Āraṇyaka" occupies pp. 157–268 in The Upanishads in "Sacred Books of the East," Vol. I, Oxford, Clarendon Press, 1879; Vol. I, Part I, in American ed., New York, Christian Literature Society, 1897.

UPANISHADS

Bhagavat, H. R., The Upanishads. 7 vols. Poona, Astekar, 1924.

Hume, R. E., The Thirteen Principal Upanishads. London, Oxford University Press, 1921; 2d ed., revised and enlarged, 1931, also 1934.

Johnston, Charles, From the Upanishads. Dublin, Whaley, 1896; Portland, Maine, Mosher, 1897; smaller reprint, 1913.

Mascaro, Juan, Himalayas of the Soul; Translations from the Sanskrit of the Principal Upanishads. London, Murray, 1938. "Wisdom of the East."

Mead, G. R. S., and J. C. Chattopadhyaya, The Upanishads. 2 vols. London, Theosophical Publishing Society, 1896.

Milburn, R. G., The Religious Mysticism of the Upanishads. Calcutta, Cambray, 1919.

Müller, F. Max, The Upanishads. 2 vols. Oxford, Clarendon Press, 1879, 1884; American ed., Vol. I, 1897. "Sacred Books of the East," Vols. I and XV.

Röer, E., Nine Upanishads. Calcutta, Bibliotheca Indica, 1853.

Roy, Rāmmohun, Translation of Several Principal Books, Passages and Texts of the Veds. London, Parbury Allen, 1832; reprinted Calcutta, Society for the Resuscitation of Indian Literature, 1903.

Sastri, S. S., and Ganganath Jha, The Upanishads. 5 vols. Madras, Natesan, 1898–1901.

Tattvabhushan, Sitanath, The Upanishads. 2 vols. Calcutta, Som, 1900, 1904.

——— The Ten Upanishads. Calcutta, Brahma Mission Press, 1925.

Vasu, S. C., Upanishads. Allahabad, Pāṇiṇi Office, 1902. "The Sacred Books of the Hindus," Vols. I, III, XIV.

LAWS OF MANU

Bühler, Georg, The Laws of Manu. Oxford, Clarendon Press, 1896. "Sacred Books of the East," Vol. XXV.

Burnell, A. C., and E. W. Hopkins, The Ordinances of Manu. London, Trübner, 1884.

Dutt, M. N., Manu Samhīta, in The Dharma Śāstra; or, The Hindu Law Codes. Calcutta, Elysium Press, 1908, Vol. III.

Jha, Ganganath, Manu Smṛti. 7 vols. University of Calcutta, 1920–24.

Jones, William, and G. C. Haughton, Mānava-Dherma-Śāstra; or, The Institutes of Menu. Vol. II, London, Cox and Baylis, 1825.

PURĀṆAS

Agni Purāṇa

Dutt, M. N., A Prose English Translation of the Agni Purāṇam. 2 vols. Calcutta, Elysium Press, Vol. I, 1903; Vol. II, 1904.

Bhāgavata Purāṇa

Chatterjee, M. N., The Bhāgavata Purāṇam. Calcutta, S. M. Datta, 1895.

Dutt, M. N., Bhāgavata Purāṇa. Calcutta, Elysium Press, 1895–96. "Wealth of India Series."

Rau, S. S., Srimad Bhāgavatam. 2 vols. Tirupati, India, Lakshmana Rao, 1928.

Sanyal, J. M., Srimad-Bhāgavatam. Calcutta, Oriental Publishing Co., 1929.

Brahma-Vaivarta Purāṇa

Sen, R. N., Brahma-Vaivarta Purāṇa; edited by Major B. D. Basu. 2 vols. Bahadurganj, Allahabad, Sudhindra Natha Vasu, Pāṇiṇi Office, Vol. I, 1920; Vol. II, 1922. "The Sacred Books of the Hindus," Vol. XXIV, Parts 1 and 2.

Devī Bhāgavata

Swami Vijnanananda, Devī Bhāgavata; edited by Major B. D. Basu; published by Sudhindra Natha Vasu, Bahadurganj, Allahabad, Pāṇiṇi Office, 1916. "The Sacred Books of the Hindus," Vol. XXVI, Parts 1 and 2.

Garuda Purāṇa

Dutt, M. N., The Garuda Purāṇam. Calcutta, Society for the Resuscitation of Indian Literature, Elysium Press, 1908.

Mārkaṇḍeya Purāṇa

Dutt, M. N., The Mārkaṇḍeya Purāṇam. Culcutta, Elysium Press, 1896.

Pargiter, F. E., The Mārkaṇḍeya Purāṇa. Calcutta, Baptist Mission Press, and published by The Asiatic Society, 1904. "Bibliotheca Indica Series."

Matsya Purāṇa

A Taluqdar of Oudh (pseud.), The Matsya Purāṇam. Allahabad, Pāṇini Office, 1916–17. "The Sacred Books of the Hindus," Vol. XVII, Parts 1–2.

Vishṇu Purāṇa

Dutt, M. N., A Prose English Translation of the Vishṇu Purāṇam. Calcutta, Elysium Press, 1894; reprinted 1912. "Wealth of India Series."

Wilson, H. H., The Vishṇu Purāṇa, a System of Hindu Mythology and Tradition, Translated from the Original Sanskrit, and Illustrated by Notes. London, Oriental Translation Fund, 1840, containing 779 large folio pages. Edited with notes and an enlarged index by Fitzedward Hall as six volumes, containing 2003 pages, in the series, Works by the Late Horace Hayman Wilson, London, Trübner, 1864–77.

MAHĀBHĀRATA

Dutt, M. N., A Prose English Translation of the Mahabharata. 18 vols. Calcutta, Elysium Press, 1895–1903.

Dutt, R. C., Mahabharata, Epic of the Bharatas, in "The Epics and Lays of Ancient India"; Condensed into English Verse. Calcutta, Mitra, 1903, Vol. I.

——— Mahābhārata, the Epic of Ancient India; Condensed into English Verse. London, Dent, 1898. "The Temple Classics."

Muir, John, Religious and Moral Sentiments; Metrically Rendered from Sanskrit Writers. London, Williams and Norgate, 1875. Contains translations of several selections from the Mahābhārata.

Roy, P. C., The Mahābhārata of Kṛishṇa-Swaipayana Vyasa. 12 vols. Calcutta, Bharata Press, 1884–94; reprinted, 11 vols., Calcutta, Datta Bose, 1923.

BHAGAVAD GĪTĀ

Arnold, Edwin, The Song Celestial; or, Bhagavad-Gītā. Boston, Robert Bros., 1885; Boston, Little Brown, 1900. Also printed in "The Harvard Classics," XLV (Sacred Writings, Vol. II), 799–884, New York, Collier, 1910.

Barnett, L. D., Bhagavad-Gītā; or, The Lord's Song. London, Dent, 1905. "The Temple Classics."

Besant, Annie, The Bhagavad-Gītā; or, The Lord's Song. London, Theosophical Publishing Society, 1896.

Besant, Annie, and Bhagavan Das, The Bhagavad-Gītā. London and Benares, Theosophical Publishing Society, 1905.

Bower, H., The Bhagavad-gītā. Madras, Higginbotham, 1889.

Caleb, C. C., The Song Divine; or, The Bhagavad-Gītā; A Metrical Rendering. London, Luzac, 1911.

Chakravarti, J. S., Bhagavad Gītā in English Rhyme. London, Trübner; Calcutta, Lahiri, 1906.

Charan, Babu Radha, Bhagavad Gītā. Allahabad, Lalit Mohan Basu, 1928. "The Sacred Books of the Hindus," Extra Volume.

Chatterji, M. M., The Bhagavad Gītā; or, The Lord's Lay. Boston and New York, Houghton Mifflin; London, Trübner, 1887.

Crane, Arthur and Frank, The Bhagavad-gītā; or, The Battle of Life, The Ancient Poem of India. Chicago, The Abstract Society, 1918.

Davies, John, The Bhagavad Gītā; or, The Sacred Lay. 3d ed. London, Trübner, 1893.

Hill, W. D. P., The Bhagavadgītā. London, Oxford University Press, 1928.

Mukerji, D. G., The Song of God; Translation of the Bhagavad-Gītā. New York, Dutton, 1931.

Ryder, Arthur, The Bhagavad-Gītā; Translated into English Rhymed Verse. Chicago, University of Chicago Press, 1929.

RAMĀYĀṆA

Carey, William, and Joshua Marshman, Rāmāyaṇa of Valmeeki. 4 vols. Serampore, 1806.

Dutt, M. N., A Prose English Translation of the Rāmāyaṇa. Calcutta, Elysium Press, Vol. I, 1891, Vol. II, 1892; Calcutta, Deva Press, Vol. III, 1893.

Dutt, R. C., Ramayana, Epic of Rama, Prince of India. Calcutta, Mitra, 1903. "The Epics and Lays of Ancient India"; Condensed into English Verse. Vol. II.

——— The Ramayana, and The Mahabharata; Condensed into English Verse. London, Dent; New York, Dutton, 1910, 1911, 1915. "Everyman's Library."

Griffith, R. T. H., The Rāmāyan of Vālmīki; Translated into English Verse. 5 vols. Benares, Lazarus, 1870–74; reprinted in 1 vol. 1895 and 1915.

Sen, M. L., The Rāmāyaṇa; Translated from the Original of Vālmīki, A Modernised Version in English Prose. Calcutta, Datta Bose, 1927.

HINDUISM

Aiyar, K. Narayanaswami, The Purāṇas in the Light of Modern Science. Madras, Theosophical Society, 1916.

Andrews, C. F., Mahatma Gandhi, His Own Story. New York, Macmillan, 1930.

——— Gandhi at Work. New York, Macmillan, 1931.

——— Mahatma Gandhi's Ideas. New York, Macmillan, 1930.

——— The True India. London, Allen and Unwin, 1939.

Apte, V. S., English-Sanskrit Dictionary. Bombay, Mrs. Radhabai Atmaram Sagoon, 1893.

——— Sanskrit-English Dictionary. Poona, Shiralkar, 1890.

Ballou, R. O., The Bible of the World. New York, Viking Press, 1939. Selections of Hindu Scriptures occupy pp. 1–140.

Barnett, L. D., Antiquities of India. London, Philip Lee Warner, 1913.

——— Brahma-Knowledge; an Outline of the Philosophy of the Vedānta as Set Forth by the Upanishads and by Saṅkara. London, Murray; New York, Dutton, 1911. "Wisdom of the East."

——— Hinduism. London, Constable, 1906. "Religions Ancient and Modern."

——— Some Sayings from the Upanishads. London, Luzac, 1905.

Barth, Auguste, The Religions of India. London, Trübner, 1882.

Bergaigne, A. H. J., La Religion védique d'apres les hymnes du Rig-Veda. Paris, Vieweg Libraire-Editeur, Vol. I, 1878; Vols. II–III, 1883.

Besant, Annie, The Story of the Great War. Adyar, Madras, Theosophical Publishing House, 1919.

——— Shri Rama Chandra, the Ideal King. Benares and London, Theosophical Publishing Society, 1905.

Bloomfield, Maurice, A Vedic Concordance. Cambridge, Mass., Harvard University Press, 1906. "Harvard Oriental Series," Vol. X.

——— The Religion of the Veda. New York, Putnam's, 1908.

Bowman, A. H., Christian Thought and Hindu Philosophy. 2 vols. London, The Religious Tract Society, 1917.

Braden, C. S., "Tendencies in Hinduism," in Modern Tendencies in World-Religions, pp. 20–86. New York, Macmillan, 1933.

Browning, K., Notes and Index to the Bhagavad Gītā. London, Theosophical Publishing Society, 1916.

Burway, M. W., Glimpses of the Bhagawatgita and the Vedanta Philosophy. Bombay, Deole, 1916.

Butterworth, Alan, The Substance of Indian Faith. Camberley, Surrey, A. B. Butterworth, 1926.

Cambridge History of India. 6 vols. Cambridge, Cambridge University Press, 1922. Vol. I, Ancient India.

Colebrooke, H. T., Essays on the Religion and Philosophy of the Hindus. London and Edinburgh, Williams and Norgate; Paris, Duprat, 1858.

Crooke, William, The Popular Religion and Folk-Lore of Northern India. London, Constable, 1896.

Das, A. C., Ṛgvedic Culture. Calcutta and Madras, Cambray, 1925.

Das, Bhagavan, The Science of Social Organisation; or, The Laws of Manu in the Light of Theosophy. Benares and London, Theosophical Publishing Society; Adyar, Madras, The Theosophist Office, 1910.

Das, Govinda, Hinduism. Madras, Natesan, 1924.

——— Hinduism and India. London and Benares, Theosophical Publishing Society, 1908.

Deussen, Paul, The Religion and Philosophy of India: The Philosophy of the Upanishads. Edinburgh, Clark, 1906.

Dhar, M. M., Kṛishṇa the Charioteer; or, The Teachings of Bhagavad Gītā. London, The Theosophical Publishing House, 1917.

Dowson, John, A Classical Dictionary of Hindu Mythology and Religion, Geography, History, and Literature. 4th ed. London, Trübner, 1903.

Dubois, Abbé J. A., Hindu Manners, Customs, and Ceremonies. London, 1817; Oxford, Clarendon Press, 1906.

Eliot, Charles, Hinduism and Buddhism. 3 vols. London, Arnold, 1927.

Farquhar, J. N., The Crown of Hinduism. London, Oxford University Press, 1913.

——— Modern Religious Movements in India. New York, Macmillan, 1915.

——— An Outline of the Religious Literature of India. London, Oxford University Press, 1920.

——— A Primer of Hinduism. London, Oxford University Press, 1912.

Fausböll, M. V., Indian Mythology according to the Mahābhārata. London, Luzac, 1902.

Fleming, D. J., Building with India. West Medford, Mass., Missionary Education Movement of the U.S. and Canada, and the Central Committee of the United Study of Foreign Missions, 1922.

Frazer, R. W., Indian Thought, Past and Present. London, Unwin, 1915.

Friess, H. L., and H. W. Schneider, Religion in Various Cultures. New York, Holt, 1932.

Gandhi, M. K., Autobiography; the Story of My Experiments with Truth; translated from the original in Gujarati, by Mahadev Haribhai Desai and Pyarelel Nair. Ahmedabad, Navajivan Press, Vol. I, 1927; Vol. II, 1929.

Ghose, Aurobindo, Essays on the Gītā. Madras, Sastrulu, 1922.

Gough, A. E., The Philosophy of the Upanishads. London, Trübner, 1891.

Grassmann, Hermann, Wörterbuch zum Rigveda. Leipzig, Brockhaus, 1873.

Gray, L. H., "Interpretation, Vedic and Avesta," in Hasting's Encyclopaedia of Religion and Ethics, VII, 395–96.

Griswold, H. D., Insights into Modern Hinduism. New York, Holt, 1934.

——— The Religion of the Ṛigveda. London, Oxford University Press, 1923.

Hastings, James, Encyclopaedia of Religion and Ethics. New York, Scribner's, 1914. Articles on Hinduism and India.

Hillebrandt, Alfred, "Ritual-Litteratur, Vedische Opfer und Zauber," in Grundriss der Indo-Arischen Philologie. Strassburg, Trübner, 1897.

Hopkins, E. W., Epic Mythology. Strassburg, Trübner, 1915.

——— The Great Epic of India. New York, Scribner's, 1901.

——— Legends of India. New Haven, Yale University Press, 1928.

——— The Religions of India. Boston and London, Ginn, 1898.

Howell, George, The Soul of India. London, Clarke, 1913.

Hume, R. A., An Interpretation of India's Early Religious History. New York, Revell, 1911.

Hume, R. E., "The Essentials of Religion," in World Congress of Faiths, Oxford, July 23–27, The World's Need of Religion. London, Nicholson and Watson, 1937.

——— "Hinduism and War," *The American Journal of Theology,* XX (Jan., 1916), pp. 31–44.

——— "Lamaism," in World Congress of Faiths, Cambridge University, 1938, The Renascence of Religion. London, Probsthian, 1938.

——— Treasure House of the Living Religions. New York, Scribner's, 1932.

——— The World's Living Religions. New York, Scribner's, 1939.

Hypes, J. L., Spotlights on the Culture of India. Washington, D.C., Daylion, 1937.

India, Census of India, 1921. Calcutta, Superintendent Government Printing, 1924.

——— Census of India, 1931. Delhi, Central Publication Branch, Government of India, Manager of Publications, 1933.

Jolly, Julius, "Recht und Sitte," in Grundriss der Indo-Arischen Philologie. Strassburg, Trübner, 1896.

Keith, A. B., Religion and Philosophy of the Veda and Upanishads. 2 vols. Cambridge, Mass., Harvard University Press, 1925. "Harvard Oriental Series," Vols. XXXI–XXXII.

Ketkar, S. V., The History of Caste in India. Ithaca, New York, Taylor and Carpenter, 1909.

Kincaid, C. A., The Indian Heroes. London, Oxford University Press, 1915.
Macdonald, Frederika, The Iliad of the East; A Selection of Legends from Vālmīki's Sanscrit Poem, The Ramayana. London, Bodley Head; and New York, John Lane, 1908.
Macdonald, K. S., The Vedic Religion. London, Nisbet, 1881.
Macdonell, A. A., A History of Sanskrit Literature. New York, Appleton, 1929. "Literatures of the World."
——— India's Past. Oxford, Clarendon Press, 1927.
——— Vedic Mythology. Strassburg, Trübner, 1897.
Macdonell, A. A., and A. B. Keith, Vedic Index of Names and Subjects. 2 vols. London, Murray, 1912.
Macfie, J. M., Laws of Manu. Madras, The Christian Literature Society for India, 1921.
——— The Mahābhārata. Madras, The Christian Literature Society for India, 1921.
——— Myths and Legends of India. Edinburgh, Clark, 1924.
——— The Rāmāyaṇa of Vālmīki. Madras, The Christian Literature Society for India, 1923.
——— The Vishṇu Purāṇa. Madras, The Christian Literature Society for India, 1926.
Macmunn, Sir George, The Religions and Hidden Cults of India. London, Sampson Low, Marston, 1934.
Macnicol, Nicol, Indian Theism. London, Oxford University Press, 1915.
——— The Living Religions of the Indian People. London, Student Christian Movement Press, 1934.
Maitra, Harendranath, Hinduism: the World Ideal. New York, Dodd, Mead, 1916.
——— The foregoing in a second edition. New York, Temple Scott, 1922.
Meyer, J. J., Sexual Life in Ancient India. 2 vols. "The Broadway Oriental Library." London, Routledge, Vols. I and II, 1930.
Mitchell, J. Murray, Hinduism, Past and Present. London, The Religious Tract Society, 1885.
Monier-Williams, Sir Monier, Brahmanism and Hinduism; or, Religious Thought and Life in India. London, Murray, 1887.
——— Hinduism. London, Society for Propagating Christian Knowledge; and New York, Gorham. 1911. "Non-Christian Religious Systems."
——— Sanskrit-English Dictionary. Oxford, Clarendon Press, 1899.
——— Indian Wisdom. London, Luzac, 1893.
Müller, F. Max, Biographical Essays. New York, Scribner's, 1884.
——— A History of Ancient Sanskrit Literature. London, Williams and Norgate, 1859.

Müller, F. Max, India: What Can It Teach Us? London and New York, Longmans, Green, 1892. A Course of Lectures Delivered before the University of Cambridge.

Muir, John, Original Sanskrit Texts on the Origin and History of the People of India, Their Religion and Institutions. 5 vols. London, Trübner, 1868–74.

Noble, Margaret, Cradle Tales of Hinduism. New York, Longmans, 1917.

Oldenberg, Hermann, Die Religion des Veda. Berlin, Hertz, 1894.

Oman, J. C., Cults, Customs, and Superstitions of India. London, Unwin, 1908.

——— The Brahmans, Theists, and Muslims of India. London, Unwin, 1909.

——— The Mystics, Ascetics, and Saints of India. London, Unwin, 1903.

——— The Great Indian Epics: The Stories of the Ramayana and the Mahabharata. London, George Bell and Sons, 1912.

——— Struggles in the Dawn; the Stories of the Great Indian Epics. Lahore, Mitra Vilasa Press, 1893.

Otto, Rudolf, India's Religion of Grace and Christianity, Compared and Contrasted. London, Student Christian Press, 1930.

Pratt, J. B., India and Its Faiths; a Traveler's Record. Boston and New York, Houghton Mifflin, 1915.

Radhakrishnan, Sir Sarvapalli, East and West in Religion. London, Allen and Unwin, 1933.

——— Eastern Religions and Western Thought. London, Oxford University Press, 1939.

——— Hinduism. An article in "The Legacy of India," a symposium edited by G. T. Garratt. Oxford, Clarendon Press, 1937.

——— The Hindu View of Life: Upton Lectures Delivered at Manchester College, Oxford, 1926. London, Allen and Unwin, 1927. Translated into German by H. W. Schomerus under the title "Die Lebensanschauung des Hindu." Leipzig, Hinrich, 1928.

——— An Idealist View of Life; Being the Hibbert Lectures for 1929. London, Allen and Unwin, 1932.

——— Indian Philosophy. 2 vols. London, Allen and Unwin, Vol. I, 1923 and Vol. II, 1927.

——— The Philosophy of the Upanishads. London, Allen and Unwin; New York, Macmillan, 1924. A reprint of Chap. iv in his Indian Philosophy, I, 137–267.

——— The Reign of Religion in Contemporary Philosophy. London, Macmillan, 1920.

Rawlinson, H. G., India; a Short Cultural History. New York and London, Appleton-Century, 1938.

Reed, Elizabeth, Hindu Literature; or, The Ancient Books of India. Chicago, Foresman, 1907.
Rele, V. G., Bhagavad-Gītā; an Exposition. Bombay, Taraporevala Sons, 1928.
Renou, Louis, Les Maitres de la philologie védique. Paris, Librairie Orientaliste, Paul Geuthner, 1928, in Musee Guimet, Bibliotheque d'Etudes, Annales, Vols. XXXVII–XXXVIII.
Risley, Herbert, The People of India. 2d ed. London, Thacker, 1915.
Robson, John, Hinduism and Christianity. Edinburgh, Anderson, 1905.
Row, T. Subba, Philosophy of the Bhagavad Gita. Madras, The Theosophist Office, 1912.
——— Discourses on the Bhagavad Gītā. Bombay, Tatya, 1888.
Roy, Raja Rāmmohun, The English Works of Raja Rāmmohun Roy; edited by J. C. Ghose, compiled and published by E. C. Bose, Calcutta, Bhowanipore, Oriental Press, Vol. I, 1885; Vol. II, 1887.
Sampson, H. E., The Bhagavad-Gītā Interpreted. London, Rider, 1923.
Sarma, D. S., A Primer of Hinduism. London, Macmillan, 1929.
——— Introduction to the Bhagavad-Gītā. Madras, Ganesh, 1925. "Indian Renaissance Library Series," No. 4.
Sastri, A. M., The Vedic Law of Marriage, Mysore, The Government Branch Press, 1908.
Schroeder, Leopold von, Arische Religion. Leipzig, Haessel, 1914.
Sidhanta, N. K., The Heroic Age of India; a Comparative Study. London, Trübner, and New York, Knopf, 1930. "The History of Civilization."
Slater, T. E., The Higher Hinduism in Relation to Christianity. London, Eliot Stock, 1902.
Smith, V. A., The Early History of India. Oxford, Clarendon Press, 1914.
——— The Oxford History of India. Oxford, Clarendon Press, 1920.
Srinivasachariar, A. M., The Mahabharata; Condensed in the Poet's Own Words, Text in Devanagari and English Translation. Madras, G. A. Natesan, 1935.
Stevenson, Margaret, The Rites of the Twice-Born. London, Oxford University Press, 1920.
Tagore, Devendranath, The Autobiography of Maharshi Devendranath Tagore. Calcutta, Lahiri, 1909; and London, Macmillan, 1916.
Thomas, Wendel, Hinduism Invades America, New York, Beacon, 1930.
Tilak, B. G., His Writings and Speeches. Madras, B. A. Ghose, 1910.
Thompson, Edward, Suttee. London, Allen and Unwin, 1928.
Underwood, A. C., Contemporary Thought of India. New York, Knopf, 1931. "The Library of Contemporary Thought."
Vishweshvaranand, Swami, and Swami Nityanand, Indexes to Rigveda,

Yajurveda, Sāmaveda, Atharvaveda. 4 vols. Bombay, Nirnaya-Sagara Press, 1907–8.

Weber, Albrecht, Indische Studien. 4 vols. Berlin, Dümmler's Buchhandlung, Vol. I, 1850; Vol. II, 1853; Vol. III, 1855; Vol. IV, 1858.

——— The History of Indian Literature. London, Trübner, 1904.

Whitney, W. D., Index Verborum to the Published Text of the Atharva-Veda. New Haven, Tuttle, Morehouse and Taylor, 1881. An off-print from the *Journal of the American Oriental Society,* XII (1881), 1–383.

Wilkins, W. J., Hindu Mythology, Vedic and Puranic. Calcutta and London, Thacker, and Spink, 1882.

——— Modern Hinduism. Calcutta and London, Thacker, 1900.

Wilson, H. H., Essays on the Religion of the Hindus. 2 vols. London, Trübner, Vol. I, 1861; Vol. II, 1862.

——— Purāṇas. Calcutta, Elysium Press, 1898.

Winternitz, Moritz, A History of Indian Literature. 2 vols. Calcutta, University of Calcutta, 1927. Vol. I. Hindu Sanskrit Literature.

Zimmer, Heinrich, Altindisches Leben. Berlin, Weidmannsche Buchhandlung, 1879.

INDIAN WOMANHOOD

All-India Women's Conference. Report of the Eleventh Session, December 23 to 27, 1936. [Ahmedabad, Vasavada, 1937.]

Athavale, Mrs. Parvati, My Story; the Autobiography of a Hindu Widow; translated by J. E. Abbott. New York and London, Putnam, 1930.

Bader, Clarisse, Women in Ancient India. London, Kegan Paul, Trench, Trübner and Co., 1925.

Balfour, Margaret, and Ruth Young, The Work of Medical Women in India. London, Oxford University Press, 1929.

Banerjea, Surendranath, A Nation in the Making. London and New York, Oxford University Press, 1925.

Barnes, Irene H., Behind the Pardah. London, Marshall, 1897.

Baroda, Maharani of [Chimnabai II] and S. M. Mitra, The Position of Women in India. London, Longmans, 1911.

Begum of Bhopal, H[er] H[ighness], An Account of My Life. London, Murray, 1912.

Bhattacharyya, Panchanan, Ideals of Indian Womanhood. Calcutta, Goldquin, 1921.

Billington, M. F., Woman in India. London, Chapman and Hall, 1895.

Bleakley, Ethel, A Country Doctor in Bengal. London, Church of England Zenana Missionary Society, 1928.

Booth, Mrs. Winifred, Pictures from a Missionary's Album. London and Edinburgh, Marshall, 1923.

Burton, M. E., Women Workers of the Orient. West Medford, Mass., The Central Committee on the United Study of Foreign Missions, 1918.

Caton, A. R., The Key of Progress; a Survey of the Status and Conditions of Women in India. London, Oxford University Press, 1930.

Cattell, Milly, Behind the Purdah; or, The Lives and Legends of Our Hindu Sisters. Calcutta, Thacker, 1916.

Chapman, G. C. C., Sketches of Some Distinguished Indian Women. London and Calcutta, Allen, 1891.

Christlieb, M. L., An Uphill Road in India. London, Allen and Unwin, 1927.

Cooper, Elizabeth, My Lady of the Indian Purdah. New York, Stokes, 1927.

Cousins, M. E., The Awakening of Asian Womanhood. Madras, Ganesh, 1922.

Cowan, Minna G., The Education of the Women of India. New York, Revell, 1900.

Craske, M. E., Sister India; One Solution of the Problems of "Mother India." London, Religious Tract Society, 1930.

Das, Mrs. Sarangadhar, A Marriage to India. New York, Vanguard Press, 1930.

——— Purdah: the Status of Indian Women. New York, Vanguard Press, 1932.

Debenham, M. H., Girls of India. London, United Council for Missionary Education, 1923.

Dutt, G. S., A Woman of India; Being the Life of Saroj Nalini (founder of the Women's Institute Movement in India). London, Leonard and Virginia Woolf, Hogarth Press, 1929.

Edib, Halide, Inside India. London, Allen and Unwin, 1937.

Field, H. H., After Mother India. New York, Harcourt, Brace, 1929.

Fleming, D. J., "Modern Education for India's Women," extract from *Woman's Work*. XXXVI (No. 10, October, 1926), 217–20.

——— Schools with a Message in India. London, Oxford University Press, 1921.

Frazer, Sir J. G., The Golden Bough. New York, Macmillan, 1914. Passages relating to India.

Fuller, Mrs. M. B., The Wrongs of Indian Womanhood. New York, Revell, 1900.

Gedge, E. C., Women in Modern India. Bombay, Taraporewala, 1929.

Ghosha, Jogesachandra, The Daughter of Hindusthan. Calcutta, Sen, 1928.

Higginbottom, E. C., Through Teakwood Windows: Close-up views of India's Womanhood. New York, Revell, 1926.

Hinkley, Edyth, and M. L. Christlieb, Struggle for a Soul. Philadelphia, Union Press, 1907.

Hopkins, Mrs. S. A., Within the Purdah. New York, Eaton and Mains; Cincinnati, Curts and Jennings, 1898.

Indian Statutory Commission. Report. 3 vols. London, His Majesty's Stationery Office, 1930. (Vol. I. Survey. See especially Pt. 1, ch. vii, The Women of India.)

Kelman, J. H., Labour in India; a Study of the Conditions of Indian Women in Modern Industry. London, Allen and Unwin, New York, Doran, 1923.

Macnicol, Mrs. M. G. C., Poems by Indian Women; selected and rendered by various translators. Calcutta, Association Press; London and New York, Oxford University Press, 1923.

Macnicol, Nicol, India in the Dark Wood. London, Livingstone Press, 1930.

Mayo, Katherine, Mother India. New York, Harcourt, Brace, 1927.

Mukerji, D. G., Caste and Outcast. New York, Dutton, 1923.

——— A Son of Mother India Answers. New York, Dutton, 1928.

——— Visit India with Me. New York, Dutton, 1929.

Noble, Margaret, The Web of Indian Life. London, Heinemann, 1914.

Olcott, Mason, Village Schools and Teachers in India. Calcutta, Association Press, 1926.

——— Better Village Schools. Calcutta, Y.M.C.A. Publishing House, 1937.

Padfield, J. E., The Hindu at Home. London, Simpkin Marshall, 1908.

Panikkar, K. M., Hinduism and the Modern World. Allahabad, Kitabistan, 1938.

Pinch, Trevor, Stark India. London, Hutchinson, 1930.

Pym, Michael, The Power of India. New York, London, Putnam, 1930.

Ramabai Sarasvati, The High-Caste Hindu Woman. New York, Revell, 1901.

Rai, Lajpat, Unhappy India; Being a Reply to Miss Katherine Mayo's "Mother India." Calcutta, Banna, 1928.

——— The Problem of National Education in India. London, Allen and Unwin, 1920.

Ranga, I. C., Father India; a Reply to Mother India. London, Selwyn and Blount, 1927; also New York, Carrier, 1928.

Sorabji, Cornelia, Between the Twilights. London and New York, Harper, 1908.

Sorabji, Cornelia, India Calling; the Memories of Cornelia Sorabji. London, Nisbet, 1934.

——— Love and Life behind the Purdah. London, Freemantle, 1901.

——— The Purdahnashin. Calcutta, Thacker, 1917.

Thomas, P. K., Women and Marriage in India. London, Allen and Unwin, 1939.

Tinling, Christine, India's Womanhood; Forty Years' Work at Ludhiana. London, Lutterworth, 1935.

Underhill, Lillian, Extremes Meet; Some Facts about India's Women. London, Highway Press, 1934.

——— Indian Womanhood To-day. London, Highway Press, 1930.

Urquhart, Mrs. Margaret, Women of Bengal. Calcutta, Association Press, 1926.

VanDoren, A. B., Lighted to Lighten the Hope of India. West Medford, Massachusetts, The Central Committee on the United Study of Foreign Missions, 1922.

Vaughan, K. O., The Purdah System and Its Effect on Motherhood. Cambridge, Heffer, 1928.

Vickland, E. E., Women of Assam. Philadelphia, Judson Press, 1928.

Visvesvaraya, M., Reconstructing India. London, King, 1920.

Williams, G. M., Understanding India, New York, Coward-McCann, 1928.

Wilson, Margaret, Daughters of India. London, Jonathan Cape, 1928.

Wilson-Carmichael, Amy, Lotus Buds. London, Morgan and Scott, 1912.

——— Things As They Are. London, Morgan and Scott, 1903.

CITATIONS TO THE SACRED TEXTS

The italic figures following the colons are references to the pages of this book.

RIG-VEDA

1.3.10, 11, 12: *12*
1.23.18–22: *13*
1.62.11: *17*
1.72.5: *18*
1.83.3: *19*
1.89: *9, 12*
1.92.13: *24*
1.104.3: *17*
1.105.8: *17*
1.109.2: *22*
1.113.19: *9, 14*
1.115.2: *38*
1.117.7: *35*
1.119.5: *34*
1.124.7: *16, 33*
1.131.3: *16, 19*
1.167.4: *34*
1.180.2: *34*
2.3.8: *12*
2.13.12: *34*
2.15.7: *34*
2.29.1: *33*
2.30.8: *12*
2.41.16: *12*
3.1.7: *16*
3.2.2: *16*
3.16.5: *26*
3.31.1: *25*
3.38.8: *27*
3.53.2: *28*
3.53.4: *16*
3.53.20: *29*
3.54.7: *16*
4.3.2: *16*
4.5.5: *32, 33*
4.16.15: *30*
4.19.9: *34*
4.25.3: *9*
4.30.16: *34*

RIG-VEDA (*Cont.*)

4.33.2, 3: *28*
4.43.6: *34*
4.52.1–7: *15*
4.53.7: *29*
4.58.9: *22*
5.3.2: *16*
5.6.8: *29*
5.19.4: *16*
5.42.2: *9*
5.43.11: *12*
5.44.7: *30*
5.61.6: *21*
5.78.9: *25*
5.85.7, 8: *46*
6.20.8: *10*
6.49.7: *12*
6.61.4: *12*
7.4.7, 8: *25*
7.10.4: *9*
7.18.2: *17*
7.26.3: *17*
7.40.2, 4: *9*
7.45.2: *12*
7.62.6: *29, 31*
7.74.6: *29*
7.78.3: *14*
7.82.10: *9*
7.95.4, 5: *12*
7.96.1: *12*
7.103.3: *28*
7.104.17: *41*
8.17.7: *34*
8.18.6, 7: *10*
8.19.27: *28*
8.19.36: *41*
8.31.5–9: *18*
8.33.17: *21*
8.35.5: *39*
8.56.10–12: *10*

INDEX

Variant spellings of certain words are placed in parentheses following the words as spelled by this author.

To

Dr. Frederick H. Kuitems

With deep personal regards

Mildreth Worth Pinkham